The Problem of
Secret Intelligence

Series Editors: Richard J. Aldrich, Rory Cormac, Michael S. Goodman and Hugh Wilford

This series explores the full spectrum of spying and secret warfare in a globalised world.

Intelligence has changed. Secret service is no longer just about spying or passively watching a target. Espionage chiefs now command secret armies and legions of cyber warriors who can quietly shape international relations itself. Intelligence actively supports diplomacy, peacekeeping and warfare: the entire spectrum of security activities. As traditional inter-state wars become more costly, covert action, black propaganda and other forms of secret interventionism become more important. This ranges from proxy warfare to covert action; from targeted killing to disruption activity. Meanwhile, surveillance permeates communications to the point where many feel there is little privacy. Intelligence, and the accelerating technology that surrounds it, have never been more important for the citizen and the state.

Titles in the *Intelligence, Surveillance and Secret Warfare* series include:

Published:

The Arab World and Western Intelligence: Analysing the Middle East, 1956–1981
Dina Rezk

The Twilight of the British Empire: British Intelligence and Counter-Subversion in the Middle East, 1948–63
Chikara Hashimoto

Chile, the CIA and the Cold War: A Transatlantic Perspective
James Lockhart

The Clandestine Lives of Colonel David Smiley: Code Name 'Grin'
Clive Jones

The Problem of Secret Intelligence
Kjetil Anders Hatlebrekke

Outsourcing US Intelligence: Private Contractors and Government Accountability
Damien Van Puyvelde

Forthcoming:

The Snowden Era on Screen: Signals Intelligence and Digital Surveillance
James Smith

The CIA and the Pursuit of Security: History, Documents and Contexts
Hew Dylan

https://edinburghuniversitypress.com/series-intelligence-surveillance-and-secret-warfare.html

The Problem of Secret Intelligence

Kjetil Anders Hatlebrekke

EDINBURGH
University Press

Edinburgh University Press is one of the leading
university presses in the UK. We publish academic
books and journals in our selected subject areas across
the humanities and social sciences, combining cutting-
edge scholarship with high editorial and production
values to produce academic works of lasting
importance. For more information visit our website:
edinburghuniversitypress.com

Edinburgh University Press Ltd
The Tun – Holyrood Road
12(2f) Jackson's Entry
Edinburgh EH8 8PJ

First published in hardback by Edinburgh University Press 2019

Typeset in 11/13 Adobe Sabon by
IDSUK (Dataconnection) Ltd, and
printed and bound by CPI Group (UK) Ltd,
Croydon, CR0 4YY

A CIP record for this book is available from the
British Library

ISBN 978 0 7486 9183 8 (hardback)
ISBN 978 1 4744 8183 0 (paperback)
ISBN 978 0 7486 9184 5 (webready PDF)
ISBN 978 0 7486 9185 2 (epub)

Contents

Acknowledgements

This book would not have been possible without the sound, clear and wise supervision given to me by Michael Rainsborough, professor of Strategic Theory and Head of the War Studies Department, King's College London. I would also like to express my deep thanks to the editorial staff at Edinburgh University Press. Their consideration and support have been invaluable.

During the course of my studies there were many people who either generously gave of their time to meet me, or who went out of their way to facilitate my progress. In this regard, special thanks are due to the Norwegian Defence Intelligence School. The former and current Heads of School, Freddy Furulund and Espen Andersen, have given me space and time to finish my research, and I am extremely grateful to the rest of the staff, who with their personal manner and deep concern for intelligence matters have surrounded me with an environment of creativity and imagination. I also regard myself as fortunate in having the opportunity to gain advice from experienced professionals and academics in the field. In this regard, I am particularly grateful to John Lunde, Lord Robin Butler, Sir David Omand, Uri Bar-Joseph, Peter Jackson, Bill Duff, and the Dean and pro Dean at the Norwegian Defence Intelligence School, Tore Pedersen and Pia Jansen.

I would like to express my warm appreciation for the assistance I received from the Norwegian Defence University College during my time as Programme Director for the Professional Advanced Intelligence course. The College gave me the opportunity to found an intelligence course that over three years enabled me to teach highly motivated professionals, whose constructive criticisms have led me to understand a great deal more about my own work. My contact with the soldiers and officers in the Norwegian Naval Special Operations Commando and the Norwegian Intelligence Battalion has also been invaluable, and the result of my research would not have been the same without all the discussions I have had with these fine and professional soldiers. I extend my profound thanks even though, by necessity, they cannot be identified by name. I would also like to express my gratitude to the Norwegian Police University College. A special thanks to Torstein Eidet, Morten Løw Hansen and Ivar Fahsing.

Generous thanks are given to the deceased Knut Aasberg. He was the one who made me understand that intelligence is much more than methods and systems. His great interest in intelligence, his immense experience as an intelligence officer, and his curiosity, creativity and imagination demonstrated to me what intelligence professionalism really is. I am also grateful to Patrick Bury. His experience as an army officer in war has been insightful for my research. His advice and helpful comments have motivated me to carry on my research. I am grateful that he is my good friend.

I would also like to express my gratitude to Håvar Stavsetra. His interest in my research made this book possible. His personal support has always been unreserved, for which I am enormously appreciative. I hope that I will be able to justify the immense faith he has shown in me. I also would like to thank Torger, Kirsti and Elisabeth for their personal support. A warm thank you to all my friends, and a special thank you to Tanja, Guro, Henning, Runar, Kathinka, Åsmund, Robin, Anders, Halvor, Amund, Kristian A., Peter W., Peter E., Iver Johannes, Odd Martin, Pekka, Martin, Stian, Vidar, Håkon, Klaus, Sara, Torgeir, Kari-Anne, Ronny, Christina, Laila, Erlend, Stefan, Sven, Knut, Erik, Inger, Thomas, Herman, Torjus, Kristian J., Emil, Hans M., Marius H., Stig and Stein K. for being there in both the (many) good times, and the (occasional) bad ones. And of course, I wish to thank Fred, Børge and Vivian for their unreserved care and love. This book would have been impossible without them. A special thought goes to my father, who passed away in August 2015. His love, support and wisdom are irreplaceable. Warm thoughts and love go to my mother. Her love, serenity, wisdom and strength are inspiring and have given me the endurance I needed to finish this book. I would also like to thank the heart specialists and nurses at Oslo University hospital. They have increased my quality of life significantly. They have never given up, and this book would have been challenging to publish without them.

Finally, I want to thank those that I have served with on operations abroad, and a special thought goes to my friends Bjørg, Lasse and Freddy. You sacrificed the most and lost your beloved husband and brother Trond Bolle. He was killed in action in Afghanistan, and this book is dedicated to him.

KAH
Oslo
8 October 2018

Abbreviations

AMAN	Israeli Directorate of Military Intelligence
CIA	Central Intelligence Agency
CSG	Counterterrorism Security Group
CTC	Counter Terrorist Center
DCI	Director of Central Intelligence
DI	Directorate of Intelligence
DMI	Director of Military Intelligence
FBI	Federal Bureau of Investigation
Geoint	Geographical Intelligence
Humint	Human Intelligence
IDF	Israeli Defence Forces
Imint	Imagery Intelligence
JIC	Joint Intelligence Committee
NCS	National Clandestine Service
NIE	National Intelligence Estimates
NORAD	North American Aerospace Defense Command
NSA	National Security Agency
Osint	Open Source Intelligence
PDB	Presidential Daily Brief
Sigint	Signal Intelligence

Introduction

The iron curtain and cold war that used to divide Europe have been replaced by transnational threats, nonlinear war, digideceptionalisation,[1] and state-sponsored digital subversion. The threats reach beyond and transcend the boundaries given by history, and thus challenge traditional methods of intelligence.

The ultimate objective of modern intelligence is thus the cleverness and ability to divide truth from falsehood, the willingness to accept the inconceivable and the courage to share information beyond the boundaries of experience and tradition. Intelligence must therefore be built on intellectual courage, solid theory, commonly understood definitions and scientific doubt.

However, this book argues that there exists neither a proper conceptual or descriptive theory of intelligence, nor any adequate definition that can shape a cohesive appreciation of what intelligence is.[2] The lack of a rigorous understanding of intelligence has arguably increased the problem of induction and discourse failure.[3] The problem of induction is the belief that history repeats itself.[4] Discourse will for analytical purposes be understood as the level of common understanding of meaning and contexts in language and communication.[5] Discourse failure hence explains how low levels of common understanding of meaning and context in language and communication decreases intelligence institutions' ability to identify, understand, communicate and accept threats that occur in new variations.[6] The book will thus explore and illustrate how the lack of a descriptive intelligence theory has increased the problem of induction and discourse failure, and how an appreciation of intelligence as art can diminish this problem.

Many books on intelligence focus on more technical challenges presented in what they see as the practice of the intelligence profession. They often have a tendency to explore problems inherent in the basic structures of the collection, analysis and dissemination cycle. This book will, in contrast, probe beyond this understanding. It will argue that the central characteristic of intelligence is that it is a cognitive activity. The book hence argues that the essence of intelligence reflects the core principles of critical rationalism,[7] since good intelligence makes uncertain estimates less uncertain.[8] Intelligence should therefore be understood as *secretly generated wisdom beyond the limits of formal reasoning that makes uncertain estimates less uncertain, and that consequently generates political, strategic and operational advantages over adversaries.*[9]

However, this book no doubt acknowledges that formal reasoning, which is the formal 'process of drawing a conclusion from a set of premises',[10] is an important and inseparable part of high-quality intelligence production, inasmuch as the methodical approach offered by the formal methodology is a prerequisite for verifiability and accountability. That said, it also contends that the limitations caused by the strict syntactic relation between the conclusion and the premises that formal reasoning is built upon[11] increases the problem of induction, and thereby also increases discourse failure. This book thus argues that the quality of intelligence production will increase when intelligence institutions acknowledge that the problem of induction reflects the limitations of formal reasoning. Good intelligence must hence be built on a fine balance between formal reasoning, and imagination and creativity.

The relationship between human nature and intelligence therefore needs to be studied. Until now, few, if any, scholars have examined intelligence from this understanding to any great depth, and none have studied the relationship between the problem of induction, how it increases discourse failure and how intelligence failure may increase when these factors interact with a secretive intelligence culture, and the human tendency to close cognition.[12] This book will bridge this academic gap, and it will demonstrate how a deeper understanding of intelligence as the art of knowing beyond the limits of formal reasoning increases the perception of the quintessence of intelligence. Accordingly, it will marshal evidence to show that an acknowledgement of the problem of induction will diminish the effects of discourse failure, and therefore mitigate intelligence failure.

This book is therefore concerned with the relationship between human cognitive capabilities and limitations, and the challenges described in the discourse failure theory.[13] It studies whether and to what extent the limitations and capabilities of human cognition, and its connections to the problem of induction, shape intelligence production. Existing literature, especially the discourse failure theory and theories on cognitive closure, will be used to examine how human cognition, and especially the human tendency to close cognition when exposed to complexity,[14] negatively affects the intelligence cycle through a destructive reduction of discourse in intelligence communities and between these communities and society at large. Classic cases of intelligence failure will be used to examine whether the problem of induction has created a restricted language in intelligence communities that limits threat perception, and thus decreases perception and acknowledgement of threats that occur in new variations. The existing literature will be analysed against the 9/11 Commission Report, the House-Senate Joint Inquiry (Joint Inquiry) as well as against existing literature on 9/11. The reports will be examined for empirical data to critically substantiate the hypothesis of this book.

High-quality intelligence hence probes beyond the limits set by induction. It seeks to estimate the potential variations of past threats the future may emerge in. The 2004 Butler Report states:

> A hidden limitation of intelligence is its inability to transform a mystery into a secret. In principle, intelligence can be expected to uncover secrets. The enemy's order of battle may not be known, but it is knowable. The enemy's intentions may not be known, but they too are knowable. But mysteries are essentially unknowable: what a leader truly believes, or what his reaction would be in certain circumstances, cannot be known, but can only be judged.[15]

The Butler Report, which reviewed the use of intelligence pertaining to Weapons of Mass Destruction before the Iraq war, by this draws attention to the hidden limitation of intelligence, and thus to the true character of intelligence. Intelligence is essentially a qualified judgement and elucidation[16] of how the future may occur under specific circumstances. This undoubtedly makes the essence of intelligence fundamentally different from traditional intelligence analysis, since the latter is based on a formal, inductive, logical approach, that is: 'the general science of inference . . . in which a conclusion follows from a set of premises . . . [or] the way in which premises may support a conclusion without entailing it'.[17] Classic inductive intelligence analysis and its limitations therefore constitute a profound challenge to intelligence that needs to be evaluated and understood.

Woodrow Kuhns clarifies this challenge in emphasising that it is the formal inductive approach in intelligence analysis that is the problem.[18] He suggests that an opponent's belief, or his or her reaction to certain circumstances, cannot be understood through the inductive approach because the future does not necessarily need to be derived from history; this is because 'the future will be in part like the past and in part not at all like the past'.[19] The future can therefore not be predicted by using induction alone, simply because induction confirms only itself, and using it to foresee the future would therefore be the same as 'proving logic by logic'.[20] The inductive approach thus brings intelligence into a circular trap, and threats that occur in new variations are hence challenging or, at worst, impossible to foresee. Critical intelligence probing beyond the limits of formal reasoning is therefore the answer to the problem of induction, and intelligence should hereafter be understood as the art of *knowing beyond the limits of formal reasoning through the use of wise qualified judgement and elucidation*. Elucidation should be understood thus: 'the activity of analysis and assessment, throwing light on the underlying meaning behind the information that has been assessed'.[21]

However, this explanation of intelligence requires evaluation and it may be enlightening to look at the limitations of intelligence, since understanding a phenomenon's limitations also reveals its strengths and capabilities. In the following analysis, therefore, it will be essential to look at these limitations, and thus uncover the strength of intelligence as an art.

Intelligence analysis can be divided into three different but coinciding approaches: unveiling puzzles (secrets), understanding mysteries and comprehending complexities.[22] 'A secret is best thought of as information that exists, although it may be carefully hidden and protected, but which at least in theory is capable of being found out by an effective intelligence agency.'[23] Mysteries, however, are futuristic, and pertain to potential political, strategic or tactical moves that the adversary may consider. Though they have not yet materialised as events, they exist in the minds of opponents: accordingly, they consist of 'highly desirable information concerning intentions not yet crystallized into decisions or predictions of the outcome of events that have not yet taken place'.[24] Mysteries thus exist outside the realm of inductive inference which presupposes a logical conjecture between actual historical events and the future. This also sheds more light on the problem of induction which argues 'that any experience shows us only events occurring within a very restricted part of the vast spatial and temporal order about which we then come to believe things'.[25] Intelligence analysis which presupposes a rational belief in an automatic, logical inference between history and the future is thus highly problematic. However, the difference between secrets and mysteries, and whether an intelligence service chooses to focus on one or both, has implications for the way in which intelligence should be understood.

Gregory F. Treverton states that 'puzzles [secrets] have already happened'.[26] He also highlights that puzzles are '*known problems*, for which there is a unique relationship between causes and effects'.[27] This implies that secrets can be understood using classic analysis and are therefore not influenced by the problem of induction. Nonetheless, any conclusions premised on a blind belief in an automatic inference between secrets (history and present) and the future is invalid. Unveiling merely secrets hence limits intelligence production, since estimation, the essence of intelligence, presupposes an understanding of mysteries enabling judgement beyond the borders set by induction.

The thesis in this book will therefore be based on the acknowledgement of intelligence as the art of estimation *beyond* formal reasoning and secrets. Nonetheless, understanding mysteries is impossible without unveiling secrets, and the following analysis will therefore be based on the presumption that intelligence must both unveil secrets and understand mysteries to be able to make uncertain estimates less uncertain.

Treverton also emphasises that complexities are the third analytical intelligence issue. He highlights that they appear as *'mysteries-plus*, involving a wide array of causes and effects that can interact in a variety of contingent ways'.[28] This book, however, argues that mysteries will always involve complex variations of causes and effects: indeed, the term *mysteries-plus* is unhelpful and often confusing, since mysteries do not become less complex just because complexities are defined as more complex mysteries. The danger of such an understanding of mysteries is that it creates an understanding based on the assumption that mysteries can be understood mathematically if they are characterised as less complex than they are. Mysteries are therefore complex, regardless of the variations in which these complexities appear. This book therefore challenges the belief that mysteries can be understood using classic inductive intelligence analysis, and accordingly contests that mysteries only 'involve contingent relationships between a limited set of causes and effects'.[29] Mysteries should hence be understood as infinitely complex.

However, complexities are helpful for a deeper understanding of intelligence, if the phenomenon is perceived in accordance to Sherman Kent's explanation of intelligence:

> Then there is about it an extension in subtlety, for some of the problems having to do with national survival involve long-range speculations on the strength and intentions of other states, involve estimates of their probable responses to acts which we ourselves plan to initiate.[30]

R. V. Jones echoes Kent convincingly when he emphasises that 'it is almost as dangerous to concentrate entirely on the immediate and thereby prejudice the future by failing to anticipate new developments, as it is to concentrate on the future and ignore the immediate'.[31] Secrets are hence related to everything that has happened and happens. Mysteries are linked to everything we estimate might happen in the future, and complexities entail how the actions of intelligence producers and decision-makers might affect the counter-action of adversaries.

Understanding mysteries as categories that can be mapped and categorised mathematically implicitly illustrates a stringent belief in game theory. Game theory presupposes that the world can be understood as 'situations in which two or more players have a choice of decisions (strategies); where the outcome depends on all the strategies; and where each player has a set of preferences defined over the outcomes'.[32] Such an understanding of intelligence is limited, since its restrictive, mathematical categorising only increases the problem of induction. Intelligence analysis must therefore always be based on the perception that the problems it tries to understand are limitless in nature, since the future may occur in infinite variations, regardless of the way in which intelligence analysts choose to map and categorise them. Nonetheless, this study acknowledges that it is impossible for humans to perceive this infinity, and that analysis will always cover only a limited part of a limitless puzzle that appears to us as mysteries. It is therefore important for intelligence *not* to be understood as a mechanical, mathematical process capable of unveiling mysteries just by categorising them as less complex than they are. Intelligence mysteries must therefore always be understood as complex and infinite, but this does not mean that they cannot be understood. It means only that they are much more challenging to understand than secrets, and that they cannot be understood using classic inductive intelligence analysis.

It is clear that classical intelligence analysis based on induction decreases adequate threat perception because the methods used are based on a belief that a formal logical inference exists between the conclusion and historical precedents. Such an approach is restrictive and reductive, since the methods are unable to detect and identify threats occuring in new variations and hence outside of the inductive premises.

The future never copies the past: but it will often arise similarly.[33] The future will therefore always be both similar and, simultaneously, different to the past. Intelligence institutions must therefore seek to foresee possible contextual threat combinations, and it is this duality that intelligence institutions should attempt to understand and elucidate.

Intelligence is therefore the art of identifying the similarities and differences between the past and the future, and as such the ability to judge and elucidate how classical threats may occur in new contextual variations. For this reason, intelligence is the art of judging and elucidating the 'similar differences, and different similarities'[34] of possible new threat variations; intelligence institutions must thus strive to understand similar differences in threat structures and their different similarities; this entails seeking to identify what makes threats universal, and what makes these universal threats individually unique.

It is when intelligence institutions are able to identify the relation between similar differences and different similarities in threat structures that threats occurring in new variations can be detected and understood: this is the quintessence of the art of intelligence. However, the problem of induction reduces this ability, inasmuch as induction, through its self-referring approach, is unable to detect new variations between differences and similarities in threat structures. This negatively shapes the intelligence discourse and leads to discourse failure.

The intelligence discourse encapsulates the way in which language and communication in intelligence institutions and intelligence communities shape threat perception.[35] Discourse failure must therefore be understood as a reduced capacity and reduced willingness to understand, accept and communicate existing and potential threats, because the reduced and restricted language caused by induction reduces one's capacity to comprehend the wholeness and complexity of threat structures. It is therefore important to explore how discourse failure and its relation to the problem of induction decrease adequate threat perception through the limitation and reduction of the level of precision and scope of the discourse in and between intelligence institutions, and between the intelligence institutions and their consumers.

Furthermore, it will be argued that discourse is additionally reduced by what should be understood as intelligence tribal language and the level of secrecy in intelligence communities.

As a result of the above and for the purpose of analysis, intelligence institutions, intelligence operators and their consumers should focus on and be conscious of the following:

If we want to prevent another 9/11, we need to become aware of the ideological prisms through which every one of us filters reality. Inevitably, this process starts with ourselves: we all need to become more honest in questioning our own political assumptions and orthodoxies.[36]

In this quote, Peter Neumann and M. L. R. Smith attend to the human and hence mental landscape of intelligence, and thereby capture the quintessence of this book. Their discourse failure theory highlights the difficulties and profound challenges which are strongly linked to intelligence work, thereby illustrating the failure 'to identify, analyze, and accept that a significant threat [exists]'.[37] Neumann and Smith thus elucidate the significance of discourse in intelligence work, and David Bohm's illumination of healthy and progressive dialogue helps clarify the essence of enriching discourse:

Thus, in a dialogue, each person does not attempt to *make common* certain ideas or items of information that are already known to him. Rather, it may be said that the two people are making something *in common*, i.e., creating something new together.[38]

Enriching discourse, then, is progressive and allows educational communication between humans in which something new is created. Discourse probes into human cognition and its relation to intelligence failure. Many scholars have studied this relationship, arguing that the main reasons for intelligence failure are to be found in the human propensity for epistemic failure.[39] Nonetheless, the explicit relation between the problem of induction, human cognition, secrecy, intelligence tribal language and intelligence failure has drawn limited academic interest and constitutes a gap in the literature of intelligence studies.

This book aims to bridge this gap by examining the cognitive processes through which reality is filtered, and their relation to notions of discourse failure. The study explicitly attempts to explore how the nature of complex and constantly changing threats increases discourse failure through a negative relation and through the interplay between the problem of induction, human cognition, secrecy and intelligence tribal language. For analytical purposes, human cognition should be understood as the critical 'processing of experience, perception, and memory, as well as overtly verbal thinking'.[40]

The Scope of the Analysis

For the purpose of analysis, attention will be paid to three main areas. First, focus will be given to the capabilities and limitations of human cognition constituted as the problem of induction, examining the cognitive impact on discourse failure and its consequence for intelligence production. The analysis will study whether a recontextualisation of Bohm's theory of creativity and Karl Popper's principle of falsification and critical rationalism, if fused with Michael Oakeshott's critique of rationalism in politics, can help intelligence organisations comprehend that discourse failure may occur because 'the Rationalist never doubts the power of his "reason" (when properly applied) to determine the worth of a thing, the truth of an opinion or the property of an action'.[41] Rationalism thus leads to the negative triumph of reason over imagination, and makes it challenging for the rationalist to identify and accept change. It is this comprehension of the weakness of rationalism that constitutes critical rationalism, since a critical mind that does conduct critical rationalism acknowledges that 'changes are circumstances to which we have to accommodate ourselves'.[42] This understanding of the workings of a critical mind may decrease the problem of induction and discourse failure, since a critical mind in Popper's and Oakeshott's thinking does not accept habit and prejudice.[43]

A critical mind and critical rationalism would hence increase analysts' focus on imagination and creativity, and would accordingly minimise discourse failure. Critical rationalism should therefore be understood as critical induction.

Second, there is the challenge of secrecy, which creates a strong paradox for secret organisations tasked with understanding and comprehending complexity. Complexity, one would contend, presupposes healthy discourse and communication between intelligence analysts in order to be perceived and acknowledged holistically. Accordingly, how and whether secrecy influences and negatively shapes discourse in intelligence organisations will be evaluated. The book aims to demonstrate that because humans are essentially social beings, secrecy is largely alien to the human personality. Secrecy may therefore decrease imagination, creativity, discourse and, consequently, threat perception. Nevertheless, secrecy is the main and necessary characteristic of intelligence. This is because 'spying can be dangerous, unappealing, shifty and profound. It must be kept secret.'[44]

Intelligence is dangerous because it seeks to unveil secrets and understand mysteries that adversaries will do their utmost to protect, and one should therefore understand *secret intelligence* as intelligence that others are seeking to prevent you knowing, often with formidable security barriers and violent sanctions against those who cooperate with intelligence officers'.[45] Secrecy is therefore necessary.

The paradox that secrecy creates for intelligence organisations also creates another challenge related to selection and recruitment. Secrecy and the understanding and assumptions most people have of intelligence work do not necessarily attract the people that intelligence organisations need. It will be argued that someone who is attracted to secrecy, psychological dualism and mind games, is unlikely to be a persona that readily increases discourse.

This implicitly suggests that intelligence organisations are threatened by those who are attracted to what intelligence should not be.

Third, there is the problem and challenge of intelligence tribal language (an internal system language which has a kind of self-reference, meaning that it can be understood only by those who belong to the organisation using it). Eric Fromm suggests that humans have a desire for power as well as a lust for submission, and that these conditions create a deep fear of freedom.[46] It will be explored whether the interplay of these two cognitively destructive desires creates a climate for intelligence tribal language, which consequently restricts discourse and understanding.

The book seeks to analyse whether whole, imaginary and creative discourse may pose a threat to the deep human desire to resist enlightenment, and hence provide infertile soil for a self-protective intelligence tribal language.

The complexity of these three main areas and their interaction shape the thesis of this book, and the analysis aims to demonstrate how they force intelligence organisations and intelligence production into a kind of self-destructive spiral.

The Structure and Chapter Division

The book will be divided into three main parts. Part 1 consists of two chapters. Chapter 1 conceptually describes and analyses human cognition, and will aim to demonstrate that human cognition is complicated, subtle and intricate, and therefore impossible to fully comprehend. It will be argued that imagination and creativity are the two most important constituent factors in cognition. Imagination and creativity increase cognition and create a positive environment for discourse between intelligence operators, and between intelligence organisations, consumers and society at large. Intelligence organisations are trying to predict the future, an inherently challenging activity.

It will be argued that prediction can only be achieved if intelligence organisations cultivate an environment and a culture where imagination and creativity may flourish, and where operators attempt to be critically rational and where hypotheses can be falsified rather than verified. This book therefore emphasises that induction alone does not offer certainty to cognition and, consequently, does not provide certainty to intelligence production because induction without critical rationalism is limiting to thinking,[47] inasmuch as logic cannot describe holistic phenomena. Simon Blackburn clarifies this in emphasising that 'concepts gain their identity not so much through internal structure, as through their place in a larger theory or network of doctrines and practices with which they are associated'.[48]

Predicting the future hence implies that intelligence organisations should try to comprehend the world holistically and therefore assess the 'strength and intentions of other states, involve estimates of their probable responses to acts which we ourselves plan to initiate'.[49] An environment based on attentiveness, alertness, awareness and sensitivity[50] would have to be sophisticated to achieve this.

Openness and space for individuality and diversity are crucial to organisations seeking to achieve such objectives,[51] and it is important in this respect to attempt to understand why imagination and creativity so easily seem to decrease in intelligence organisations. The book will explore whether a lack of openness and decreased room for individuality, combined with habits and routines, decrease cognition and thus also reduce discourse and rational self-criticism of the mind. The chapter concludes by demonstrating how a re-contextualising of Bohm's theory on creativity and Popper's principle of falsification, if fused with Oakeshott's critique of rationalism in politics, may increase intelligence institutions' consciousness of the problem of induction, and as such help diminish discourse failure.

In Chapter 2, intelligence, intelligence failure in general and discourse failure in particular will be described and analysed. For the purpose of analysis, attention will be given to the interaction of these three factors. Human cognitive capacity and its limitations and possibilities for intelligence will be analysed, and classical intelligence failures and their relation to notions of discourse failure will be conceptually examined.

Intelligence and intelligence failure can neither be understood nor described without a deep comprehension of threat perception and the substantial nature of threats. The examination of intelligence, intelligence failure and discourse failure will therefore be analysed and weighed up against the nature of threats, and threat perception as such. Intelligence will be described fourfold,[52] and the chapter seeks to examine why and how intelligence activity increases the need for cognitive closure. Chapter 2 will end with a presentation of the way in which intelligence can be better understood through twelve images existing among the phenomenon, method and science on the one hand, and the subject matter, product, activity and function of intelligence on the other.

Part 2 will conceptually and reflectively analyse the challenges and problems related to secrecy and intelligence tribal language. Part 2 consists of one chapter – Chapter 3 – which analyses secrecy and describes and explores the negative impact of secrecy on imagination, creativity and discourse in intelligence organisations. It also explores intelligence tribal language and aims to demonstrate that misunderstood secrecy and cognitive closure decrease imagination, creativity and, consequently, discourse. This cultivates an environment that increases the possibilities for dualism and psychological mind games. The negative consequence of this environment may emerge as intelligence tribal language that decreases critical rationalism and creativity. Decreased imagination, creativity, critical rationalism and discourse increase insecurity in operators and between intelligence organisations and the intelligence consumers, and the book explores here whether and to what extent these factors decrease threat perception.

Part 3 is divided into Chapters 4 to 7. The problem of induction, the nature of threats, human cognition, intelligence tribal language and secrecy, and their impact on discourse failure are analysed against the specific factors in the intelligence cycle. This cycle involves collection, analysis, dissemination and action/decision by the intelligence consumer.[53]

The assessment contained in these chapters uses the case of the 9/11 attacks on the United States as a demonstrative case study.

The Literature on the Relationship between Human Cognition and Intelligence Failure

This book examines the ideological prisms through which reality is filtered. The study will be based on the following notion:

> Intelligence needs to move beyond 'established' practice to become an authentic profession. To do that, it needs to find ways to open itself to and ultimately embrace the importance of empirical studies and methodical self-reflection – not as a peripheral matter but rather in the essential interest of intelligence itself.[54]

The book hence seeks to move beyond classic intelligence studies. It challenges established views on intelligence, and argues that intelligence failures can be reduced when intelligence is properly understood, and when this understanding is integrated with an acknowledgement of the way in which human nature shapes the nature of intelligence practice. Jennifer Sims illustrates below the importance of a positive relation between intelligence theory and the adequate perception of intelligence failure and success:

> One fundamental premise is that intelligence cannot usefully be reformed without a good grasp of the theory behind what intelligence is or should be about. Good theory helps one understand causation and thus should, in the intelligence context, help identify the sources of success and failure before they occur.[55]

Good intelligence theory should thus reflect the relation between human capabilities and fallibilities, and their impact on intelligence failure and success, since humans are the most important resource of intelligence organisations and also their weakest link. Predicting and understanding the future are the inherent tasks of an intelligence service, and are undoubtedly among the most difficult and challenging human endeavours today. Intelligence employees face the daily challenge of analysing developments in an extremely complex world.[56] This complexity is increased because intelligence organisations also seek to comprehend cultures and societies that are fundamentally dissimilar to their own. Not only do intelligence operators need to comprehend dissimilarities between cultures, they also need to comprehend and be aware of the complexity of the world more generally, a complexity that no doubt exceeds the human cognitive capacity. Intelligence operators are therefore exposed to a challenge, which is explained by Popper:

> The reason why all description is selective is, roughly speaking, the infinite wealth and variety of the possible aspects of the facts of our world. In order to describe this infinite wealth, we have at our disposal only a finite number of finite series of words.[57]

The disparities and the multiplicity of the 'possible aspects of the facts of our world'[58] are additionally amplified by the dissimilarities between cultures. Because comprehending the world is complicated and challenging, and humans arguably have cognitive limitations to process this complexity, one has to be more aware and critical of what one perceives and how this complexity is perceived. One has to ask where the main challenge to human comprehension of the world is to be found. Ludwig Wittgenstein highlights this, asking:

> 'What is a question?' – Is it the statement that I do not know such-and-such, or the statement that I wish the other person would tell me . . . ? Or is it the description of my mental state of uncertainty? – And is the cry 'Help!' such a description?[59]

This book argues that the mental state of uncertainty, and the substantial human need for 'help' to deal with this uncertainty, constitutes the most challenging factor that negatively affects intelligence production and intelligence institutions today. Furthermore, it aims to demonstrate that this substantial human weakness shapes human action and interaction, and consequently intelligence production, and constitutes intelligence failure.

'An intelligence failure is essentially a misunderstanding of the situation that leads a government (or its military forces) to take actions that are inappropriate and counterproductive to its own interests.'[60] Scholars such as Michael Herman, Neumann, Smith, Kuhns, Richards J. Heuer, Uri Bar-Joseph, George Friedman, Michael Handel, Abraham Shulsky, Gary J. Schmitt, James J. Wirtz, Michael A. Turner and Walter Laqueur all emphasise that intelligence is a human cognitive product. They implicitly suggest that the reason for intelligence failure is to be found in human cognitive propensities. However, few scholars have analysed the impact of the relation between the problem of induction, human cognition, intelligence tribal language and secrecy, and the impact of this relation on discourse failure and intelligence production. However, Kuhns has drawn attention to the important relation between epistemology and forecasting in his work on the negative relation between the problem of induction and intelligence analysis. In this he asks whether there is 'an epistemological or methodological reason that these [intelligence] failures occur?'[61]

Kuhns' contribution to the study of intelligence failure has been invaluable. Nevertheless, he does not evaluate whether and how the possible relation between the problem of induction and fore-casting shapes the intelligence tribal language, and consequently the intelligence discourse. That said, Neumann's, Smith's and Heuer's works elucidate the important link between the weakness in human cognition and intelligence production. Heuer demon-strates this link in emphasising the following: 'because of limits in human mental capacity, he [Herbert Simon] argued, the mind cannot cope directly with the complexity of the world. Rather, we construct a simplified mental model of reality and then work with this model.'[62]

However, although scholars have studied intelligence failure deeply,[63] and some, such as Neuman, Smith, Heuer and Kuhns, have detected the relation between human cognitive propensities to failure and its notion to intelligence failure, it still seems to be challenging to use this knowledge to improve intelligence, and diminish intelligence failures. This problem therefore needs more analysis.

As Richard Betts has emphasised: 'development of a normative theory of intelligence has been inhibited because lessons of hind-sight do not guarantee improvement in foresight, and hypotheti-cal solutions to failure only occasionally produce improvement in practice'.[64] Betts thereby illustrates two of the most important hindrances to the improvement of intelligence. The first is that no good, generic understanding of what intelligence essentially is exists, and the second follows from the first, and is the orthodox focus on hindsight, and a form of hindsight that often focuses on organisational explanations, explanations that seem not to 'mea-surably reduce failure'.[65]

All this suggests that because intelligence is not properly under-stood and defined, it becomes challenging to evaluate when intel-ligence fails and why. This is because 'there are no clear indicators of what the ratio of failure to success in intelligence is'.[66] The explanation for this challenge also reveals how it can be solved, since 'theories are critical for metrics because intelligence failures are a result of failed theories'.[67] One should therefore explore why no theory of intelligence exists, and what the consequences are for the understanding of intelligence in general, and for a deeper understanding of intelligence and discourse failure as such.

First, let it be clear that this book will not suggest that intelligence failure can be eliminated. It is the contention, nevertheless, that intelligence failure can be further understood and hence reduced. Nonetheless, this understanding is only possible if one understands intelligence; that intelligence is reciprocal, and does not exist in a vacuum; that opponents will do what they can to deceive their counterparts; that they will do their utmost to win, and intelligence institutions should therefore accept that they may lose from time to time, and as such have an inherent 'tolerance for disaster'.[68]

The effect of such an understanding is that intelligence must not, under any circumstances, be understood as mere facts. Intelligence operates in uncertainty, and the institutions operate against similar counterparts. The information that is presented to the intelligence consumer should thus be understood as uncertain estimates that are made less uncertain through the intelligence production process.[69] However, this does not lend more clarity as to why the wholeness of intelligence is so difficult to understand, and what the consequences have been for intelligence activity and the understanding of intelligence failure.

Michael Warner at the Office of the Director of National Intelligence in the US emphasises that one needs a definition before one can 'derive a theory'.[70] He continues, saying that 'intelligence means many things to many people'.[71] Warner thereby highlights the complexity of intelligence. It is a phenomenon that covers many aspects of human cognition as well as many parts of both social and public life in a society. As such it becomes difficult to define, and intelligence must thus be understood through its holistic complexity. Even so, this complexity must be comprehended in the wholeness in which it operates. The complexity can certainly and consequently be understood, and it is when this holistic complexity is understood that intelligence can be properly comprehended and acknowledged.

The argument in this book is therefore based on the notion that complexity presupposes wholeness, since wholeness cannot be understood without understanding the parts on which it is constructed, and that these parts in their complexity cannot be understood if the wholeness they construct is not acknowledged. It is from this viewpoint that intelligence must be approached. One must understand the small and constructive parts of intelligence in their overall complexity, and the relation between the overall complexity and the parts on which they are built. It is therefore the complexity of intelligence and the wholeness in which it operates that needs to be examined towards a deeper comprehension of intelligence.

Based on the above, it might be argued that Warner is right in emphasising that it is difficult to define intelligence because intelligence means so many things to so many people. But he errs in claiming that one needs a definition to develop a theory, and this affects the rest of his argument. A definition of anything initially presupposes a clear understanding of the phenomenon or the thing defined, and Warner seems to suggest that a theory can only be established when the phenomenon has been defined. This book counters this argument, arguing that a definition can first be established when an idea and a phenomenon is properly understood. That said, it is clear that one often needs to experiment with many definitions. These definitions, as hypotheses, need to be tested, and it is only when sufficient tests have been conducted on enough hypothetical definitions that one can conclude that this specific definition seems to elucidate the acknowledgment of the idea of intelligence.

This implies that a definition is impossible to make of anything unless a deeply rooted idea and a theory of what a specific phenomenon is exists. This implies that Warner's argument of a negative interplay between different opinions about intelligence and difficulties to define it is weak, since the confusion between different intelligence scholars and practitioners is arguably caused by the lack of understanding and definition in the first place.

Intelligence is therefore not difficult to understand or define because scholars and practitioners disagree, but because they do not know what they disagree about.

A proper discussion of the understanding of intelligence in general, and intelligence theory, should therefore start with a clarification of why intelligence exists in the first place, and what the idea of intelligence is essentially. Peter Gill poses the salient question: 'What is the point?'[72] He continues: 'a good theory *of intelligence* should, by definition, be useful *for intelligence*'.[73] This means that the theory must be useful for practitioners and consumers. It must encapsulate the complexity and wholeness of intelligence, and as such elucidate why it exists, how it is conducted and, most importantly, the interests that intelligence serves.

The RAND Corporation's Workshop Report on Intelligence Theory concludes 'that a good definition is a prerequisite for a good theory, as well as for comparative study . . . [but also states that] the definitions offered ranged from the discursive to the terse'.[74] This undoubtedly demonstrates that RAND's conclusion is challenging, and the diversity which exists concerning the way in which intelligence should be defined supports this viewpoint. One must first discuss and agree about why intelligence in general exists, what kind of role it consequently serves or should serve, and how it is to be conducted to serve this role before attempting to define intelligence.

Kevin O'Connell emphasizes that 'The United States has been obsessed with data, and that has come at the expense of judgment. Rather than maintaining the ideal of speaking the truth to power, intelligence has focused on gathering information.'[75] This has no doubt shaped an intelligence community which in the US and Europe has been characterised by its focus on collection. O'Connell continues and describes how this focus on collection has resulted in an overemphasis on data: as a result, a 'temptation to turn mysteries into puzzles, with the presumption that all the pieces can be found'[76] has emerged. Thus, the US Intelligence Community may understand intelligence as omniscient.[77]

This misunderstanding of intelligence is harmful, since it fails to comprehend the weaknesses of intelligence. Any organisation that does not understand its own limitations and weaknesses is not only a danger to itself, but more importantly a danger to those it serves. This also explains why intelligence failure has been so challenging to understand and to explain, since it is difficult to understand failure in an environment in which there is an understanding of intelligence as persistent omniscience. One therefore needs to ask how intelligence should be understood.

20

How Intelligence Should Be Understood

The argument above illustrates that intelligence failure is not properly understood because intelligence is inaccurately perceived and, consequently, inadequately defined: but how should intelligence be understood? Sun Tzu offers a straightforward, helpful philosophy here: the way to victory is ensured because the achievements of the enlightened prince and the wise general presuppose that their forms of knowledge 'surpass those of ordinary men [because they are based on] foreknowledge'.[78]

The Secret and Reciprocal Nature of Intelligence

This Chinese war philosophy thereby highlights the reciprocal nature of intelligence. Intelligence is not linked only to the production of knowledge, but more importantly to the production of knowledge that needs to surpass the knowledge of one's adversary. Intelligence needs to be kept secret, simply because the power of intelligence knowledge will be diminished or, at worst, vanish if the adversary knows what the opponent knows or does not know. As Sims has stated:

> . . . *intelligence necessarily involves secrecy.* This assumption is important because it implies that the most important information about our adversaries is secret and must be stolen.[79]

This introduces the fact that intelligence is the art of knowing the current and possible strengths and capabilities of the adversary; but there is more to intelligence than this, and Ernest R. May is helpful in stating the following:

> Alas, two intelligence successes of note, those by the Germans of 1940 and al Qaeda in 2001, have been accomplished by people we would have preferred to see fail. The two share one common theme: They both understood their adversary's vulnerabilities.[80]

May differs from most intelligence scholars in that he asks why the enemy succeeded, instead of asking why the US intelligence community failed. He thereby acknowledges the reciprocal nature of intelligence, and its complexity. His approach to intelligence failure also reveals that he possesses a deeper understanding of the complexity and wholeness of intelligence than is usual in intelligence studies. He understands the interplay that develops between those who will do their utmost to know, and others who will do their utmost to conceal the knowledge, which they deem others wish to possess. This implies that intelligence gathering and the intelligence product must be kept secret, but it also introduces another factor shaping the essence of intelligence:

The Importance of Imagination

The complex, holistic and reciprocal nature between adversaries presupposes imagination, and one constantly needs to ask 'what if?' This should by no means be new to officers. Army officers, for example, have always been trained to ask: what if the enemy is doing this or that? Excellent army officers have hence always been good at understanding their enemies and have planned their operations accordingly. May elucidates the importance of foresight and imagination in stating the following:

> Asking these 'what ifs' needs to be done regularly and routinely in all steps of military and political planning. It was done on a regular basis during the cold war, a practice that needs to be reinstituted.[81]

It has now been demonstrated that the essence of intelligence is its predictive and imaginary character. However, intelligence should not of course be unfocused and based on fantasy, creativity and imagination alone. It must be shaped by the goals of the intelligence consumers.

The Close Relationship to State Power

Ideally, intelligence should be driven by political priorities, though not politicised. Intelligence activity should therefore be managed and directed with a clear focus but without any direct interference from the intelligence consumer. The intelligence consumer should only communicate intelligence needs and make political priorities that form the basis of intelligence requirements and priorities. Intelligence must therefore serve political objectives indirectly through its status as an objective, knowledgeable servant of the state. Intelligence services thus provide decision-making support to decision-makers. This support should be based on the intelligence needs and priorities voiced by the intelligence consumer or decision-maker, but it must also be based on creativity and imagination, since the intelligence service has a responsibility to protect the state: as a result, it also should communicate to the intelligence consumer what the consumer should focus on. Intelligence institutions should therefore not only try to understand and communicate existing threats to the state, but also estimate and foresee possible prospective threats. It is only when the intelligence producer is able to perform this advisory role as well that the intelligence institution can call itself an adequate intelligence service.

The Service Role of Intelligence

Based on the arguments presented above, one might argue that intelligence services are services because they perform duties that protect the state. They are meant to do a job and perform duties that no one else can or should do, because these duties potentially imply a deep insight into the secrets of the state, and because they presuppose the use of techniques and methods that can reduce the freedom of the members of the state that the intelligence services are meant to protect.

The service role of intelligence and its necessarily secret character thus constitute the specialness of intelligence. Philip H. Davies illustrates the essence of this specialness in stating that 'governments do not need intelligence agencies to read newspapers, journals, or the like'.[82] Politicians, generals and other state operatives can read newspapers themselves. They can watch television, and they can search on the internet. Intelligence services, however, exist to obtain the knowledge that is unavailable without using the methods of Signals Intelligence (Sigint), Human Intelligence (Humint), Open Source Intelligence (Osint) and Geographical Intelligence (Imint). This introduces:

The Specialness of Intelligence

Arguably, however, the argument presented above does not reflect reality, since, 'according to most estimates, about 90 percent of the information used in intelligence analysis today comes from open sources'.[83] But what does that mean? Does this imply that analysts collect the data from the internet? Does this mean that analysts read newspapers and then use what they find in their analysis? One would hope not, and it is probably not so. Open-source intelligence is not called 'open source' because it is collected randomly and in the open, but because it is collected from open sources. But the actual collection is not open. Moreover, the internet is also reciprocal: the adversary is also on the net, attempting to track opponents. Consequently, it is as important here, as indeed it is everywhere where intelligence organisations operate, to hide the tracks made by collection. An intelligence service should do its utmost to protect its objectives, methods, sources and capacities. Nonetheless, open sources are not in themselves enough. It is when this information can be confirmed and acknowledged by human intelligence, signals intelligence and geographical intelligence that intelligence reaches its true potential, as 'covertly gathered information may "add value"'[84] to intelligence. It is therefore the relative outcome between different types of data and information, openly and clandestinely collected, that shapes good intelligence. But there is always a danger that clandestinely collected data of potential intelligence value will overshadow the importance of data collected from open sources. At worst, the result may be as described by Sims:

> Focusing on clandestine collection diminishes the perceived value of technologies related to processing and exploitation, which are regarded as more mundane and thus less critical to the enterprise. There is also an analytical bias toward intelligence that comes with higher classification.[85]

The conclusion to draw based on these challenges should be that a high-quality intelligence institution should focus on both clandestine and open methods and sources. It should search for the information where it exists. Whether this is from the internet or from a human source is unimportant, since it is the fused product that counts. Good intelligence is collected from different and multiple sources. It is quality-assured, confirmed and tested. Intelligence should accordingly and principally never be based on a single source, but on a wide range of sources, be they technical or human. This is to ensure that intelligence services do not nurture and focus solely on secrecy and its clandestine character, a danger that at worst may lead to an introvert culture with a reduced ability to predict adequately what may occur in the future. Sims is again instructive in emphasising the following:

> The more secret some piece of information is, the 'better' and thus the weightier it is assumed to be. After all, what is harder to get must have been more 'hidden' by the adversary and thus more crucial to understanding the threat. This is wrongheaded. The sensitivity of the collection method, a key determinant of classification, does not necessarily correlate with the quality of the product. Assuming that good intelligence involves information collected principally through secret means renders the United States particularly vulnerable to manipulation and deception.[86]

This illustrates that the factors that have been discussed and analysed above – the necessarily secret character of intelligence, the importance of imagination, the reciprocal nature, the close relationship to state power, and the service role and specialness of intelligence – start revealing the true essence of intelligence. But there is more to it than this. One also needs to evaluate the producer/consumer relationship more closely, since the way it is understood and performed undoubtedly shapes intelligence. Sims argues that one:

> . . . implication here is that the decisionmaker is not part of the process, but rather a master to be served. In fact, decisionmakers must play a role in identifying critical policy decisions that require intelligence support, informing collectors of the pace of policy and requirements for timeliness, and providing feedback on where intelligence is helping and where it needs improvement. Decisionmakers must be educated to their role in the intelligence process and assume their share of responsibility for both its successes and failures.[87]

The Producer/Consumer Relationship

This book will argue that decision-makers undoubtedly are and should be a part of the intelligence process, but that they should not be directly involved in the production of intelligence. That does not imply that they should be on the outside, and passively receive the finished product. It is their needs which shape and focus intelligence collection, processing and analysis. A close, intimate relationship between policymakers and the intelligence producer is therefore called for. It can certainly be claimed that this sort of close relationship may easily lead to the politicising of intelligence. But that can be countered by arguing that it is precisely this close relationship, based on a mutual understanding of concepts, methods and limitations, that reduces the danger of politicising and intelligence failures.

The relationship between the decision-maker and the intelligence producer is hence the last factor that should form a theory of intelligence, and I will in the following analyse the characteristics of a good intelligence theory.

The Characteristics of a Good Intelligence Theory

Bohm states that the:

> word 'theory' . . . has the same root as 'theater,' in a verb meaning 'to view' or 'to make a spectacle.' This suggests that the theory is to be regarded primarily as a way of looking at the world through the mind, so that it is a form of insight (and not a form of knowledge of what the world is).[88]

Intelligence theory should therefore be an insightful cognitive perception and presentation of the spectacle of what intelligence essentially is, and Bohm's explanation supports the notion that a theory must exist before the theoretical concept can be encapsulated by a definition. Bohm's elucidation of a theory also illustrates that a theory is a restricted description of a specific understanding of a concept. This is because 'theories are ways of looking which are neither true nor false, but rather clear and fruitful in certain domains, and unclear and unfruitful when extended beyond these domains'.[89]

Theories on intelligence are therefore clear and fruitful if they are used to communicate an understanding of intelligence that is common to those who use the definition. Bohm's clarification of theories implicitly illustrates that theories are only clear and fruitful if they communicate certain, and thus restricted and limited, domains; in addition, those who perceive the theories through definitions must weigh up these definitions against the same and commonly understood theories. They hence become unclear and confusing when extended beyond their domains. This also implies that definitions of theories become unfruitful when they are used to explain domains that exist beyond the borders of the domains that the theory explains.

Definitions of intelligence are thus unclear and unfruitful if they are used to explain factors that exist beyond the theoretical understanding of intelligence, and when such an understanding does not exist, or in a situation where one definition is being used to explain different theoretical schools.

It is therefore essential for there to exist a common understanding of intelligence, and for this understanding to be used when attempting to explain and define intelligence. This book will argue that it is the absence of such a common appreciation of intelligence that has made it almost impossible to theorise on and define intelligence. But there is more to it than this. Intelligence covers a wide variety of concepts, and it is challenging to develop a theory that embraces and encapsulates this complex wholeness without creating confusion and misunderstanding.

It is the complexity created by a holistic phenomenon, limited theories and often confusing definitions that has made understanding intelligence difficult. This book will consequently attempt to bridge this gap, and present a theory of intelligence describing the complexity of intelligence as method and science, as well as appreciating the wholeness of the phenomenon as art. This theory will be presented and analysed in Chapter 2, but the thinking and philosophy that form the quintessence of the theory will, for the purpose of analysis, be presented below.

Intelligence as Method, Science and Art

It has now been established that intelligence is the art of knowing beyond the limits of formal reasoning. This explanation reflects the notion that intelligence is an art probing beyond classic analysis. It seeks to understand complex concepts and estimate the future. This is doubtless an activity existing outside of the classical borders of induction, and as such it is an activity existing between the

sciences and the arts. The essential character of intelligence therefore arises as result of, and between, intelligence as an art, science
and method. It is this fusion which creates the complex identity of
intelligence, and shapes its wholeness. This complexity undoubtedly evolves simultaneously with the complexity of human nature,
since 'human beings are much more complicated than atoms and it
will take us [long] to unravel the secrets of intelligence behavior'.[90]

The nature of intelligence is a fusion of science, art and method
because it seeks to understand secrets, mysteries and complexities.
Intelligence attempts to understand the actions of other humans
and, at best, predicts future actions. This would place intelligence
in the arts, since the future can only exist in the minds of humans,
and one might ask whether art can ever be defined or substantially
understood. Here, the understanding of the relationship between
the complexity and wholeness of intelligence becomes important,
and the thesis in this book will thus be based on the notion that
intelligence must be explained and understood both holistically
and through its complexity. Nonetheless, this alone does not provide any new insight into intelligence studies. This book will therefore present a theory of the nature of intelligence that encapsulates
and reflects the interplay between the wholeness of intelligence as
art, and the complexity of intelligence as art, science and method.
This implies that the theory is based on the notion that intelligence
is holistic in character, resulting from the interplay between intelligence as art, science and method, as well as from the individual
and complex interaction between these factors.

However, how can this interaction between wholeness and
complexity be analysed, explained and understood? The three
factors need to be weighed up against Herman's fourfold understanding of intelligence: intelligence as *activity, product, function and subject matter* (subjects).[91] It is in the interplay between
intelligence as art, science, method, activity, product, function
and subject matter that the following characteristic images of
intelligence evolve: *power, wisdom, service, intuition, truth, elucidation, objectivity, falsification and critical rationalism, cleverness, experience, staff function and collection*. These images
will be analysed and described in more detail in Chapter 2. The
twelve images and their relation to intelligence as phenomenon,

science, method, activity, product, function and subject matter are illustrated in Table I.1 below:

Table I.1 The Twelve Images of Intelligence

	Phenomenon	Science	Method
Subject Matter	Power	Truth	Cleverness
Product	Wisdom	Elucidation	Experience
Function	Service	Objectivity	Staff function
Activity	Intuition	Falsification Critical rationalism	Collection

This book will argue that it is when one understands the individual character of these images, and the way in which they interact in a complex interplay, that the wholeness of intelligence is disclosed and becomes understandable. When one comprehends this quintessential character, one may properly appreciate why intelligence is the art of knowing beyond the limits of induction, and this acknowledgement shapes and forms the basis for a new theory of intelligence.

The Lack of Intelligence Theory and the Originality of This Book

The lack of a general and common understanding of intelligence has undoubtedly increased the problem of induction and discourse failure, since a lack of understanding of concept and meaning may decrease the human ability to withdraw from an orthodox belief in a logical inference between history and future. This again has arguably shaped an intelligence culture that has hindered an adequate understanding of the nature of threats, and thus the ability to detect slowly changing threat structures.

A deeper understanding of intelligence as the art of knowing beyond the limits of formal reasoning would arguably reduce this problem, since this comprehension in itself opens up for imagination and creativity. It communicates that intelligence should constantly be on its toes; to change and surprise. Some scholars, and especially Handel, have studied the nature of surprise, and stated that 'procedural, analytical and methodological difficulties constitute only a small fraction of the problems involved in the intelligence estimation process'.[92] Handel thereby implicitly highlights that one needs to understand more than organisational challenges if one is seeking to understand intelligence failure. Handel's thinking has not only been important to the understanding of surprise; more importantly, it has shaped modern intelligence studies. Nevertheless, no theory of intelligence exists which probes to the essence of its nature, and, 'if we are to understand the relationship among intelligence, threat, and power, a consensus on what intelligence is and a terminology to describe its central characteristics is essential'.[93] The central characteristic of intelligence is that it is a cognitive activity. It is not only thinking, but it is highly sophisticated and critical thinking, and the relationship between human nature and intelligence therefore needs to be studied.

The originality in this book, therefore, lies in its attempt to evaluate, analyse and present an understanding of intelligence as a complex phenomenon that needs to be understood holistically. Existing theories on intelligence have not been advanced enough,[94] and this lack of a proper holistic theory, which describes the human factor in intelligence and its relation to secrecy and intelligence tribal language, has decreased the ability of intelligence scholars and professionals to reflect on intelligence as a predominantly cognitive activity.

Herman lends support to this thesis in emphasising that 'experience of failure tends to focus less on innate propensities to misperception, and more on specific fallibilities in organization and direction, particularly of multi-organization operations'.[95] The consequence of Herman's argument is that intelligence failures can be diminished only when intelligence organisations focus their attention on human psychology and especially on the limitations and capabilities of human cognition. Only then can the quality of threat perception increase. This is wholly in line with the discourse failure theory. Wirtz sums up this point in reminding us that 'surprise is about human cognition, perception, and psychology'.[96]

Neuman, Smith, Herman, Heuer and Wirtz all argue that the causes of intelligence failure can be found in and explained by human cognition. Handel's theory on strategic surprise is also based on this assumption, and he indirectly emphasises the importance of a deep understanding of human cognition in the following: *'the more alert one is to deception, the more likely one is to become its victim.'*[97] These few words reveal the problems and challenges that are so deeply linked to intelligence work and they imply that intelligence services are substantially threatened by the complexity[98] of the threats they are supposed to comprehend and foresee.

The Nature of Threats and Their Relation to the Problem of Induction

Threats change continuously, and 'new *orders of* [*threat structures*] are always emerging'.[99] The primary task of an intelligence service is to detect and identify such changes. The detection of changes in threat structures makes uncertainty less uncertain, and it thus becomes easier for intelligence institutions to 'maximize damage limitation'.[100] The threat structures these organisations must understand are by definition hypothetical in nature. It follows from this that the real threats are those that have not yet been understood, and those that have not yet materialised. A classical logical approach thus has limited value.[101] Intelligence operators, intelligence organisations and their consumers may therefore start to manage reality only when they have the courage to acknowledge the changing identity of threat structures, instead of seeking solutions in the realm of a preconceived reality.

Intelligence work in general and threat perception in particular are hence cognitive activities, and ones that are threatened by the mental alertness created by the threats that intelligence organisations are supposed to foresee and comprehend. Handel's warning above is demonstrative as it illustrates that institutions attempting to detect deception can easily find themselves its victim, 'since the deceiver intends to present noise as highly trustworthy information,' and because the intelligence analysts are 'psychologically predisposed to believe it . . . until proven otherwise'.[102] Intelligence work is therefore threatened by threat perception itself: the search for threats, and the belief that one will be deceived by the adversary, increase the possibility of one finding the answers one is unconsciously seeking. A profound comprehension of Handel's theory of surprise illustrates the reciprocal nature of intelligence, and demonstrates that the search for threats in some instances could be a greater threat than the potential threat, inasmuch as political assumptions and orthodoxies clutter human cognition.[103]

Accordingly, the greatest enemy of intelligence is self-fulfilling prophecies identified as discourse failure. Heuer calls attention to this possibility in emphasising that '[analysts] start with certain assumptions – often about foreign capabilities and intent – that have been developed through education, training, and experience'.[104] For this reason, analysts are threatened by their own political assumptions, orthodoxies, religious beliefs, limited education and national history. These factors and their interaction influence and colour the analyses, and the most negative consequence may be that threats are underestimated or overlooked entirely.

Oakeshott provides a helpful perspective on this issue when he describes how rationalists embrace 'half-knowledge', and how a rationalist 'sincerely believes that a training in technical knowledge is the only education worth while, because [rationalism] is moved by the faith that there is no knowledge, in the proper sense, except technical knowledge'.[105] Intelligence production should hence avoid this sort of half-knowledge, since it decreases the detection of change, and as such increases the development of political orthodoxies, and consequently cognitive closure.

Cognitive Closure

Humility and self-criticism in relation to intellectual activity and intelligence analysis have been demonstrated to be crucial, since intelligence and threat perception are complicated analyses involving complex cognitive processes that improve thinking but which may, nevertheless, deceive it. These cognitive processes therefore need introduction, and their limitations and capabilities must be understood. Thus, this book argues that discourse failure increases because a flaw easily arises in the cognitive process in intelligence operators, intelligence organisations and especially intelligence consumers. Why operators, organisations and intelligence consumers seem to overlook major threats must therefore be examined.

Arie W. Kruglanski's theory on cognitive closure is valuable in answering this question. He clarifies that humans and consequently also intelligence organisations need to be aware of and prepared for the danger of cognitive closure. Cognitive closure decreases discourse because:

> The need for nonspecific closure represents the desire for a definite answer on some topic, *any* answer as opposed to confusion and ambiguity. Such need thus represents a quest for assured knowledge that affords predictability and a base for action.[106]

Turner lends support to Kruglanski in stating that 'the human element, however, has as much to do with the failures of secret intelligence as do structural factors, if not more'.[107] The world that intelligence operators, organisations and consumers should seek to understand is complicated, and cognitive closure therefore needs to be understood as a natural defence mechanism and mental counterweight to the uncertainty that this complexity creates. Bar-Joseph supports these viewpoints: according to him, humans unconsciously protect themselves against uncertainty.[108] The need for cognitive closure consequently increases from threat perception itself, and this suggests that threat perception in itself poses a threat to threat perception.

Cognition will be analysed in more detail in Chapter 1, and cognitive closure and its negative impact on intelligence will be evaluated in Chapter 2.

The Threat from Threat Perception to Threat Perception

This book will examine the assumption that it is threat perception in itself, and not so much the threats themselves, which increases the unconscious need for cognitive closure. This theory reflects the need to scrutinise threat perception, rather than focus solely on the nature of threats. These factors are nevertheless interconnected. The weaknesses of threat perception cannot be understood without knowledge and comprehension of the substantial nature of threats. This book will therefore focus on the human cognitive processes in threat perception, and for the purpose of a reflective analysis, these processes will be weighed up against findings, which crystallised after 9/11.

Shulsky and Schmitt lend support to the arguments presented in pointing out that 'the heart of the problem of intelligence failure, [is] the thought processes of the individual analyst'.[109] Kuhns also highlights that 'intelligence failures are rarely a problem of collection but generally one of interpretation'.[110] Friedman elucidates these challenges related to threat perception and the comprehension of complex situations, and highlights how these problems make intelligence organisations almost analytically handicapped:

> An event that breaks the paradigm of an era and that cannot be covertly sourced is what the CIA is worse at. Broad historical events that are visible to everyone, but which requires an ability to intuit the deep trend, is something the CIA simply doesn't do very well. When that broad historical event violates all conventional expectations, the CIA is fairly helpless.[111]

The cognitive challenge demonstrated by Friedman is probably not only true for the CIA, but for everyone involved with sophisticated thinking and estimation. The arguments presented in this book are therefore illustrative beyond the example presented by Friedman. The case of 9/11, and the high-quality investigations that followed, just happen to be a good demonstrative case for discourse failure and cognitive closure. The US intelligence community is the biggest in the world. It is arguably also one of the best, since high quality in anything is often accompanied by self-criticism and self-awareness. The US intelligence community is undoubtedly humble and self-critical, and it is this self-criticism and self-awareness that make inquiries and books like this possible. These factors undoubtedly increase intelligence discourse and decrease discourse failure.

Discourse is therefore a necessity when intelligence services are seeking to comprehend threats, and crucial for intellectual activity, and hence essential in intelligence production. The nature of intelligence and the nature of threat perception in particular increase the unconscious need for cognitive closure, which again decreases discourse and increases discourse failure. Laqueur elucidates why human cognition creates such a huge challenge for intelligence organisations in stating the following: 'by and large, the arguments can be summarized as follows: analysts cannot interpret information without hypotheses or a belief system. But this system may be wrong in the first place . . .'[112] Discourse failure cannot thus be diminished without a comprehension and embracing of the capabilities of human cognition.

Conclusion

Intelligence can never be truths, only uncertain theories about the future. Intelligence organisations should therefore seek to develop individual and organisational thinking that embraces imagination and creativity. Qualified intelligence work is, accordingly, ideas that lead to theories about the future. These theories should always seek to explain a comprehension of the wholeness of threats. The hypothesis derived from these theories must thereafter be tested, as tests that make the theories less uncertain. This implies that intelligence never can be anything but uncertain theories about the future that are made less uncertain through scientific, critical tests of hypotheses derived from those theories.

Intelligence production and adequate threat perception can only be increased when intelligence organisations understand that humans are social beings burdened by their individual and collective history. Intelligence operators whose task is to comprehend other cultures, often fundamentally different from their own, must be given room and freedom to understand themselves and their own culture before they even attempt to comprehend other cultures. Intelligence work is profoundly mental, and the process is therefore extremely vulnerable. Intelligence organisations must never forget that their qualities, negative and positive, are reflected in the sum of their human capital. The quality of intelligence products is therefore always a mirror of how these organisations are directed and run.

Open and free intelligence institutions that take freedom, creativity and fantasy seriously, also take diversity, inequality, individuality and criticism seriously. Consequently, it is likely that such organisations are more qualified to comprehend and predict threats beyond the limits of induction. By contrast, closed and politicised intelligence organisations characterised by their secrecy, orthodoxies, political assumptions, mental insecurity, subtleties, cognitive closure and careerism decrease cognition and discourse. This unhealthy cognitive climate creates an atmosphere of suspicion and distrust. It is likely that such an institutional atmosphere reduces the institutional self-comprehension and, consequently, the organisations' capability to comprehend their allies, and their potential enemies and counterparts. The inevitable result of such institutionalised psychology is that everyone is a potential enemy. This psychology makes such organisations unfocused and cognitively unaware, leading to a self-destructive paranoia that makes imaginable and creative estimates about the future difficult and even impossible to produce.

If intelligence organisations want to be able to counter perceived threats, they need to comprehend the strength of their human capital, as well as analyse and understand the ideological prisms that exist and develop in the realm of secrecy and intelligence tribal language.

Part I

Critical Thinking and Intelligence

1   Cognition

If [the intelligence operator] thinks of the totality as constituted of independent fragments, then that is how his mind will tend to operate, but if he can include everything coherently and harmoniously in an overall whole that is undivided, unbroken, and without a border (for every border is a division or break) then his mind will tend to move in a similar way, and from this will flow an orderly action within the whole.[1]

Intelligence operators must comprehend the wholeness and harmony of their minds, and of the larger context in which they operate. Only then can they understand the complete dynamics and wholeness of threats. Critics may argue that this sounds ideal and ethereal, and they are right: it is idealistic, and it is probably highly challenging and even impossible to achieve. However, high quality in anything is difficult to attain unless one aims for ideals. Full wholeness and harmony of mind is impossible to achieve, but intelligence institutions should nonetheless create a culture that stimulates and reward operators who, through a critical understanding of their own minds, attempt to comprehend the wholeness and complexity of threat structures.

It has been established that intelligence lacks a proper theory. A good theory needs to be based on a prudent idea, one that originates in a philosophy and ethos that shape the underlying thinking of intelligence institutions. This chapter aims to describe and evaluate this philosophy, and implicitly illustrates that it is the lack of intelligence philosophy that has made the development of intelligence theory challenging. This chapter is hence based on the assumption that high-quality intelligence requires intellectual and mental refinement.

The key to successful intelligence work is understanding the coherence, wholeness and harmony of threats. Divided minds can comprehend only division and fragments, while undivided minds comprehend coherence, wholeness and harmony. This chapter will thus investigate human cognition, illustrating it as a force that may positively shape threat perception if it is properly understood and cultivated. The study also demonstrates how cognitive limitations decrease discourse in intelligence organisations, and between them and the societies they serve. The chapter proposes how these challenges could be minimised.

Division in mind implies that one cognitively perceives the world as independent fragments operating separately from the totality they constitute, and this leads to division in thinking, resulting in a threat perception that views threat structures as fragments that exist independently of the threat wholeness they constitute.[2] The damaging effect of such thinking is evident, and Bohm illustrates how confined thinking will disastrously decrease the quality of intelligence analysis in writing the following: 'to avoid [failure], the [analyst] whose *first* aim was pleasure would tend to overlook weak points in his work (as indeed does unfortunately tend to happen with surprising frequency)'.[3]

Bohm captures the limitations of human cognition, and lends support to Popper, Neumann and Smith. The human propensity for failure is inevitable. That said, these cognitive limitations may reduce discourse failure if they are explored, understood and accepted. Accordingly, it is not the reduction of cognitive limitations in itself that reduces discourse failure, but the constant quest for a deep comprehension of the capabilities and limitations in human cognition.

Cognition is the 'processing of experience, perception, and memory, as well as overtly verbal thinking'.[4] It is therefore the human processes that are 'responsible for knowledge and awareness'.[5] Although this philosophical definition is good, it is not comprehensive enough to provide us with the insight necessary to understand cognition. One therefore needs to think more about thinking. Thinking about thinking is no doubt challenging, and so too is intelligence because it is deeply involved with both thinking and thinking about thinking.

Humans are survivors and thinking is, in its purest and most essential form, a process performed to survive. Thinking in its more sophisticated and scientific form is arguably developed from this instinctive type of thinking. Nevertheless, the swift quick thinking performed to survive a potential traffic accident is not that different from the thinking performed in science. Both forms of thinking, the pure and instinctive, and the more sophisticated and scientific, presuppose two important factors – imagination and creativity – because they '[require] consideration of hypothetical possibilities'.[6] Hypotheses are essentially always substantially futuristic, and therefore presuppose creativity and imagination.

Bohm captures the important relationship between creativity, imagination, reason and thought: 'it is evident, then, that we have to consider the relationship between imagination and reason if we wish to obtain an adequate account of the operation of the process of thought'.[7] One important question is whether it is possible to think adequately and rationally about the future, since rational reasoning implies that 'when we see the reason for something, we are aware of a totality of interrelated ratios or properties of that thing'.[8] This quote highlights two important factors. Reasoning is a part of a formal and classical thinking process, but imaginary thinking does not necessarily imply classical reasoning, since imagination and creativity dispel the borders of formal reasoning, inasmuch as formal reasoning presupposes that there already exists a situation or a 'thing' that can be understood.

The future only exists in human minds, and can therefore not be comprehended through rational reasoning alone. Intelligence institutions are meant to produce foreknowledge, and 'foreknowledge is especially difficult to obtain, since it concerns things that no one can see'.[9] The future therefore needs to be thought about through thinking that exists beyond formal reasoning. The type of thinking intelligence organisations need to perform is therefore a form of imaginary insight expressed as a form of wisdom that goes beyond classic formal reasoning. This is because it helps humans to comprehend:

> . . . a whole range of differences, similarities, connections, disconnections, totalities of universal and particular ratio or proportion, and so forth. This insight, which is of the essential quality of intelligence,

cannot ultimately be a mere product of memory and training, because in each case it has to be seen anew. Rather, it is an act of *perception through the mind* (essentially what was called 'nous' by the ancient Greeks). As such, it is a particular case of perception as a whole. This latter includes not only perception through the mind, but also sense perception, aesthetic perception, and emotional perception (perception through feelings).[10]

Estimation of the future thus demands thinking and cognition that go beyond rationality in its classical structure. Bohm captures the kind of thinking intelligence institutions must embrace to be able to conceive of the wholeness of what they attempt to comprehend. They need to create a culture and a discourse that stimulate and develop creative and imaginary holistic perception that synthesises rational perception, sense perception, aesthetic perception and emotional perception expressed as critical intelligence cognition.

However, imagination, and thus creativity, are often 'wrongly thought of as opposed to reason'.[11] This thesis holds that imagination and creativity are not substantially different or contrastive to reason as such. It argues instead that these two important human properties provide an important enlargement of reason in its more classic, methodical form. Imagination and creativity are therefore not indifferent to reasoning.[12] But they do, however, differ from formal reason, which is built upon a strict syntactic relation between the conclusion and the premises.[13] However, this argument may imply that intelligence production is a kind of instinctive sensation free of methodical rationality. That is not the case, and the following illustrative example demonstrates how cognition in intelligence operators should be understood.

It can probably be contended that actions performed by a driver to avoid a traffic accident are purely instinctive, and not a result of thinking. However, this study counters this argument, holding that the seemingly instinctive reactions the driver must perform are the result of thinking. Driving a car presupposes training and experience, and the process performed to survive a traffic accident undoubtedly presupposes that the driver knows the various dangers involved. The driver therefore needs experience, education and training to be able to take the right actions in specific situations. The faster the driver is able to react, the better, and the more likely the driver will survive. But this is not instinct – it is rather a fast operational 'processing of experience, perception, and memory'.[14]

The driver performs intuition constituted as quick operational cognition. The rapid and intuitive thought process performed to survive would not have been possible without imagination and creativity, in the sense that the driver must use his or her experience and quickly assess different outcomes likely to occur as a result of the driver's intuitive, swift choice.

Imagination and creativity are the two human properties that constitute survival and consequently human progression. However, imagination and creativity alone are not enough. Humans learn from experience, and convert experience into innovation and development. Cognition is therefore the human ability to learn from experience, perception and memory, and the theoretical and practical capability to fuse experience with imagination and creativity, and use the result to comprehend the multidimensional objectives of human life. This is the straightforward and simplified explanation, and the term 'thinking' therefore needs more thinking and closer analysis.

The philosophical definition of formal reasoning states that it is the 'process of drawing a conclusion from a set of premises'.[15] Formal reasoning is therefore an inductive process, since induction is the 'process of reasoning that takes us from empirical premises to empirical conclusions supported by the premises'.[16] Induction is thus the essence of formal reasoning. It has caused endless debates in philosophy, and many scientists have been encouraged to solve its problem, which is that 'any evidence-transcending belief is unreasonable'.[17] Inductive thinking thus never regards the future as part of the premises, simply because induction is empirical, and therefore essentially historicism, inasmuch as it 'attempts to tie knowledge to experience'.[18]

Nevertheless, intelligence organisations and their employees certainly need to know and understand history, but they should not produce any estimates about the future based on history alone. Intelligence work in general, and intelligence estimation as such, should be based on wisdom and cleverness. Wise and clever intelligence services are therefore able to estimate potential variations of previous threats. Healthy and productive intelligence discourse and cognition must thus be based on 'a quality of insight going beyond any particular fixed form of reaction and associated reflective thought. *This insight must be free of conditioning to previous existing patterns, otherwise it will, of course, ultimately be just an extension of mechanical reaction.*'[19]

Imagination and creativity thus go beyond mechanical reactions and particular fixed theories, and provide thinking with doubt, an immensely important factor since thinking 'begins with doubt'.[20] The following analysis will therefore focus on the capability of imagination and creativity in human cognition, and explore whether and how decreased imagination and creativity increase discourse failure.

Imagination and creativity are necessary for intelligence production because the aim of intelligence should be to 'learn something new that has a certain fundamental kind of significance: a hitherto unknown lawfulness in the order of nature, which exhibits *unity* in a *broad range* of phenomena'.[21] Intelligence organisations thus have to seek to comprehend the as yet unexperienced. Ideal intelligence analysis should accordingly search for a holistic insight into the future, and a kind of specific insight needed and required by their consumers. The subject matter of useful and professional intelligence is hence the search for a kind of wisdom that can guide the intelligence consumer into the future.[22] Such wisdom is probably unattainable unless intelligence organisations have the cognitive capability to think beyond the limits of experience. Any weakness in human cognition that reduces such holistic oneness[23] needs to be diminished. Bohm elucidates this in writing that 'the power to imagine things that have not been actually experienced has, on the one hand, commonly been regarded as a key aspect of creative and intelligent thought'.[24]

The Analysis and Its Structure

The following analysis will be divided into two main parts. The first will argue that imagination and creativity presuppose attentiveness, alertness, awareness and sensitivity.[25] These are all mainly individual qualities. On an organisational level, openness and space for individuality and diversity are crucial. It will be suggested that an intelligence-focused comprehension of Bohm's theory can help intelligence organisations to be attentive to the cognitive qualities of their operators, and give them space to flourish intellectually, and it will be argued that individual and collective imagination and creativity increase discourse and intellectuality, and the quality of the intelligence product will thus increase. Decreased attentiveness, alertness, awareness and sensitivity thus reduce discourse and increase discourse failure.

The analysis seeks to demonstrate that it is when intelligence operators are attentive to and aware of the limitations and thus to the capabilities of their own cognitive capacity, that it is likely that they will also be more alert and sensitive to the imaginary and creative qualities of others. This, no doubt, increases discourse, collective imagination and creativity, which should be the highest goal of intelligence organisations.

The second part deals with and briefly demonstrates that a re-contextualising of Bohm's theory on creativity and Popper's principle of falsification, if fused with Oakeshott's critique of rationalism in politics, may increase intelligence institutions' consciousness of the problem of induction, and as such help diminish discourse failure.

This chapter and its description and exploration of human cognition serve as an introduction to the challenges that the negative synergy between the limitations of human cognition, misunderstood secrecy and intelligence tribal language offer to intelligence. The analysis focuses on the positive force of human cognition, since a clear comprehension of the advantages of critical thinking increases the understanding of the consequences if such thinking is decreased by a lack of qualitative discourse.

The Quest for Imagination and Creativity

Imagination and creativity arguably presuppose intellectual freedom. Intelligence operators therefore need psychological space and intellectual freedom to be able to think beyond the limits of experience. Attentiveness, alertness, awareness and sensitivity in and between intelligence operators increase freedom and therefore imagination and creativity. Imagination and creativity are not a concept, which comes into being by itself. It is a human treasure that is hidden in all humans, and one that must be constantly cultivated to flourish. Intelligence organisations must therefore create a culture facilitating such cultivation. The organisational discourse must hence be open, and space for individuality and diversity must be achievable.

Attentiveness, alertness, awareness, sensitivity, openness, individuality and diversity will be analysed in the following, and the book will demonstrate how the different factors and their interaction increase imagination and creativity. This chapter aims to demonstrate that any reduction in the possibility of developing individual and collective imagination and creativity in intelligence organisations creates a cognitively suppressing culture, and a limited and restrictive language, that in sum greatly increase discourse failure and reduce the quality of the intelligence products.

The analysis will explore the unity of attentiveness, alertness, awareness, sensitivity, openness, individuality and diversity on an individual level, and thereafter investigate whether and how these factors on a collective level may decrease discourse if they are not comprehended and cultivated.

The Unity of Attentiveness, Alertness, Awareness, Sensitivity, Openness, Individuality and Diversity on the Individual Level

Mary Midgley draws one's attention to the cognitive power inside each human in stating the following: 'freedom is the chance to develop *what you have it in you to be* – your talents, your capacities, your natural feelings. If you had no such particular potentials in you for a start, you could have no use for freedom and it could not concern you.'[26] She illustrates that each human needs to be attentive to and aware of the imaginary and creative cognitive force inside him or herself. Intelligence operators therefore need to be given both personal and professional freedom: only then can they and their institutions hope to achieve individual and collective imagination and creativity. Midgley by this captures the force of human cognition, and implicitly also echoes Bohm's understanding of the negative energy of a fragmented and divided mind.[27] Attentiveness, alertness, awareness and sensitivity among intelligence operators arguably diminish cognitive fragmentation and division. However, the cognitive energy inside each human is fragile and can easily be misunderstood. It is, therefore, a treasure that needs to be found and cultivated through prudent self-examination. Intelligence operators therefore need to be treated with care and sensitivity and be given opportunities to fulfil their intellectual potential and achieve sentiment. They therefore need to be given opportunities and challenges outside their own defined trade. Humans who are supposed to comprehend the wholeness of threats need to comprehend their own cognitive wholeness. Such wholeness can probably only be attained when humans are attentive to their own and others' cognitive force, and to the culture, discourse and nature around themselves. That is the essence of the kind of intellectual sentiment needed by an organisation seeking to understand others.

Bohm accordingly highlights that wholeness is integrity,[28] and he thereby illustrates the true essence of human wholeness. Integrity is no doubt the most important factor for successful intelligence activity, and any intelligence institution that wants to fulfil its true function should do everything it can to develop individual and collective integrity.

Intelligence operators should be given space to attentively develop their own cognitive wholeness. They must therefore be given the opportunity to stimulate their mental awareness and alertness to their own intellectual capacity, and they must hence be urged to read their own countries' classical and contemporary literature, since it is important to 'know your own history and culture'[29] to be able to understand others, and 'it is important that analysts study the philosophy, literature, and key thinkers of whatever country they work on'.[30] In this they can diminish the negative effect of their individual and collective history and increase their ability to comprehend wholeness of threats. To be able to understand this wholeness, intelligence operators must be attentive to the differences and similarities between cultures. Mircea Eliade highlights why this is so challenging:

> For our purpose it is enough to observe that desacralization pervades the entire experience of the nonreligious man of modern societies and that, in consequence, he finds it increasingly difficult to rediscover the existential dimensions of religious man in the archaic societies.[31]

It is therefore necessary to explore how intelligence institutions could create an environment that stimulates the development of their operators' attentiveness to other cultures, and consequently also to the wholeness of threats. It follows from this that those intelligence institutions that are negatively bureaucratic and unwilling to stimulate a culture that embraces free creative thinking, consequently do not develop the human capital needed to foresee and comprehend changing threat structures. It is therefore essential to explore and demonstrate how cultivation of cognition reduces discourse failure, and thus what the result may be if such cultivation does not exist.

Discourse failure theory provides an insight and an understanding of the importance of the language that intelligence uses to communicate internally, with other intelligence producers and with intelligence consumers. The theory also emphasises the force of intelligence discourse on the intelligence culture, and how a restrictive culture decreases the quality of communication between humans and organisations and contributes to discourse failure. It is important to explore the interplay between the individual human being and the intelligence organisation to be able to analyse and comprehend the negative force of a limiting and unhealthy intelligence culture and intelligence discourse on human cognition. Open and imaginary cognition presupposes freedom. An unfree human cannot think freely, and a human unable to think freely can neither speculate constructively about the future, nor think of the unthinkable.

Intelligence organisations in general and intelligence work itself are not activities that bring immediate attention to wisdom, speculation, imagination and creativity. Popular literature has created an impression of intelligence as secrecy, spy hunts and trickery, in many instances accompanied and facilitated by a lack of morality. This kind of fiction is not only misleading – it is also, more importantly, damaging to what high-quality intelligence is and should be. Intelligence is a highly demanding activity, both intellectually and mentally. It deals with uncertainty and often with danger. Few operatives are directly involved in danger, and fewer still risk their lives, but most intelligence operatives feel the burden of responsibility in assessing possible threats to their own society and providing intelligence briefs to a patrol of soldiers preparing for an operation. Intelligence officers who have seen soldiers prepare for battle know the feeling of accountability, and the burden on their shoulders. Those intelligence operatives who have never felt such pressure, or do not understand it, should not be involved with intelligence.

Intelligence, whether it is on a political or tactical level, therefore demands humility, integrity and honesty. Anything else could, at the extreme end of the scale, be life-threatening to those who use the intelligence. Intelligence operatives must therefore be loyal to their duties. They must do their utmost to produce quality. Intelligence work is therefore intellectually challenging and mentally straining. Few factors can be weighed and measured, the product can in some cases separate life from death, and intelligence work is therefore extremely mentally demanding.

All these factors illustrate that the human factor is crucial to understanding both for intelligence professionals and intelligence scholars. However, there are surprisingly few scholars interested in this field of study. The reasons for such limited scientific interest are difficult to evaluate, though it is likely that the difficulties involved in analysing the complexity of the human interrelationship within intelligence organisations provide some explanation.

Discourse failure theory, however, has opened up a new window of comprehension, because the theory draws attention to the importance of humility, integrity and a sense of self-comprehension and self-criticism in threat perception.[32] Neumann and Smith elucidate that humans are often predetermined to submit to cognitive closure, meaning that they are unwilling to understand or accept any information that threatens their preconceived political assumptions and orthodoxies. Intelligence operatives and intelligence institutions therefore need to be aware of the negative force of cognitive closure and discourse failure, and they hence need to be cognitively, mentally and morally self-aware.[33]

The 9/11 Commission Report illustrates the importance of high-quality cognition expressed as mental and moral self-awareness, and its evidential contrast with bureaucracy, in stating that 'imagination is not a gift usually associated with bureaucracies'.[34] This quote implicitly stresses freedom as the most important prerequisite for cognitive self-awareness, and thus the challenges that arise when intelligence institutions attempt to bureaucratise creativity and imagination.

Attentiveness, alertness, awareness, sensitivity, openness, individuality and diversity are qualities that do not easily lend themselves to institutionalisation or bureaucratisation, and this is a huge challenge for intelligence organisations. Intelligence is, in its most essential form, a creative activity. Nevertheless, it can certainly not be carried out without direction and management. Intelligence requirements are indeed needed, and these requirements must be prioritised, and the collected material requires proper and adequate handling by a qualified workforce that conducts its duties in a highly professional organisation.

These facts demonstrate that intelligence organisations are constantly torn between their apparent need for systems, methods and organisation on the one hand, and the essential need for creativity and imagination on the other. This conflicting identity shapes intelligence organisations, creating a culture that is both demanding and highly challenging for humans, and especially for creative people and for imaginary thinking, since imagination is 'the ability to create and rehearse possible situations, to combine knowledge in unusual ways, or to invent thought experiments'.[35] This creates a challenge for intelligence organisations since it is difficult for systems and specific methodologies to intercept thought experiments, inasmuch as thought experiments (in contrast to normal experiments) exist in the minds of humans.[36]

Thought experiments and suppositions hence only exist as imagination in the observer's mind, and there are few systems or methods that can properly process them, since classical methods used in political analysis are limited to observation and analysis of existing scientific material or situations.[37] Thought experiments and thus imagination therefore demand an approach that is flexible with a readiness to change. Systems and methods are developed by humans, and they can only be changed by humans. These systems and methods therefore require humans who are able to change them when the situation demands it.

The problem for intelligence organisations arises since humans do not easily adapt to changes, given that these changes are often comprehended as threatening to one's preconceived apprehension of the world. Humans will therefore in many cases react with cognitive closure.[38]

It is when this human psychological need for predictability and security melds with misunderstood secrecy and a limited intelligence tribal language that discourse failure arises and develops, since misunderstood and misused secrecy which operates with a restricted intelligence tribal language can seriously decrease the human ability to be creative and carry out thought experiments. This negative interaction will be analysed more deeply in Chapter 3.

Intelligence institutions therefore need to do their utmost to oppose and work against the negative force of cognitive closure and discourse failure. Freedom and openness are the two most important conditions for a healthy and creative intelligence culture, and it is when this organisational trait is established that attentiveness, alertness, awareness, sensitivity, individuality and diversity can flourish and develop. This illustrates that creativity presupposes freedom, and institutions in general, and intelligence organisations as such threaten creativity, as organisations and bureaucracies do not necessarily or easily stimulate attentiveness, alertness, awareness, sensitivity, openness, individuality or diversity. It therefore becomes challenging to exist as an autonomous and creative human being in an intelligence organisation, and to produce intelligence that contradicts the established political assumptions and orthodoxies.

Intelligence organisations thus have a self-destructive character that easily decreases the operator's opportunity and willingness to develop cognitively and, as a result, to take intellectual chances. The result of such conservatism is evidential, as it decreases the organisation's overall ability to foresee and accept what is challenging to imagine. The 9/11 Commission Report elucidates this in stating the following:

> The CTC [Counter Terrorist Center] did not analyze how an aircraft, hijacked or explosives-laden, might be used as a weapon. It did not perform this kind of analysis from the enemy's perspective ('red team' analysis), even though suicide terrorism had become a principal tactic of Middle Eastern terrorists. If it had done so, we believe such an analysis would soon have spotlighted a critical constraint for the terrorists – finding a suicide operative able to fly large jet aircraft. They had never done so before 9/11.[39]

The indications that the United States (US) was under immediate threat from al Qaeda were overwhelming, and even President Bush referred to the August 6 Presidential Daily Brief (PDB), stating that 'the August 6 report was historical in nature. President Bush said the article told him that al Qaeda was dangerous, which he said he had known since he had become President'.[40] The August 6 Presidential Daily Brief stated that 'a Bin Ladin attack in the United States remained both current and serious'.[41]

One important question to ask is therefore why no one in the Bush administration or in the intelligence community managed to synthesise the various reports into a lucid threat picture that could have accumulated appropriate and lethal action against the al Qaeda terrorists. The answers to this question are complex, although one important factor crystallises. There was one important and dangerous weakness in the US intelligence focus, since 'there was a clear disparity in the levels of response to foreign versus domestic threats'.[42] This created a huge window of opportunity for al Qaeda, an opportunity that was made even bigger in that 'domestic agencies never mobilized in response to the threat. They did not have direction, and did not have a plan to institute.'[43]

This lack of a holistic understanding of the enemy, direction or a plan to follow made it difficult for the US intelligence community as a whole to comprehend and consequently react sufficiently against the threat. The attackers could therefore continue to plan undisturbed their deadly actions because the transnational security sphere was not sufficiently understood or monitored by the US intelligence community. Intelligence that indicated a domestic terrorist threat from foreign terrorists was thus neither understood nor accepted and constitutes a classic discourse failure, since the community, despite intelligence indicating a threat, was not able 'to identify, analyze, and accept that a significant threat existed'.[44] This was made possible because 'the terrorists exploited deep institutional failings within [the US] government'.[45] Wirtz is illustrative in highlighting that 'while there was a unified command structure in the Persian Gulf to address the local terrorist threat, organizational responsibilities in the US government largely diverged at the water's edge'.[46]

The 9/11 attackers not only discovered institutional failings within the US government, they also exploited a cultural weakness within the US intelligence community. The community overlooked the immensely important lesson that Pearl Harbor had provided, since 'both incidents were preceded by clear indications that the United States faced an imminent threat'.[47] Current trends, let alone the future, are extremely difficult to understand, although the lessons from Pearl Harbor should have shaped a US intelligence community more prepared for 9/11 than it was. However, discourse failure demonstrates that the objects of human existence are infinite, and manifest themselves in a number of variations inconceivable within the limited language available to humans. Intelligence operatives and intelligence institutions must deal with such uncertainty on a daily basis. It is challenging and mentally straining, and it easily creates a culture that lends itself to cognitive closure and thus limited and restrictive discourse.

This is a weakness that arguably identifies and shapes most intelligence organisations around the world. Roberta Wohlstetter elucidates this in concluding in her study of the Pearl Harbor that surprise attack, and consequently intelligence failure, lie 'in the conditions of human perception and [stem] from uncertainties so basic that they are not likely to be eliminated'.[48] It is when intelligence institutions forget this that cognitive closure arises and discourse failure ensues. Wohlstetter continues: 'no magic, in code or otherwise, will provide certainty. Our plans must work without it.'[49]

Intelligence work will therefore always be based on uncertainty, a lesson that is not easy for humans to adjust to. Uncertainty may create intelligence cultures that oppose and disclose the reality of uncertainty, simply because uncertainty is too challenging for humans to live with over time. This again creates a culture that does not easily lend itself to open creative thinking, speculation, discussion and constructive criticism. Cooperation in such organisations is challenging, and often impossible. If an organisation has problems with internal cooperation it is even more difficult for that organisation to cooperate with others. A lack of cooperation between the different intelligence organisations in the US was one of the main problems prior to 9/11, and 'relationships at the mid- and upper-management levels of those agencies [CIA and NSA] were often strained'.[50]

However, the cooperation between operatives 'at the working level had often been very good'.[51] This indicates that humans are by their nature cooperative, although they seem to easily become more competitive and introverted as they become institutionalised by the organisations to which they belong. This is not unique to intelligence organisations, although it can be argued that the secrecy that surrounds intelligence and the consequent intelligence tribal language shape and create a limited intelligence discourse that easily leads these organisations to cognitive closure. The problems and challenges created by the interplay between secrecy and intelligence tribal language will be analysed in Chapter 3.

The findings in the Joint Inquiry detected that a lack of cooperation was a challenge prior to 9/11. It is also indicated that this problem was organisational rather than human. This book challenges this view, and holds that the problems that cause intelligence failures are not organisational. Organisations are not separate from the humans who create them. Organisations are not autonomous organisms that live their own lives, although they often create their own dynamics. These dynamics are challenging for humans to control or change. The explanations therefore need to be explored in the interplay between human cognition and cultural and organisational characteristics unique to intelligence institutions. These characteristics are secrecy and a distinctive intelligence tribal language. It is therefore worth looking at the negative interplay between collective cognition and secrecy and intelligence tribal language.

Collective Cognition versus Secrecy and Intelligence Tribal Language

Intelligence institutions are often huge institutions, identified and characterised by their bureaucracy, history and secrecy. They are typically difficult to change, and their traditions and secrecy-driven culture place the burden of development on both the individual and collective level. Daniel Patrick Moynihan's description is illustrative:

> . . . secrets had become assets; organizations hoarded them, revealing them sparingly and only in return for some consideration. Such as these wanted no part of some central security office busying itself with their internal affairs. This, of course, is conjecture, but it is certainly true that no central security office emerged.[52]

Moynihan demonstrates how secrecy can become a problem, and how it can decrease collective intelligence cognition through its decentralisation of intelligence. This undoubtedly facilitates decreased cooperation and communication, and cognition, certainly, presupposes communication between humans. Two institutional weaknesses and threats to collective cognition thus seem to crystallise: the uncontrolled and rapid growth of intelligence institutions, and the lack of communication and cooperation between them.

The US had sixteen intelligence institutions in 2001. The CIA is one of them, and one of the biggest intelligence institutions in the world. Arguably, the growth and development of intelligence communities have created their own dynamic outside human control, and one should ask whether growth necessarily increases the effectiveness of intelligence institutions, and can prevent a new 9/11. Former associate deputy director for operations in the CIA John MacGaffin elucidates this in stating that 'simply changing bureaucratic structures, increasing personnel, and even diversifying HUMINT cadres will not solve HUMINT's current weakness'.[53] MacGaffin indicates that the main problem of Humint is that it has left its first principle as the 'final and critical option',[54] and should hence only be 'employed when it is clear that no other option is available or has a real possibility to succeed'.[55] An increase in personnel therefore does not solve the problem, since the main problem of Humint is not related to a lack of workforce but to a misconception of its merits and capacity. This example illustrates that weakness evolving from other problems than whether organisations have enough people or not, are nevertheless often solved by increasing manning. But this is unhelpful if the problem is a question of human quality rather than quantity.

Finding 5 in the Excerpts from the Joint Inquiry Report on 9/11 is illustrative in highlighting that the quality of counterterrorism analysis prior to 9/11 was inconsistent, since the analysts were unqualified.[56] However, this poor quality was a result of the reduction of the analytical workforce after the Cold War,[57] and it is often the case that organisations lose their best employees as result of workforce reduction. The aftermath of 9/11 caused an increase in the communities' workforce to compensate, but with no focus on quality: this has resulted in a 'less experienced analytic cadre today than, say, in the 1970s and 1980s'.[58]

Constant and unfocused changes in structures and organisations therefore do not necessarily increase the quality of intelligence analysis; they are more likely to decrease quality. Humans are social individuals who arguably adapt steadily and slowly to their social and cultural environments. It is therefore likely that rapid and constant change in these environments decreases human alertness to cognitive wholeness. This implies that humans who foresee developments and changes in threats should be given opportunities to exist in an environment with organisational tranquillity.

Intelligence institutions should therefore stimulate and create dynamic but stable organisational structures. These organisational structures need to stimulate innovation, and they must give the intelligence operators intellectual stability. They need to be variable, but at the same time predictable for the personnel working in these organisations. Intelligence institutions hence need to give tranquillity to their operators, so these operators are able to develop and comprehend their own cognitive capabilities. Only then can these operators hope to detect and comprehend differences in already perceived and known orders of threats. Such organisations are better equipped to foresee and comprehend the development of different sets of orders of threats, their relation and possible conflict with each other, and as a result produce intelligence that may reduce discourse failure.

For example, the Director of Military Intelligence in Israel in 1973, General Eli Zeira, did not act as if he understood the importance of intellectual freedom for his intelligence operators. He did not accept any analysis that indicated possible Egyptian attacks against Israel, and he stated that 'those officers who estimated in spring 1973 that war was likely should not expect promotion'.[59] The result of such leadership is evident. The Israeli intelligence community was cognitively handicapped, and therefore unable to conduct its proper function as an information specialist.

Collective cognition is therefore an institutional asset that must be built slowly and carefully. The institutions must make sure that they select and recruit the right personnel, who must be educated and properly trained. It is with this challenge that Bohm, Popper and Oakeshott might provide help.

Bohm's, Popper's and Oakeshott's Theories and Their Consequences for Cognition

Bohm, Popper and Oakeshott are all thinkers who have embraced freedom and openness. Their work has been dedicated to critical thinking, and they have all been advocates of open societies and personal freedom. Bohm's theories on the importance of creativity, Popper's defence of the open society and falsification and critical rationalism are ideas and theories which, if melded with Oakeshott's critique of rationalism in politics and his consequent embracing of a critical rationalism, may increase both individual and collective cognition in intelligence institutions.

Bohm's ideas about creativity have been analysed earlier in this chapter: accordingly, in the following I will describe only briefly how his theories may provide support to Popper's theories of falsification and critical rationalism. Popper's theories and the problem of induction will be analysed in Chapter 5, so they too are only outlined briefly in this chapter, since this presentation only seeks to illustrate the substance of the theories and how, if fused with Bohm and Oakeshott, they may increase and stimulate cognition.

Arguably, cognition will increase if Bohm's creativity is embraced and fused with Popper's theories on falsification and critical rationalism, because the critical thinker, in contrast to the rationalist (according to Oakeshott) acknowledges that it takes at least two generations to learn a profession.[60] Good political education therefore:

> ... begins in the enjoyment of a tradition, in the observation and imitation of the behaviour of our elders, and there is little or nothing in the world which comes before us as we open our eyes which does not contribute to it.[61]

Nevertheless, Oakeshott also emphasises that nothing in life is static or constant, including the knowledge acquired through lifelong education. Education and tradition should therefore constantly be critically examined. It is exactly this approach to learning that constitutes critical rationalism, since the approach embraces that nothing in life 'is immune to change'.[62] Critical rationalism is therefore based on an unwillingness to accept habit and prejudice.

Intelligence operators who are trained and educated in the spirit of Bohm's attentive creativity and Popper's critical rationalism are therefore, in theory, less vulnerable to orthodoxies and political assumptions, since integrity and creativity are inseparable. Creativity is arguably also freedom, and therefore presupposes openness and an atmosphere free from prejudice, orthodoxy and political assumptions. Bohm, as described earlier, highlights that integrity is wholeness,[63] and integrity, like creativity, is therefore something substantial and indivisible. One can conclude from this that integrity presupposes freedom, and that freedom facilitates creativity. Creativity without integrity is therefore highly challenging and even impossible, since integrity marshals creativity. Freedom, integrity and creativity are therefore essential to high-quality intelligence production, which is why Popper, Bohm and Oakeshott may provide a solution to the challenges posed by cognitive closure and discourse failure.

This book argues that it is the problem of induction that facilitates cognitive closure and consequently discourse failure. The problem of induction will be presented and analysed in Chapter 5, but will nevertheless be described and discussed in the following for the purpose of introductory analysis.

First, induction is the way people think. Humans reach their conclusions based on empirical observations, and induction can, in short, be defined as the method of 'inferring universal statements from singular ones'.[64] This seems at first sight to be logical, and it is, formally. But it is not necessarily logical beyond the premises used, since the universal statement is only a conclusion based on selected premises, and as such only describes that selection, or 'can in the first place be only a singular statement and not a universal one'.[65] The result, if the observer takes the conclusion as a valid description of nature, is dogmatic thinking,[66] and dogmatic thinking no doubt leads to a uniform belief in nature.[67] Dogmatic thinking and a uniform belief in nature facilitate cognitive closure, and one can therefore conclude that the problem of induction, the belief that there exists a compelling inference between the past and the future,[68] certainly facilitates cognitive closure and discourse failure.

Popper, Bohm and Oakeshott may provide a solution to this problem. Popper advocates our forsaking 'the way of justification in favour of the way of criticism'.[69] He thereby introduces falsification and critical rationalism as a solution to the problem of induction. He argues that a hypothesis should be tested through refutation instead of through verification, and highlights that it is when a hypothesis stands up to refutation that it is a good hypothesis, since it 'stands up to our efforts to criticize it. Then this fact is a good reason to believe H, tentatively and for the time being, *though it is not a reason for the hypothesis H itself*.[70] Popper's critical rationalism and his falsification theory can therefore provide necessary scepticism and criticism to intelligence cultures, and if fused with Bohm's theory of creativity, thereby facilitate critical thinking.

The danger of induction to threat perception is that the method does not lend itself to change, and the result may be that because foreign terrorists have never attacked the US domestically using airplanes as suicides weapons, it is unlikely that anyone will do so in the future. 9/11 demonstrates the fallacy of such conclusions. Nevertheless, this is the only conclusion that induction would lead to, a fact that forcefully illustrates the immense danger of induction. Critical rationalism and Bohm's holistic creativity are therefore called for.

Intelligence must therefore accept that there is not any necessary inference between the past and the future. Of course, the future will sometimes and often resemble the past, but the point is that it does not need to, as threats are essentially threats because they occur in new orders and variations. Threats that are known, acknowledged and reacted against are also threats, but less dangerous than those that are not understood and accepted, and an understanding of the discourse failure theory is therefore essential if one wants to diminish intelligence failure. Bohm's contention of creativity as the ability to understand reality holistically is therefore essential to intelligence, since it implies that intelligence can only hope to comprehend threat structures if intelligence institutions try to understand the holistic order and variations of these structures. This presupposes an ideal combination of Bohm's creativity, Popper's critical rationalism and Oakeshott's critique of rationalism in politics, but there are challenges.

Popper's theory of falsification and critical rationalism has its weaknesses. It suggests that refutation may provide a solution to induction, since verification ultimately may lead to dogmatic thinking and, at worst, discourse failure. However, falsification through refutation is also based on induction, since the source of the refutation is based on corroboration, which is essentially a form of verification. This implies that thinking substantially is inductive, and that critical rationalism, consequently, is critical induction.

Popper would probably counter such an understanding, but this book suggests that it is the understanding of critical rationalism as critical induction that could truly diminish the problem of induction, and thus the problem of discourse failure.

Popper introduced critical rationalism and falsification as tools to solve, or at least diminish, the problem of induction, and the argument set down here certainly supports the idea that these methods may provide a solution to the problems of induction. Nonetheless, this book also acknowledges that Popper's methods are based on corroboration, and that history and collective and individual understanding of this history form the corroboration and as such the critical rationalism. Critical rationalism is therefore not dissimilar to induction, although it is, unlike induction, critical to historical premises, and that is its strength.

Popper did acknowledge that corroboration did not demonstrate whether a hypothesis is true or probable, but that 'it is a reason for believing the hypothesis'.[71] This illustrates that critical rationalism is based on inherited thought structures, and that the way in which we understand the world around us is influenced by our subjective experiences and the perceptions of these experiences. The Norwegian thinker and poet Stein Mehren is supportive in portraying human beings threatened by their limited comprehension of human life, and their restrictive understanding of the world.[72] Oakeshott elucidates this, stating that '[the rationalist] is something also of an individualist, finding it difficult to believe that anyone who can think honestly and clearly will think differently from himself'.[73]

These examples suggest that humans are essentially inductive in their thinking, and that escaping it is extremely challenging if not impossible. However, Popper's critical rationalism is a solution, since its methodical structure reduces the possibilities for cognitive closure and discourse failure, in that the critical method stimulates the intelligence institution to look for swans that are not white.[74]

The traditional thought process, which is based on induction, constitutes that humans would look for those swans that verify that all swans are white, and analysis that is based on such an approach would fail to capitalise on contextual premises that exist outside the syntax of the inductive argument.[75] Intelligence institutions that embrace Popper's critical rationalism and Oakeshott's ideas on critical thinking therefore reduce the inductive problem, since the approach reduces 'our [propensities] to look out for regularities, and to impose laws upon nature'.[76] Instead of searching for answers that verify the hypothesis, intelligence institutions should hence search for answers that refute them; or the institutions could make hypotheses that contradict what they search for, and verify these. In other words, if intelligence institutions want to know whether all swans are white, they should stop searching for white swans, and instead look for those that are not white. Such an approach is certainly also more cost-effective.

Critical rationalism and falsification are, although based on cor-roboration, also a counterweight to the danger of self-corroboration, and consequently to orthodoxies, political assumptions and preju-dice, since critical rationalism and falsification ensure self-corrective criticism of the thought process, although this does not entail self-criticism of the perception of the conclusion.

The result of a deep and critical acknowledgement of Popper's theories is that it is easier to fuse them with Bohm's theories on creativity. A deep understanding of Popper's theories also makes it easier to comprehend that Bohm's creativity can help intelligence institutions see the importance of a holistic approach to threat per-ception. It is when these theories are understood and fused that Oakeshott's philosophy of a critical mind can be embraced, and it becomes easier to develop intelligence operatives with a thought system that is shaped by doubt. The ultimate and positive result of the tripartite fusion of Popper's, Bohm's and Oakeshott's theories is that the problem of induction has fewer chances, and dogmatic thinking, orthodoxy, political assumption and discourse failure diminish.

Conclusion

Intelligence institutions that want to increase the quality of their work must ensure their intelligence operatives are given a chance to develop their minds. They must be given freedom and oppor-tunities to develop their creativity and as such their integrity, and intelligence organisations, intelligence operatives and consumers therefore need to be attentive, alert, aware and sensitive to the reality of the holistic complexity of threats. The comprehension of this oneness and totality may help intelligence communities to analyse threat structures deeply and understand their order. Ideology, organisation, leadership, manning, funding, supporters and potential breeding grounds for threats are all factors needing exploration. Special attention should be given to the relation and structure of these factors. They must never be analysed separately. It is the interplay of the holistic complexity of threats that needs to be understood.

Comprehending future threats is probably one of the most difficult cognitive challenges on which humans and organisations can embark. Intelligence organisations therefore need to be attentive to the capabilities and limitations of human cognition. Human imagination and creativity need to be embraced. Only then can discourse failure be diminished, and the structures and the harmony of threats properly understood. Attentive, alert, aware and sensitive intelligence operators cooperate better. Increased cooperation improves discourse, and increased discourse develops pleasure and a true love for intelligence work. It is when such pleasure and love have been established that operators will explore weak points in their work, instead of overlooking them. Intelligence is therefore a phenomenon that seeks to explore and comprehend the complex structured order of threats. This is a cognitive activity more than a mathematical process. 'Certain kinds of things can be achieved by techniques and formulae, but originality and creativity are not among these. The act of seeing deeply (and not merely verbally or intellectually) is also the act in which originality and creativity can be born.'[77]

Intelligence institutions should therefore stimulate and develop thinking and creativity that probe beyond the limits of formal reasoning, so that they are able to comprehend the wholeness of threats. The next chapter analyses and describes this multidimensional task.

2   Intelligence and Discourse Failure

> If one approaches another man with a fixed 'theory' about him as
> an 'enemy' against whom one must defend oneself, he will respond
> similarly, and thus one's 'theory' will apparently be confirmed by
> experience.[1]

Intelligence is a delicate, challenging process that can produce its
own self-referential dynamic. Bohm accurately illustrates this in
implicitly pointing out that predetermined intelligence theories
about the enemy will be confirmed by experience.[2] Bohm thus
exposes the main challenge of intelligence. Threats that intelligence
organisations are meant to comprehend are complex and individually unique, and arguably also universal in their structures. However, it is important to remember that social phenomena do 'not
tend to approach a state of complete statistical regularity or sym-
metry'.[3] Intelligence is therefore an activity challenged by human
orthodoxies and preconceived political assumptions.[4] Intelligence
organisations should hence seek to understand threats beyond the
boundaries of induction, and this book therefore suggests that the
complex structures of threats may be comprehended through their
unique similar differences.[5]

Intelligence organisations therefore need to comprehend what
they can understand and accept what they cannot conceive of.
Understanding the similarities and differences between a curve and
a circle is helpful, and it is important to remember that curves are
lines. The segments of a curve vary in position and are similar in
direction. And likewise with a circle: the segments vary, while the
angles are similar. The difference between the curve and the circle
are thus similar. But 'the *similarities* defining the circle are *different*

from those defining the straight line. This, in fact, is the essential *difference* between the two curves.'[6]

What can be learned from this, and which ideas may be transferable to threat perception? Intelligence organisations must experience and learn what is individually unique to threats, and thus what is universally different, and they have to look for the similar differences between threats. These similar differences manifest themselves as threats, which are individually unique, and with a universal difference that appears as their slowly and constantly varying character. Their varying character is their similar difference, and thus their similarity. A threat will therefore always challenge the existing language and threat discourse, and threats are primarily threats because no language exists with which to conceive of them. This implies that intelligence organisations need to '[develop] a language that can describe the quality of [the order of threats] properly'.[7]

This book hence suggests that threats to societies possess a contradictory complexity that makes them inherently challenging to foresee and comprehend. It is when this complexity interacts with the synthesis of secrecy, intelligence tribal language and cognitive closure that discourse failure develops. This chapter will demonstrate the existence of an innate and potentially self-destructive nature to intelligence, and that this identity increases when intelligence organisations seek to understand and comprehend threats.

The Analysis and its Structure

For the purpose of analysis, this chapter will be divided into four parts. The first part focuses on a conceptual, fourfold description of intelligence. Part two explores whether intelligence organisations are more exposed to cognitive closure than other state organisations, and how this possibly self-destructive nature of intelligence increases discourse failure. Part three is a conceptual and general analysis of intelligence failure and a conceptual and specific analysis of discourse failure. Part four analyses how intelligence can better be understood through twelve images derived from the interplay between intelligence as art and phenomenon, science, method, activity, product, function and subject matter.

When seeking to comprehend the complexity of threat perception, it is important to be attentive and alert to the changing nature of threat structures. Bohm makes it clear that 'new *orders of [structures]* are always emerging'.[8] Nevertheless, he implicitly elucidates a factor that intelligence organisations should be aware of and sensitive to: the orders of structures in the threats that are to be comprehended develop slowly.[9] Intelligence organisations should therefore consider the universal structure in threats,[10] and that this universal character develops and changes its structures slowly and imperceptibly. It is in terms of this development that intelligence organisations should prioritise their analytical efforts.

A Fourfold Description of Intelligence

Intelligence is a subtle, multidimensional subject. It is in its subtleties, its different dimensions and their interaction, that a deep, holistic understanding of the phenomenon can be found. The word 'phenomenon' is used deliberately, as it shapes the understanding and comprehension of the subject. Sun Tzu's philosophy provides thinking that to a certain degree outweighs the lack of intelligence theory and definition. His philosophy warns of the consequences of actions based on ignorance, and emphasises that '[response] to conflict with massed aggression is severely damaging'.[11] This is especially true if the grounds for political decision-making are poor. It is also here that the quest for a deeper understanding of the quintessence of intelligence can be found, since Sun Tzu illustrates that intelligence is a political phenomenon. It exists because someone has a need for superior knowledge, and Sun Tzu encapsulates this comprehension in stating that it is 'when the general knows taking whole, deception can be a part of genuineness'.[12] Intelligence is genuine and special, and it therefore needs to be kept secret. Intelligence is knowledge about something or someone that probes the inner life of humans. Herman has provided intelligence studies with comprehensive descriptions of intelligence and its mental identity. He elucidates the relation of intelligence to wisdom and genuineness in stating that intelligence is a ruler's tool with which to 'search for preternatural wisdom'.[13] This chapter aims to analyse and demonstrate that high-quality intelligence is a kind of superior, preternatural wisdom. However, in this context preternatural wisdom must not be understood as something mystical, but rather as a form of insight that goes beyond formal reasoning.

This examination of intelligence obtains its scientific support from Popper's theories of critical rationalism,[14] and intelligence must hence not be understood as conclusions that arise as a result of linear premises in a classical formal logical argument. Such conclusions do not ensure the holistic dimensional understanding of situations and threats, as the syntax in calculative logic is superior to meaning and context.[15] Intelligence must therefore always seek to produce knowledge, which ensures a comprehension of the wholeness of the contextual complexities of the threats and the situations which intelligence organisations aim to comprehend. Intelligence is therefore a form of knowledge that is multidimensional and abstract. Intelligence work should thus never be static or linear; it should be comprehended as an endless, dynamic process. The intelligence process is strictly speaking a form of profound insight that explores the correspondence between thought and reality, rather than a 'form of *knowledge* of how the world is'.[16] This statement may sound radical and problematic because intelligence is normally understood as an activity seeking to comprehend the world. Intelligence organisations do often aim to comprehend the world, without taking into account that any analysis is influenced by the mindset of the analysts.[17] Their analyses are therefore often inadequate, simply because the intelligence organisations try to achieve too much. Intelligence requirements develop because the intelligence consumer has a need. This need develops into ideas that are transformed into theories, and it is from these theories that hypotheses can be expanded.[18] This explanation of the relationship between intelligence requirements and hypotheses is ideal, and does not necessarily correspond with the daily life and reality of many intelligence institutions. Intelligence is a phenomenon. It is science, but it is also a profession, and this threefold identity makes it not only difficult to comprehend, but, most importantly, difficult to direct as an art, science and a trade. Intelligence is therefore, more than anything else, a form of theoretical insight, a way of *trying* to understand how the world acts, and not necessarily an accurate comprehension of how the world is.[19] However, the most important aim for intelligence institutions is hence to reduce the potential imbalance between the conclusions derived from our theoretical perceptions of reality, and reality as it is.

Herman calls attention to this abstractive and multidimensional identity in pointing out that intelligence can be understood both 'in general usage and in formal [description]'.[20] Intelligence therefore needs to be understood conceptually and reflectively. It is also important for analysis to distinguish between national intelligence and any other form of information production and gathering. National intelligence should be understood as both the product and the production organisation that has been established and which exists for national governmental purposes. Herman encapsulates this idea in explaining 'government intelligence' as 'the specialised organizations that have the name [intelligence service], and what they do and produce'.[21]

Nations, states and governments exercise power, and this power needs to be maintained and protected. Other political players' intentions and aims need to be understood, and this is what gives national intelligence its distinct character and identity as an indirect, powerful political-information specialist. The indirect political role of national intelligence organisations highlights the 'service role' of these institutions, a very important characteristic to be discussed and examined later in this chapter.

In short, national intelligence is the product and the organisation that produces this product, and these organisations exist for political purposes; an intelligence organisation 'is [thus] torn between its twin skills of collecting information and evaluating it'.[22] This characteristic also encapsulates its distinctive identity. National intelligence services have to collect information of possible intelligence value, and evaluate and analyse this information to form a kind of distinct, superior knowledge that gives the intelligence consumer political power. This is because 'those with better intelligence have a better understanding of power relationship and, therefore, superior means to adapt to the environment in which they operate'.[23] This important character trait is vividly illustrated by Herman, who titled one of his books *Intelligence Power in Peace and War*. In short, therefore, national intelligence can be defined and understood as national political intelligence power.

Sun Tzu explicates the superiority of such intelligence, calling it foreknowledge.[24] The philosophy explains that foreknowledge needs to be attained to assure victory: 'the key to skilful action is in knowing those things that make up the environment and then arranging them so that their power becomes available.'[25] This explanation is an excellent guide for high-quality intelligence analysis inasmuch as it goes beyond formal reasoning. It ensures a critical and rational examination of threat structures, and it is this kind of investigation that is essential for adequate intelligence analysis. The foundation for the following analysis is that intelligence is power, and that national intelligence may assure political advantage for the intelligence consumer.[26]

The best description of intelligence has been provided by Kent. He explains intelligence as a specific kind of knowledge, expressed as an intelligence product, the organisation that produces this product, and the activities performed by the intelligence organisation to produce this product expressed as knowledge.[27] Kent continues and states that 'intelligence work remains the simple, natural endeavor to get the sort of knowledge upon which a successful course of action can be rested'.[28] Herman has elaborated on Kent's explanation, and points out that intelligence needs to be understood fourfold. These four parts are: *activity, product, functions* and *subject matter*.[29] It is through a comprehension of the relationship and reciprocal interaction of these constituent parts that an adequate understanding of intelligence may be found. The different parts and their relationship and interaction will be explored in the following analysis.

By investigating activity, product, functions, subject matter, their relationship to state power and their mutual interaction, it will be demonstrated that intelligence is the production of holistic insight, an insight aiming to give the intelligence consumer political power. This realisation captures the distinct service role of national intelligence organisations, a consciousness that furthermore shapes the understanding of national intelligence as something that is fundamentally different from all other forms of information activities.

Activity

Intelligence activity should be understood as those activities that aim to collect, process and evaluate information of possible intelligence value. These activities serve the same role, though they are fundamentally different, an important distinction to which one should be attentive. Collection is creative, demanding and can sometimes even be life-threatening. It is also politically sensitive. Intelligence services therefore require operators who are able to understand and accommodate this sensitivity. In addition, intelligence services also need personnel who have a kind of character that is able to exist in a mental environment torn between boring routines and creative cleverness and imagination.[30] Real intelligence collection aspires to gather information that adversaries do not want to part with. Loch K. Johnson illustrates the consequent reciprocal nature of intelligence:

> . . . the United States has established intelligence agencies to ferret out the secret information the nation needs to enhance its security and its quest for political and economic opportunities. Moreover, nations seek to shield their own secrets from the prying eyes of adversaries; therefore, they create a counterintelligence service.[31]

Intelligence collection therefore operates in an environment of deception, subversion, security and suspicion. This creates a reciprocal character which, in peacetime at least, is characterised by intelligence services often focusing excessively on secrecy:[32] 'and with the vast expansion in bureaucratization [of the US Intelligence Community] came a remarkable routinization of secrecy'.[33] There are, of course, good reasons for such caution. Intelligence organisations operate in an environment that could best be described as the dark side of human psychology.[34] Intelligence therefore

The intelligence product is therefore essentially the consumer's understanding of the information presented, rather than the substance of the information itself – a perspective that highlights the importance of a good relationship between the intelligence producer and the intelligence consumer. This good relationship should express itself as healthy intelligence discourse between intelligence institutions and intelligence consumers, a relationship that 'entails an awareness of user needs through contact with them'.[41]

Optimal collection should therefore be identified by its positive aggressiveness, creativity, cleverness and its core methodical and reflective character. The collector is courageous, intelligent and patient. High-quality analysis is methodical. Nevertheless, it is based on a prepared and creative mind, exploring all available possibilities, and 'it will not ignore its intuition when something does not quite feel right about a complex analytical situation'.[42] Analysis is hard work, requiring a patient, steady hand. The analyst should be highly intelligent, as well as ideally possessing a character almost free of prejudice, political assumptions and orthodoxies.

Intelligence collection and intelligence analysis are separate activities and require both equal and unequal qualifications. But one could not exist without the other, and they are thus twin skills.[43] High-quality intelligence analysis could not, therefore, exist without highly trained and experienced intelligence collectors who can provide analysts with qualitative raw information. Nevertheless, it is the intelligence analysts who create and shape the core character of intelligence, insofar as they transform the raw information into estimates that are presented as a product that may give the intelligence consumer vital knowledge.

Product

At first sight, it may seem easy to understand the intelligence product narrowly as written products, disseminated to the intelligence consumer as formal briefs or reports. This book argues that the true intelligence product is substantially the service intelligence organisations provide to the societies of which they form a part.[44] This service is best understood through a comprehension of the importance of intelligence dialogue between the intelligence producer and the intelligence consumer on the one hand, and the identity of intelligence as knowledge and wisdom probing beyond formal reasoning on the other. Whether intelligence products are given to a platoon commander in an operational theatre or a government, they all serve the same purpose; they are meant to provide the consumer with vital knowledge that may help optimise tactical, operational, strategic and political efforts, inputs and possible outputs and gains. Former UK Security and Intelligence Coordinator Sir David Omand elucidates this in stating that the ultimate purpose of intelligence is:

> . . . to enable action to be optimized by reducing ignorance; and of secret intelligence to achieve this objective in respect of information that others wish to remain hidden. Thus stated, the purpose of intelligence is not linked simply to knowledge for its own sake but to organized information that can be put to use.[45]

Numerous commentators from the age of Sun Tzu onwards have explained and tried to define intelligence,[46] though few explanations or definitions sufficiently illuminate the consumer's requirements; the intelligence activities; and the very important dialogue between producers and between these producers and the intelligence consumers. That defining intelligence seems to be so challenging is in itself a description of the core essence of intelligence. Intelligence is multidimensional in its nature, and Kent has rightly observed and described to a certain degree this plural and holistic character.[47] Herman's fourfold description complements Kent's definition, as it appreciates the multiple identities of intelligence and its connection to state power. Omand comprehends the obstacles of this character in emphasising the limitations of classic intelligence analysis. He holds that analysis fails to comprehend complex future situations, and suggests that intelligence organisations should instead use elucidation in their production of estimates.[48] The essence and importance of his argument will be discussed in Chapter 5. Herman's fourfold explanation of intelligence, adumbrated with Omand's understanding of the limitations of classic intelligence analysis and his consequent focus on elucidation, crystallise intelligence as activities expressed as collection, elucidation and estimation to produce knowledge and insight beyond formal reasoning. Intelligence therefore ultimately articulates a service product that increases the consumer's tactical, operational, strategic and political advantage that may 'result in improved decisions'.[49] The service product should hence be understood as the sum of high-quality estimates, the communication of this product to the intelligence consumer and the consumer's comprehension of this product, ultimately expressed in the service role of high-performance intelligence organisations. It is therefore important to explore the service function of intelligence services.

Function

Herman holds that the function of intelligence refers to intelligence as a 'staff' function rather than a 'line' function, as intelligence services should not 'propose decisions, take them or execute them'.[50] Herman captures the true essence of intelligence activity, and he clarifies that intelligence is not substantially operational, nor should it be directly involved in policy-making. It should hence be as close to the policy-makers as possible, though without jeopardising its objective and advisory service role. The question of whether intelligence should strive to be as objective as possible, or whether it should be closer, or even more directly involved in policy-making (the Kent versus Gates debate)[51] is probably one of the most important debates in intelligence studies, and is a continuation of the debate between Kent and Kendall.[52] Gates advocates that intelligence services must be as close to policy-makers as possible 'in order to intimately know what [is] on their policy plates'.[53] The thesis in this book is based on the assumption that a close relationship based on healthy intelligence dialogue with policy-makers is called for. However, Kent's view is still valid, since it reminds us that intelligence services must protect their important objectivity. Intelligence requirements are always political, and for this very reason intelligence institutions should do their utmost to avoid colouring the intelligence process. Kent therefore highlighted that intelligence should seek to be purely advisory in its character, 'lest their analyses [become] tainted by policy interests'.[54] This certainly increases its reliability, and most importantly its credibility.

Those scholars who support Kent's view argue that the quality of intelligence, and its resistance to politicisation, depend on 'the appropriate distance and independence that intelligence should have from policy making'.[55] It is no doubt a question of independence, though it is not a question of distance as such, which implies that embracing Kent's view does not imply that the communication between the intelligence producer and the intelligence consumer is less effective than it would have been if one had embraced the Gates model. It is easy to understand independence, objectivity and the service role of intelligence services as factors decreasing dialogue between the intelligence producer and the intelligence consumer, and it is also here that the classic debate has gone astray, since the debate arguably has been a question of distance and the extent of objectivity, and not of the character and the quality of the discourse between the intelligence organisation and the policy-maker. The debate should focus on this discourse, as it is the quality of this discourse and its communicative form that increase or decrease the level of the reliability and credibility of intelligence services and the intelligence product.

The ultimate result of such healthy discourse is productive sharing of information, and the 9/11 Commission holds that qualitative information sharing 'is a powerful tool'.[56] The report elucidates the damaging results of decreased communication and decreased sharing, arguably expressed as discourse failure, powerfully illustrating it with 'examples of information that could be accessed – like the undistributed NSA information that would have helped identify Nawaf al Hazmi in January 2000. But someone had to ask for it. In that case, no one did.'[57] The result was that Hazmi was able to board the American Airlines flight 77[58] that took off from Washington Dulles on 9/11 at 8:20 for Los Angeles. The flight carried fifty-eight passengers, and crashed into the Pentagon at 9:37:46. Everybody on board died, and many staff members in the Pentagon were injured or killed.[59]

This example demonstrates the importance of good discourse between the intelligence producer and consumer, and the classic television series *Upstairs, Downstairs* provides an ultimate image and illustration of high-performance intelligence services and their healthy, reliable and productive discourse with those whom they serve.

Upstairs, Downstairs describes the daily life of masters and servants in a London townhouse. They live and breathe in the same house, though they live and work separately – the masters upstairs, the servants downstairs. Although they move in different spheres they are mutually dependent, and one could not live without the other. The butler is the link between the two different but dependent worlds. He conducts the dialogue, and ensures the smooth running of the house. His role is a good metaphor for that of a perfect intelligence coordinator, who will ensure that any requirements are handed down to the servants for them to execute, and that the finished product is presented to the master in a proper and conceivable manner.

Ideally he or she should do more than that, and this perspective is the art of being a good butler – or intelligence coordinator. He or she should therefore, through high-quality intelligence dialogue, know the needs and character of the master: this presupposes 'a good rapport between ministers and intelligence chiefs, that at a crucial point the former will ask the latter, well, what do you think we should do next?'[60] Good intelligence dialogue is therefore based on mutual respect, impartiality and integrity,[61] and facilitates the communication of requirements and the dissemination of the product between master and servants. Qualitative intelligence production therefore requires an intelligence dialogue based on open and critical discourse, both in intelligence institutions and between these institutions and their decision-makers. Healthy discourse expressed as high-quality intelligence dialogue enables the intelligence producer to conduct its most important task: the service role. The service role is the function of intelligence, since it is good intelligence dialogue expressed as healthy discourse between the producer and the decision-maker that presupposes and ensures production of intelligence beyond the limits of formal reasoning, and that this insight is disseminated to and understood by the decision-maker. The butler and the intelligence coordinator constitute, accordingly, the indispensable connection between two separate but interdependent worlds.

Intelligence services conduct the same role as the servants and the butler: they provide a service function for their masters as independent, objective and advisory information specialists.[62] A deeper understanding of this role is also to be found in the dialectics in the argument presented. The connection, communication and discourse between the servants, the butler and their master are also a service, since service in its dialectical character can also be understood as the connection between two parties. This illustrates that the intelligence product comes into being as a result of the relationship that arises between the intelligence producer and the intelligence consumer. The image of such a good relationship is reflected in the butler providing his master with an umbrella: not because it is raining, or because the master asks for it, but because the servants and the butler assess that there is a possibility that it may start raining. This is also the decisive role of high-quality and high-performance intelligence work, and it illustrates that intelligence depends on a proper understanding of roles and functions, and therefore also on dialogue and discourse, rather than on appropriate distance.

The service function of intelligence therefore depends upon an intimate but separate and distinct relationship between the intelligence institutions and the policy-maker, and intelligence services should always remember that they serve the constitution through their service to the politicians. This service role is the subject matter of intelligence.

Subject Matter

Omand emphasises that intelligence optimises actions through the reduction of ignorance.[63] However, reduction of ignorance and production of knowledge are not in themselves its pure objective. Intelligence services exist as counterparts that have valuable information they do everything to hide,[64] most importantly because this information 'can be put to use'[65] by the adversary's intelligence consumer. This illustrates that the value of this information reflects the core role of decision-makers as protectors of the state. Intelligence organisations serve policy-makers, and these masters operate in a political climate where everyone tries to fulfil their political inputs and potential outputs and gains. Intelligence organisations therefore serve policy-makers who serve the state, and it is in this climate of political games and power struggles that intelligence organisations perform their duties. Nevertheless, policy and intelligence do not exist merely for the sake of political games and trickery. Politics is as difficult to define as intelligence, probably because the two have the same origin; the essence and origin of the state. Politics, and intelligence institutions' place in it, will therefore be explored in the following.

Politics is deeply cognitive and hence a mental phenomenon, and it dialectically originates from the Greek word *polis*, which 'was the basic unit for political organization throughout the Graeco-Roman world'.[66] Political activity is conducted among citizens of a political identity, in most cases called a state, and 'participation in the life of the polis gave moral development to the citizen, organized their religion, provided their culture, and was the overriding duty of the citizen or even the metic (non-citizen but legally resident alien)'.[67] *Polis* can therefore in its deepest form refer to the mental and physical force that protects the political, social, cultural and religious conduct of a state and its members. *Polis* and accordingly politics must therefore be understood both as a mindset and as an act. The Acropolis in Athens is an image of *polis*, and can metaphorically be understood as the highest moral and mental form of the state, both as individual and collective moral development, and as an image of the identity that protects the development of a human and moral society. This was the place where state citizens could seek physical protection, and it was also a temple, portraying the whole idea of the state.

The word 'politics' is in everyday use by most people, though few are able to define it or explain its essence, and 'the definition of politics is highly, perhaps essentially, contested'.[68] That is understandable, since politics is a holistic phenomenon that not only shapes human interaction, but more than anything else constitutes and originates from the human need for security and human development.

Humans constantly seek an understanding of themselves and the world they live in, as well as physical security. This deep wish and search for wisdom and security constitutes politics, and consequently also shapes the discourse between humans.

Politics is therefore the experience and consciousness of being human, as well as the enterprise to improve this state securely. The pure and essential purpose of intelligence should therefore be to serve politics and decision-makers in the enhancement of the human condition, as 'politics makes a call upon knowledge'.[69] This, no doubt, illustrates the role of high-performance and in-depth intelligence production. Intelligence organisations serve this political search for undisclosed knowledge, and the core purpose of intelligence is, hence, the hunt for information that others do not want to disclose, since 'intelligence is the agency through which states seek to protect or extend their relative advantage'.[70] The relative political advantage that intelligence institutions constitute towards counterparts is also the subject matter of intelligence, given that 'intelligence is targeted on "them" not "us", with espionage'.[71] Intelligence will therefore always face counterparts that are mutually unwilling to reveal their secrets, and adversaries are therefore 'organized so as to secure *relative advantage.*'[72] Intelligence organisations' antagonism towards their counterparts, and the hunt for their hidden knowledge, shape the essential character and identity of intelligence, as well as the methods they use to obtain this information. The reciprocal condition between intelligence organisations and their counterparts illustrates the image of the 'specialness' of intelligence, as 'secrecy and subjects combine to make it in some way "special"'.[73] Sir Percy Cradock, former chairman of the British Joint Intelligence Committee (JIC) from 1985 to 1992, vividly describes this 'special' and distorted character, and states that the reality of intelligence is:

> The hard world of shocks and accidents, threats and crises . . . Here the news was usually bad, more about the errors, less about the achievements. It was the dark side of the moon, history pre-eminently as the record of the crimes and follies of mankind.[74]

Intelligence services serve states that ultimately exist to improve the conditions of their citizens by distributing security, responsibility and benefits. The 'crimes and follies of mankind'[75] are the greatest threat to this development, and the subject matter of intelligence is therefore the protection of the society it serves against ignorance and cognitive closure. The next section argues that intelligence has an innately self-destructive character, and that this character is fuelled by the force of cognitive closure.

The Force of Cognitive Closure on Intelligence

Intelligence is, firstly, an activity. Secondly, it is the product expressed as the service provided to the intelligence consumer. It is thirdly the staff rather than the line function, and fourthly it is the sum of these three factors and their mutual interaction expressed as intelligence power. That is the subject matter and essence of intelligence.[76] However, there is something more to intelligence, something undefined, plural and blurred. Intelligence is a holistic phenomenon, and it constitutes intelligence activity as an art, since 'phenomena can be studied only subjectively'.[77] The understanding of intelligence is therefore mental, individual and often diffuse, a diffusion that has shaped the blurred understanding of intelligence that exists today, as the current comprehension of intelligence does not 'isolate the relevant factors and highlight the relationship between them, [and] thereby [fails in] constructing a theoretical reality'[78] of intelligence. The uncertainty that this vague situation creates arguably increases the self-destructive character of intelligence, since intelligence therefore does not immediately lend itself to comprehensible answers.

Analysts must trust their fantasy, imagination and intuition and defend themselves from prejudice, orthodoxies and political assumptions. These limiting factors are increased by the human tendency to acquiesce to cognitive closure, and Clausewitz is illustrative in clarifying that commanders, and implicitly also intelligence operatives, must trust their sound judgement 'and stand like a rock on which the waves break in vain'.[79] The future and the estimates about it are as vague and unintelligible as war, and intelligence therefore easily lends itself to the force of cognitive closure and discourse failure. Cognitive closure and consequently discourse failure therefore constitute the element of friction in intelligence work, since 'this difficulty of *accurate recognition* constitutes one of the most serious sources of friction in war, by making things appear entirely different from what one had expected'.[80]

However, this book holds that the human tendency to surrender to the habitual,[81] without sufficiently accurate recognition of how things might appear in the future, illustrates the negative force of cognitive closure. Sufficiently accurate recognition should not be confused with induction, since induction does not accurately recognise the unexpected,[82] and as such only fuels further misjudgement of the future. Clausewitz's theory of accurate recognition should thus be understood as professional intelligence intuition. Uncertainty and the unknown facilitate cognitive closure and thus decrease this intuitive force, and it is therefore worth analysing the phenomenon more closely.

Cognitive Closure

Humans prefer predictability and security.[83] Human development and progress undoubtedly presuppose fantasy, imagination and the courage and willingness to challenge orthodoxies and political assumptions. Cognitive closure 'represents the desire for a definite answer on some topic, any answer as opposed to confusion and ambiguity'.[84] It therefore contrasts mental growth, since mental growth presupposes creativity and freedom, and in its nature threatens the human desire for orthodoxy and non-specific cognitive closure. The ability to comprehend threats to a society therefore presupposes the ability to challenge the human tendency to suppress fantasy and imagination, and cognitive closure is therefore the greatest enemy of threat perceptions and, consequently, of intelligence.

The intelligence failure of the Yom Kippur war of 1973 is a classic demonstration of the negative force of cognitive closure on intelligence, and how the phenomenon decreased threat perception and ultimately led to intelligence failure. The war came as a huge surprise to the Israelis. Arguably, Israel saw itself as the leading military power in the Middle East at that time, and consequently believed that Egypt would be deterred from attacking; as a result, 'by favoring the doctrine of deterrence and early warning, Israel left itself vulnerable in the Yom Kippur War'.[85] Cognitive closure will be examined against this backdrop.

Intelligence failure, cognitive closure and consequently discourse failure are deeply mental phenomena. Self-image is therefore a factor that undoubtedly shapes and fuels cognitive closure.
Discourse failure is not only the inability to comprehend threats,
but also and more importantly the unwillingness to accept the
apparent. It is here that it mirrors cognitive closure. This implies
that it is difficult for anyone to believe something that they have
decided not to believe, or something that challenges or threatens
orthodox worldviews. Cognitive closure is therefore intensified in
situations where much is at stake, or where the situational make-
up is cognitively challenging. Bar-Joseph illustrates this:

> Situational variables that increase the need for closure include: time
> pressure, concrete deadline, and need for action; exogenous aspects
> such as environmental noise, and endogenous aspects such as a per-
> ception of information processing as effortful, dull, and unattractive;
> the perceiver's organismic state, primarily the state of fatigue; attribu-
> tion of high value to closure by significant other; and a requirement
> for judgement on the topic under discussion.[86]

In intelligence, the intellectual and personal stakes are often
high. Pride, honour and prestige shape intelligence as they do
everywhere else, but it is when such cultures are fused with
secrecy and intelligence tribal language that cognitive closure may
increase. A person who has put his or her reputation at stake will
probably close cognition, even when it is clear that he or she is
wrong, and this study argues that the force of cognitive closure
is likely to increase as a result of the negative force of strong personalities who put their intellectual and professional reputation
on the line.

The result in the case of the Yom Kippur War was that leading
figures in the Israeli Directorate of Military Intelligence (AMAN)
refused to accept that Israel was under immediate threat, despite
the fact that a Military Intelligence Review distributed on
5 October 1973 – twenty-four hours before the war started –
clearly indicated that Israel was under immediate threat from
Egypt because 'five of out of the six senior analysts of Syrian and
Egyptian affairs in AMAN's Research Division estimated that war

83

was either certain or highly likely'.[87] However, leading figures in AMAN, despite clear indicators of an attack, refused to accept the estimations.[88] The estimation that was presented to the policy-makers made it clear, contrary to the indicators, that 'to the best of our estimate no change took place in Egypt's estimate of the balance of forces with the IDF [Israeli Defence Forces]. Therefore, the probability that they intend to resume fighting is low.'[89] The consequence of this estimate was that military leaders and policy-makers did not obtain any warning or adequate estimations that reflected the seriousness of the threat.

One central question arises as a result of the above. Why were estimates that reflected the real magnitude of the threat not communicated to the consumers? Bar-Joseph is illustrative in asking: 'Why did some of the agency's analysts estimate the situation correctly and regard war's probability as high or even certain, while others (mostly in higher ranks) erred completely?'[90] That it was mostly higher-ranking officers who refused to accept the apparent suggests that their self-image, and its relation to their perception of Israel as the dominant military power in the region, influenced their beliefs. Such a supposition is supported in that the estimates provided to the consumers focused more on the 'balance of forces with the IDF'[91] than on the essential threat from Egypt. This suggests that these officers regarded themselves as soldiers in the strongest army in the Middle East and thus found it difficult to believe or accept that Egypt would dare attack. Bar-Joseph argues that the answers to why it went so disastrously wrong are to be found in the 'idiosyncratic behaviour of two intelligence officers'.[92]

It was Major General Eli Zeira and Lieutenant Colonel Yona Bandman who were responsible for the Israeli estimates. Zeira was Director of Military Intelligence (DMI), and as such also military intelligence advisor to the Israeli government; Bandman was head of the Egyptian and North African Affairs Branch of AMAN's (Israeli's Directorate of Military Intelligence) Research Division. Their unwillingness to accept the apparent and listen to divergent opinions crystallised itself as cognitive closure and discloses analytical parallels with the case of 9/11, where strong individuals such as Paul Wolfowitz stated that the National Coordinator for Counter Terrorism, Richard Clarke, gave 'bin Laden too much credit'.[93] These parallels illustrate that the force of cognitive closure in both cases decreased discourse and as such increased discourse failure, although these conformities operated on different strategic levels.

The reasons for cognitive closure in Israel in 1973 may be explained by a complex interplay of different factors: the politicisation of the intelligence process and a strong belief in received opinion that led to an underestimation of the enemies' capability and willingness to attack. The last and most important factor is the human tendency to overstate the ability to understand human cognition, and consequently the world in general. This tendency increases when humans throw overboard Socratic humility.[94] Bar-Joseph vividly illustrates this factor, stating that 'a combination of over-confidence, a unique *Weltanschauung* of professional duties and dogmatic beliefs concerning Arab war intentions, led Zeira to a professionally unacceptable and damaging form of conduct'.[95]

Arguably, Zeira's and Bandman's unwillingness to accept the apparent melded with their willingness to tell the politicians what they believed they wanted to hear. The result was the politicisation of the intelligence cycle stemming from cognitive closure. Zeira's and Bandman's personal involvement, and more importantly the prestige they invested in themselves, created a self-destructive psychological cycle, although estimates indicated that they were actually wrong. It is difficult admitting that one is wrong, particularly if one feels that one's reputation and career are at stake.

The operational consequence of Zeira's and Bandman's behaviour was that Major General Shmuel Gonen, the commander of the Southern Command, slowed down operational planning for war. This 'gave the Egyptians the best conditions to start the war – better than they ever dreamed about'.[96]

Both Yom Kippur and 9/11 illustrate the force of cognitive closure, and consequently also the force of discourse failure. In both cases information clearly indicated that the threat was imminent and lethal, and in both cases the understanding of this information was misunderstood, not accepted or, at worst, overlooked.[97] The two cases illustrate the power of individuals on the intelligence process, and the consequences if these individuals decide what they believe, and continue to do so despite estimates indicating that they should question their beliefs. Bar-Joseph writes that the 'unprofessional interference of DMI Zeira with the intelligence cycle on the eve of the war was, probably, the most devastating factor that prevented Israel from being ready when it came'.[98]

The cases of 9/11 and Yom Kippur both demonstrate that cognitive closure easily develops in an atmosphere where strong and powerful individuals refuse to question their orthodoxies and political assumptions. These examples also highlight that human cognition and its weaknesses provide the most important explanation for intelligence failure.

Intelligence Failure and Discourse Failure

Intelligence failure is the inability to comprehend the changing structures of threats and the consequent unwillingness to accept the apparent, as the word 'failure' implies that something significant and obvious has been misjudged or overlooked. Intelligence failure is for that reason a situation where evidential connections or indications have not been perceived and accepted, and discourse failure thus elucidates the nature of intelligence failure, since it 'explains how communication and language shape the comprehension of threats'.[99]

Intelligence failure manifests itself as discourse failure when intelligence operatives are unwilling to constantly scrutinise their own orthodoxies and political assumptions, and when this reluctance makes it difficult for them to accept the apparent, and impossible for them to imagine the challenging. High-quality intelligence work therefore calls for humility, wisdom, critical rationalism, cognitive awareness and endurance, as well as an extremely sound and creative mind. Wilhelm Agrell elucidates this: 'if there is an emerging science of intelligence somewhere ahead, it is hoped that the main component will be a radically improved ability for innovative thinking, for dealing with, learning from, and utilising anomalies for the benefit of the guesswork'.[100] It is when these cognitive qualities are reduced or closed that discourse failure develops. Intelligence failure manifested as discourse failure will therefore be described and analysed.

Intelligence failure '[involves] a misunderstanding that is revealed quickly once one side or the other takes action'.[101] Intelligence failure therefore reflects the reciprocal nature of intelligence, in that the ultimate consequence of one party's misjudgement will be the success of the other. Intelligence failure is thus always someone else's intelligence success, and it has four primary causes: subordination of intelligence to policy; unavailability of information when and where needed; received opinion governing a strong belief in 'conventional wisdom' without sufficient evidence; and mirror-imaging in which unfamiliar situations are judged 'on the basis of familiar ones'.[102]

The discourse failure theory provides another explanation for intelligence failure and suggests that it must be understood as a phenomenon stemming from individuals and their relation to their society, as well as to the organisation they are a part of. Discourse failure must hence be understood as failure that arises and develops from an interaction between human cognition and organisational cultures such as secrecy and intelligence tribal language. This book thus argues that it is the tripartite force between cognition, secrecy and intelligence tribal language that negatively shapes intelligence discourse, and as such facilitates discourse failure. This will be analysed in the next chapter.

Discourse failure is therefore a mental, psychological, cultural, social and political phenomenon that probably cannot be eliminated, since intelligence successes and intelligence failures are reciprocally interwoven. Nonetheless, it is clear that a consciousness of discourse failure's mechanisms and effects reduces its negative consequences. Humans, on the contrary, facilitate failure if they believe that it is possible to defeat failure in general and discourse failure. This implies that humility, integrity and self-criticism are factors that may reduce discourse failure, since these factors secure an understanding of discourse failure through an appreciation and understanding of the possibilities and limitations of human cognition. As Socrates has elucidated:

And surely it is the most blameworthy ignorance to believe that one knows what one does not know. It is perhaps on this point and in this respect, gentlemen, that I differ from the majority of men, and if

> I were to claim that I am wiser than anyone in anything, it would be in this, that, as I have no adequate knowledge of things in the underworld, so I do not think I have.[103]

Socrates thereby declares that an understanding of life and the objects around us presupposes humility and self-criticism. Sun Tzu encapsulates this understanding: 'simply being oneself brings about a power often lost in the rush to be something else.'[104] The essence of these classical quotes, and their view of the human condition, highlight the core of the discourse failure theory and illustrate that the opposite might elucidate itself as cognitive closure, as it demonstrates what the consequence might be when human fallibility interacts with the infinite complexity of life, and the consequent insecurity this creates. It is this very complexity Plato wants humans to be aware of. It is when such humility is displaced or cognitively closed that discourse failure arises.

The discourse failure theory therefore draws attention to the instrumentality between humans and their surroundings, and to the collective dynamic between intelligence operators, between these operators and the organisations they are in, between intelligence organisations, and between intelligence organisations and their consumers. It is the negative discourse that arises and develops in these interactions that facilitates discourse failure. One must therefore analyse and understand the interaction between the possibilities and limitations of human cognition and its interaction with intelligence discourses that stem from a secrecy-driven culture identified by its distinct intelligence tribal language. It is in this interaction that a specific and often restrictive and limiting discourse can develop, and it is this discourse that facilitates cognitive closure and consequently discourse failure. However, these cultures are not a result of how intelligence should be. They develop as reactions to the uncertainty that identifies the essence of intelligence. In the following section, I will therefore describe through twelve intelligence images how this uncertainty could be met. They are therefore ideal images pertaining to how intelligence must be if one aspires to reduce discourse failure and produce high-quality intelligence.

The Twelve Images of Intelligence

Intelligence can be comprehended through twelve images derived from and existing between the phenomenon, method and science on the one hand, and the subject matter, product, activity and function of intelligence on the other. These images will be presented and explored in the following. They are: intelligence power, wisdom, service, intuition, truth, elucidation, objectivity, falsification and critical rationalism, cleverness, experience, staff function and collection. It is through a comprehension of these twelve images and their relationship and interplay that intelligence can be better understood.

Power as the Phenomenon and Subject Matter of Intelligence

National intelligence is national intelligence because of its close connection to policy, and because it exists to protect the state. That is its subject matter as a social and political phenomenon, and it is in this sphere that intelligence power exists. Intelligence power is hence the force to reduce ignorance[105] and the political ability to implement in policy the knowledge provided, as power is 'the ability to make people (or things) do what they would not otherwise have done'.[106] However, this does not under any circumstances imply that intelligence as a tool for politics ultimately seeks to implement unwanted and oppressive policies on society. Intelligence services in many tyrannical regimes often serve politics for the sake of power itself, and it is therefore understandable if both intelligence and power are understood as something repressive and negative. But intelligence should be understood in its essential form as a servant of knowledge, enlightenment, openness and freedom, and power in this respect should be understood as a tool for a positive end in itself. Intelligence power must therefore be comprehended as 'the production of intended effects'.[107] These positive intended effects constitute a politics that ultimately seeks to reduce ignorance and thus protect and improve the society that both the intelligence operatives and the politicians serve.

Intelligence power therefore refers to the political effects that decision-makers can deduce from the wisdom and insight that high-quality intelligence has given them, since intelligence is the ability to support the implementation of politics through the production of intelligence that constitutes political knowledge and, as such, supports political decisions.

Wisdom as the Phenomenon of the Intelligence Product

Intelligence intends to support the quality of sound policy through the provision of a high-quality and wise intelligence product that provides 'superior knowledge of the rules or of the capabilities, strategies, quirks, and proclivities of the other players'.[108] Intelligence wisdom is hence the ability to apply intuition in the thought process, and the soundness to recognise the almost imperceptible and slowly working transformations in the order of threats, and that 'a sensitive and discriminated judgement is called for; a skilled intelligence to scent out the truth'.[109]

Intelligence operators, whether they are desk officers or field officers, need the same qualities as the ideal officers to whom Clausewitz alludes: 'great strength, however, is not easily produced where there is no emotion.'[110] Wisdom must accordingly be understood as a form of operational gut feeling expressed as estimation. In Chapter 5 on analysis, estimation will be described as the evaluation of observations and experiences and the assessments of these observations and experiences against trends.[111] Estimation can therefore be understood as the fast, methodical 'processing of experience, perception, and memory',[112] performed as intuitive operational cognition. Intelligence wisdom is therefore the emotional and cognitive ability to perform estimation, and intuitively to deduce different possibilities from the estimation process and present these to the decision-maker, so that these possibilities increase the decision-maker's ability to discern truth from deception.[113] Intelligence wisdom expressed as intuitive operational cognition introduces intelligence service as the intelligence function.

Service as the Phenomenon of the Intelligence Function

The service of intelligence is the product of intelligence, and it elucidates intelligence as a staff rather than a line function.[114] This understanding of intelligence is essential, since the objectivity of intelligence is its strength, a notion highlighted by Olav Riste:

> Ultimately, the best insurance against overt politicization of intelligence is for the intelligence community to demonstrate independence and integrity, by standing by its assessments even when they are at variance with the public assertions of its political masters.[115]

It is difficult, if not impossible, to advise if one simultaneously directly belongs to the decision process, and 'much of what will be necessary to defend objectivity when policy-making and analysis are in closer proximity will become clear only when that situation actually develops'.[116] It is when this thin line between decision-makers and intelligence producers is crossed that the politicising of intelligence can occur, and this 'is a reminder of the importance of ensuring that there is integrity in presenting intelligence to customers . . . the customer must have complete confidence in the integrity of the system that delivered it'.[117] K. L. Gardiner echoes this, emphasising that 'placing analysts in closer contact with policy-makers, even if indirectly through liaison officers, increases the danger that analysis will become politicized'.[118] However, the integrity, objectivity and advisory role of intelligence does not imply that the nature of an intelligence service does not involve having opinions and giving clear advice, which implies that intelligence services should conduct '"marketing", but not sales'.[119] Anything else would make intelligence sexless and reduce its importance and role as a service that should tell decision-makers unwelcome news.[120] Intelligence organisations therefore become services when they communicate intelligence that challenges the decision-makers' current worldviews. Intelligence services should thus be the humble and discreet servants of the constitution. The organisations and their members should operate in the shadows and serve decision-makers that are elected by their people. It is the constitutional service role that implies that intelligence services must conduct their obligations with integrity, dignity and objectivity.

It follows from this that intelligence services must not be directly involved in the decision process, since they ultimately serve the people and the nation, and not the politicians directly. The intelligence services must therefore also tell the decision-makers what they do not necessarily want to hear, because intelligence services are servants of the constitution and should thus serve the state beyond party politics. Intelligence is therefore protection of the formation of the state, and the population that forms this state. Ignorance threatening the construction of the state must be countered, and intelligence should therefore serve the truth. It does not follow from this that the truth necessarily serves the nation, but it serves the nation through its enlightened character and as an enemy of ignorance, political assumptions and orthodoxies.

The service function of intelligence is therefore to protect the constitution through the production of timely, relevant and reliable intelligence.[121] Sims is illustrative: 'the test for intelligence is relevance and timeliness'.[122] These quality characteristics must be developed, maintained and provided through a service function that is based on a relationship between the intelligence service and the elected decision-makers, which in turn is based on a mutual understanding of functions and responsibility. This implies that the decision-makers understand that the intelligence service does not serve them, but the constitution. Both the intelligence producer and the decision-maker must therefore remember that they serve the same nation. It is this common comprehension and agreement that serve the nation, and that reduce the possibility of the politicisation of intelligence.

It has now been demonstrated that the service function of national intelligence implies that intelligence should serve the constitution of the nation through the production of sound intelligence. Such production presupposes high-quality methods, and these methods that seek to help the intelligence services predict the future and reduce uncertainty are intuitive in their character.

Intuition as the Phenomenon of Intelligence Activity

Intelligence intuition can be understood as operational accurate recognition, through the fast operational and methodical 'processing of experience, perception, and memory'.[123] This fast process facilitates intuitive operational cognition. Intuition is therefore the one factor that constitutes wisdom and cleverness, and intuition hence encapsulates intelligence both as a thought process and as knowledge beyond formal reasoning, since 'the deep source of intelligence is the unknown and indefinable totality from which all perception originates'.[124] Intelligence quality is thus a question of wisdom, cleverness, experience and cognitive awareness, since intuition is 'immediate awareness, either of the truth of some proposition, or of an object of apprehension such as a concept'.[125] Threats that are slowly and constantly changing constitute such a concept, and intelligence operators must hence develop an accurate recognition that develops into 'an empirical form, covering the sensible apprehension of things, and as pure intuition it is that which structures sensation into the experience of things in space and time'.[126]

Intuition is thus not mystical, even though it 'is frequently regarded with suspicion'.[127] Intelligence services, however, have to detect and perceive new variations of threats, and their slowly changing and almost unobservable character creates a cognitive distance between them and the intelligence institution. These threats are essentially always in front of the intelligence operatives, and intuition provides, if not a solution, then at least a useful tool that makes being aware of these threats less challenging so that they can be detected and countered in time.

So far this description of intuition has been philosophical, and it has not described intuition as an effective, practical intelligence capability. Intelligence is a deeply cognitive phenomenon which involves perception, and Handel emphasises that:

> human perceptions are ethnocentric. They see the external world inside out, which typically involves the projection of one's own belief systems, and by definition causes the underestimation, if not denigration, of the opponent's culture; motivation; intentions; material and technological achievements; and capacity to identify with others.[128]

Intelligence institutions try to perceive threats and disclose deception, and Handel's point highlights that intelligence organisations must not only guard against deception from adversaries, but also from self-deception. Intelligence is therefore cognitively complex as well as reciprocal, and this character fuels its blurred and pluralistic nature. It can doubtless be argued that intelligence work in its deepest form is intuitive. Intuition is a form of cognition, since 'cognitive processes are those responsible for knowledge and awareness. They include the processing of experience, perception, and memory, as well as overtly verbal thinking.'[129] Intelligence intuition is therefore rapid operational perception, memory and experience that are constituted as accurate and aware recognition, and intelligence intuition as such encapsulates the essence of intelligence forecasting and estimation. Intelligence intuition must therefore not be mixed with induction, although both induction and intuition derive from experience. However, intuition captures the context and wholeness of threats, since it enables one, through the methodical use of estimation, to go beyond the challenges posed by the problem of induction. The problem of induction and the force of estimation will be explained thoroughly in Chapter 5.

It has now been illustrated that intuition identifies intelligence as activity. It elucidates the synthesis of estimation, wisdom and cognition, as it encapsulates the fast, operational and methodical relation between perception, experience and memory. Intuition therefore facilitates the ability to divide truth from falsehood, and it is therefore important to evaluate the identity of truth as the subject matter of intelligence science.

Truth as the Subject Matter of Intelligence Science

Truth is the enemy of ignorance, and therefore it is the vision of intelligence. Winston Churchill vividly highlighted the essence of intelligence: 'in wartime, truth is so precious that she should always be attended by a bodyguard of lies.'[130] Churchill thereby also elucidates the reciprocal and deeply challenging character of intelligence.

Intelligence operatives conduct their service function in a deeply uncertain and complex environment[131] where the truths are hidden in lies, and the lies are camouflaged as truths. Opponents will do everything to deceive their adversaries, and will nurture their ignorance.[132] Ignorance, orthodoxies, political assumptions, misunderstood secrecy and an entrenched intelligence tribal language therefore serve ignorance and are the enemies of truth. Intelligence institutions should therefore:

. . . give up the idea of ultimate sources of knowledge, and admit that all knowledge is human; that it is mixed with our errors, our prejudices, our dreams, and our hopes; that all we can do is to grope for truth even though it be beyond our reach.[133]

Popper's elucidation of the challenges related to knowledge suggests that truths do exist, but intelligence institutions must remember that they are interwoven in human perception and as such human discourse. Intelligence institutions must therefore critically ask themselves how they shall know that what they believe to be true is actually true. Bertrand Russell elucidates this, asking whether there is any 'knowledge in the world which is so certain that no reasonable man could doubt it?'[134] Russell thereby highlights that truths are difficult to find; if we find them it is challenging to identify and acknowledge their existence, and to separate them from lies.

The character of intelligence deception does not make this search any easier, and doubt in intelligence is therefore extremely important. But all this does not explain what truth is, and what truth is as the subject matter of science. Nevertheless, it highlights the challenges that are so deeply linked to truth-searching in a landscape that is as full of deception as the intelligence environment, and it thus illustrates the competing relationship between ignorance and truth, and the danger that cognitive closure and discourse failure pose to the accuracy of intelligence production.

The nature of truth has been discussed and analysed for centuries. These discussions will not be brought into this book. Nonetheless, it is important to be clear that the concept is challenging, and that the understanding of the word shapes the organisation that uses it. This book supports the view that truths are very difficult to detect and disclose. It demands that the observed objects, their environment and social context are properly identified and understood. However, the complexity of social situations implies that such inquiries are difficult, if not impossible. This book therefore suggests that intelligence institutions should relate to truths as the possibilities that can be considered when uncertain estimates are made less uncertain by using elucidation in the estimation process.

Elucidation as Science and Product

Classic inductive intelligence analysis clearly has its distinct limitations and weaknesses, since humans tend to believe what they believe based on observations of the past and the present. However, 'it is far from obvious, from a logical point of view, that we are justified in inferring universal statements from singular ones'.[135] Popper's point is simply that there is no logical inference between singular observations from the past and universal or singular statements that humans believe they can infer from these observations. Intelligence institutions must therefore find another approach to intelligence processing, and elucidation is a good alternative.[136]

Elucidation is a process that aims to shed a coherent light on the underlying information that is being assessed[137] to understand the complexity of a situation or a threat. Estimation and elucidation are good and effective alternatives to classic formal analysis since the two concepts in combination manage to free themselves from the inductive boundaries of induction, and as a result catch the context and wholeness of a threat beyond the limits set by formal reasoning. Elucidation is therefore a characteristic of intelligence as science and product. These concepts will be discussed and analysed in detail in Chapter 5, but it is nonetheless worthwhile to evaluate the necessity of objectivity in intelligence production.

Objectivity as Science and Intelligence Function

An intelligence institution's ultimate task is the production of estimates that can give the decision-makers competitive[138] insight and wisdom; truths must therefore be extracted from their camouflage of lies, and objective standards of inquiry are therefore called for. Popper is illustrative here:

> If we thus admit that there is no authority beyond the reach of criticism to be found within the whole province of our knowledge, however far it may have penetrated into the unknown, then we can retain, without danger, the idea that truth is beyond human authority. And we must retain it. For without this idea there can be no objective standards of inquiry; no criticism of our conjectures; no groping for the unknown; no quest for knowledge.[139]

Popper's acknowledgement of the limitations of the search for truth elucidates that such inquiry is possible only if humans approach it with integrity, humility and objectivity. His philosophy calls for critical rationalism and acknowledges that it can never be entirely objective. Humans are not objective. They are shaped by their experiences, perceptions and memories, and so is intelligence and science, since 'neither science nor rationality are universal measures of excellence. They are particular traditions, unaware of their historical grounding'.[140] Experience, perception and memory shape human discourse, and thus also human knowledge and how humans understand and communicate 'truths'. These problems increase when intelligence institutions try to understand cultures that are fundamentally different from their own, since these cultures and their inhabitants have their own distinct cultures, histories and ways of thinking. Their experiences are therefore often fundamentally different from the experiences of the spectator.

Popper's philosophy undoubtedly clarifies that truths do exist. It also highlights that these truths can be disclosed. However, the philosophy also asks for humility and realism in the search for truth. Intelligence institutions must therefore never forget that all knowledge and truths are perceived by humans who filter their understanding of the world through all sorts of implicit and explicit ideological prisms. The intelligence product is therefore not only a result of the collected information; it is also a result of the secrecy, the intelligence tribal language, the communication, the thought processes and the discourses inside the intelligence institutions. Objectivity is therefore important – not because human objectivity in intelligence production is possible, but because aspiring to it sustains critical rationalism of the conjectures and refutations of intelligence production, and this introduces falsification and critical rationalism as science and intelligence activity.

Falsification and Critical Rationalism as Science and Intelligence Activity

The classic inductive analytical approach in intelligence production is based on verification.[141] It shapes the whole intelligence process, both the collection and the analysis, and consequently also the dialogue between the intelligence producer and the intelligence consumer. The relative effects between the different collection assets are as a result managed and directed based on a need for constant verification of collected information. The intelligence institutions seek to 'connect the dots', and they seek data and information that can expand the knowledge that is based on earlier verification. This process ultimately leads intelligence institutions deeper into the problem of induction.[142] The problem of induction can further be increased if the collection of dots occurs in an unfocused manner and without sufficient connection and validation.[143] The problem of induction derives from the belief that there is a rational inference between empirical premises from the past and prospective empirical conclusions that can be made and supported by the premises observed in the past.[144] Induction may by accident, of course, lead intelligence institutions to make valid conclusions. However, induction may also, and more likely, lead to intelligence failure, since verification only increases a belief in the uniformity of nature, since induction and consequently verification facilitate habit and routine.[145] Verification is therefore self-referential, and the method can hence not defend itself against the problem of induction. Falsification and critical rationalism are therefore called for.

Falsification, critical rationalism, estimation and elucidation must be understood as interwoven, since it is in understanding their interaction that the problem of induction can be diminished, as arguably the verification of hypotheses facilitates the problem of induction. Falsification on the other hand is a method where one tests whether hypotheses can resist refutation by evidence, and falsification 'is not, therefore, the mechanical induction of generalizations from accumulated data, but the formation of bold hypotheses that are then subjected to rigorous test: a method of conjectures and refutations'.[146]

Popper, the standard-bearer of falsification, vividly describes how the problem of induction facilitates a restricted belief in nature and dogmatic thinking: he highlights how 'our propensity to look out for regularities, and to impose laws upon nature, leads to the psychological phenomenon of *dogmatic thinking* or, more generally, dogmatic behaviour'.[147] It is this uniform and dogmatic understanding of nature and social phenomena such as threats that must be attacked with falsification and critical rationalism, since threats prevail against inductive orthodoxies and political assumptions. Falsification and critical rationalism shape the doubt of intelligence, and doubt is certainly an attribute that identifies and facilitates intelligence cleverness, which is the subject matter of intelligence method.

Cleverness as the Subject Matter of Intelligence Method

Intelligence cleverness is the ability to imagine complexity, the willingness to accept the inconceivable and the courage to share information. The 9/11 Commission Report holds that the classic need-to-know principle seriously hampered the intelligence community's ability to comprehend the forthcoming threat to the United States, and it introduces the need-to-share principle.[148] However, this research suggests that the need-to-share principle does not offer a comforting solution to the problems and challenges related to sharing information, because arguably sharing is not the most marked human tendency. Most humans hold highest what is closest to themselves. They are egoists, and Midgley illustrates this: 'the foundations of Spinoza's ethics is Egoism. For him, each of us seeks merely his own. Each can only be concerned with what is like himself, and only in so far as it is like himself.'[149] It can thus be argued that a deep human unwillingness exists to sharing anything if it is not needed or does not produce immediate benefits, and that this also influences the willingness to share intelligence.[150] This is, though, a very negative view of the human condition, and it does not offer a solution to the challenge related to information sharing. Midgley thus asks: 'what would a world be like in which we only cared for others in proportion as they were like ourselves . . . ?'[151] Her rhetorical question illustrates that egoism is reciprocal and can only exist in its resonance to human communication.

Egoism is thus a phenomenon that arises between humans, and it cannot exist independently from human interaction. It is actually in the nature of human egoism that the answer to the intelligence-sharing challenge can be found. Humans want to be seen, humans want to be recognised and they want to be successful. Intelligence operatives must therefore be stimulated to be courageously imaginative and open-minded, and Bar-Joseph and Rose McDermott demonstrate this in stating that the CIA 'needs to work harder to recruit and promote "open minded" personal, especially for analytical positions'.[152] They must experience through reward and promotion that the organisations they work for appreciate imagination and intellectual courage. Midgley implicitly elucidates the consequent positive power of human egoism in emphasising that Spinoza's philosophy essentially 'claim[s] that, in promoting the welfare of others, we are promoting our own'.[153] Intelligence services should therefore use human egoism to their benefit, and stimulate a culture where sharing information produces immediate and visible recognition.

Intelligence operatives, intelligence organisations and intelligence consumers should therefore embrace a new principle: the courage-to-share. This implies that the intelligence community as a whole must not only understand and use human egoism: it must also simultaneously embrace and appreciate the complexity in the order of changing threat structures, and develop and maintain a capability to disseminate their comprehension of this complexity clearly to the consumer. Clarity in this respect does not involve clear-cut answers or comforting explanations as to the structures of threats appearing in new variations, or whether and how they might or can be countered. However, the courage-to-share principle involves and is constituted from a comprehension and appreciation of the fact that threat structures constantly change, and that these structures are constantly ahead of our imagination. Intelligence organisations and operators must therefore be willing to take intellectual chances. They must be responsible and provide policy-makers with valuable intelligence that is perceivable, and they must accordingly be prepared to be wrong. Garret Jones illustrates this:

> while it may be human nature and bureaucratically wise for the DI [Directorate of Intelligence] to try to give an extensive answer to every question posed, it is also intellectually dishonest and a disservice to the policymaker. 'We don't know' can be a valuable answer, even if it is not what the questioner wants to hear.[154]

It follows from this that the consumers must understand and accept that intelligence by its nature can never be accurate or prophetic, and 'it has no access to revealed truths: the days of "Magic" are over in more sense than one'.[155] This understanding of threats in general and therefore intelligence must be implemented not only in the organisational structures of the intelligence cycle, but also in the culture of the intelligence community, and become a positive factor that shapes healthy, positive and qualitative intelligence discourse.

The sort of healthy and humble discourse that the courage-to-share principle presupposes is not possible if no willingness exists to accept the problem of induction and the challenges that discourse failure creates, as well as the capability to imagine complexity. Complexity can only be understood and acknowledged through identification, observation and a keen understanding of the wholeness of the threat. The threat must therefore be seen and understood in its context.[156] That demands intuition, wisdom and experience, and intelligence experience and its relation to cleverness, and consequently to intuition and wisdom, will thus be described in the following.

Experience as the Methodical Product of Intelligence

Herman highlights that high-quality intelligence is characterised by its cleverness.[157] Cleverness is not an ability that can be taught, but something that must be developed and polished through years of experience and dedication, and this elucidates intelligence as a special trade, very different from many other jobs, especially in government services. Laqueur lends support to this notion:

> In some important respects intelligence differs from other branches of government. Deeper motivation is needed; a merely perfunctory interest in one's job will not do. Senior officials in many government departments will not be effective if they restrict their activities to normal office hours. This refers with special force to intelligence, but by no means only at the very senior level.[158]

Intelligence is hence a life choice, and cleverness and profound judgment presuppose long-standing experience and dedication.

The organisational culture of intelligence must therefore be built on integrity, loyalty, safety, confidence and professional predictability. Intelligence operatives should not feel unsafe about their professional future, and the 9/11 Commission Report demonstrates this in recommending that 'agents and analysts should then specialize in one of these disciplines and have the option to work such matters for their entire career'.[159] Being an intelligence employee should offer a safe and steady income. Nevertheless, this does not imply that intelligence work should be a job for safety seekers, traditionalists or other types of people who seek a job for the sake of a comforting social and economic future.

Intelligence operatives must enjoy the unpredictable and embrace the imaginary. However, unpredictability and imagination characterise classic creative work, while creativity, fantasy and imagination in intelligence presuppose a working environment that is protective and predictable, as the intelligence operative must be able to use all their creative and intellectual aptitude for their tasks. The working conditions for intelligence employees must therefore offer tranquillity, occupational predictability and security, and 'Congress should ensure that analysts are afforded training and career opportunities on a par with those offered analysts in other intelligence community agencies'.[160]

The recommendation of the 9/11 Commission Report reflects how seriously intelligence operators' working conditions should be taken and illustrates that intelligence experience is a quality that must be methodically nurtured and developed over years. Yet, the tranquillity, occupational predictability and security facilitated by sound leadership are not in themselves enough. The complex nature of the threat offers few chances for cognitive relaxation, and the psychosocial working conditions must therefore be as free as possible from complexity other than that created by the nature of the analytical work itself, since the intricate situations that intelligence operatives try to comprehend offer more than enough complexity in themselves. The intelligence services should therefore do their utmost to avoid the nature of the threats they try to comprehend from shaping the intelligence discourse and culture. The operatives must hence be of the highest moral and intellectual standard, and should possess a kind of wisdom that probes beyond the wisdom given by literary and academic knowledge. Education alone does not necessarily build a strong character with integrity. That is something that comes with life experience, since '[young recruits] are unlikely to know their own minds sufficiently, nor is it easy to assess someone accurately before he has been exposed to the turbulence of "real life"; it is unlikely that [their] character has already been fully formed'.[161]

Morality, wisdom and the ability to take right and profound decisions when needed are fundamental to intelligence work on all levels, and prior to 9/11, 'many analysts were inexperienced, unqualified, under-trained, and without access to critical information'.[162] The aftermath of 9/11 led to a massive expansion in intelligence, although few intelligence services built their workforce on operatives who had dedicated their life to the service, and many of the services have hence suffered professionally from the rapid development of the intelligence community. The swift expansion of Western intelligence services since 9/11 has hampered the quality of intelligence. More intelligence operatives do not necessarily equate to better intelligence services; nor is more intelligence necessarily better intelligence. Clarke encapsulates this paradoxical problem:

> Just as the CIA doubled the number of US spies after 9/11, it also doubled the number of analysts. As a result, the average CIA analyst today has, according to General Michael Hayden (the CIA director), fewer than five years' experience. Many have less. Was there really a need for twice as many analysts? The idea of doubling the staff seems unlikely to have been derived from a precise human resources requirements study.[163]

The quality of an intelligence product is not measured in quantity. Intelligence quality is measured by its ability to support decision-making through its reduction of uncertainty. Intelligence production is therefore highly cognitively challenging, and 'analysts and policy-makers must transform fragmented and weak data into a coherent vision of the future – a task that challenges even the best minds. Their imagination must leap, discerning a future threat where none existed in the past'.[164] Laqueur also highlights the importance of creativity and wisdom, and emphasised already in 1993 that those intelligence 'organizations that have prospered did so because decisions at critical junctures were based on creativity, foresight, and common sense'.[165]

Intelligence experience must therefore develop slowly and steadily. Intelligence services should thus recruit gifted and talented people and offer them a challenging, lifelong and prosperous professional future. Laqueur elucidates this:

> But if there are not enough competent and experienced people, if initiative, quick communication, and secrecy cannot be assured in a big organization, a good case can be made for employing fewer people. Lower standards may not mean just less intelligence. It could mean wrong intelligence.[166]

Clarke echoes Laqueur, and illustrates the negative consequences for intelligence services if they are not developed slowly and with care: 'assigning bright and eager new staff from good graduate schools to study second-order capillaries creates poor morale and eventually produces an organizational reputation that makes recruiting other good staff more difficult.'[167] Intelligence services should and need to be attractive to the best people, and they must be given intellectual challenges that stimulate and develop their cognitive capacity. Only then can they perform a proper staff function as national experts on future threats to the societies they serve.

Staff Function as the Methodical Function of Intelligence

The staff function will in the following be explained as the methodical function of intelligence activity, since it is this function that ensures that intelligence always seeks to be methodically objective and advisory. Herman elucidates the important objective and advisory identity of intelligence: 'the role of Operational Intelligence is to provide commanders and their staffs with the fullest possible understanding of the adversary and of the operational environment . . . in order that they can plan and conduct operations successfully'.[168] Herman by this brings attention to the fact that intelligence supports policy-makers. The staff function of intelligence hence serves political, strategic and operational objectives, and this service function is thoroughly explained earlier in this chapter. This servant image also highlights the necessary close relationship between intelligence producers and policy-makers. However, this closeness also increases the possibilities for politicisation. It is therefore essential to preserve the important objectivity and staff function of intelligence the closer one gets to policy-makers, as Sir Percy Cradock argues. He highlights that the relationship between intelligence and policy:

> . . . should be close but distinct. Too distinct and assessments become an in-growing, self-regarding activity producing little or no work of interest to the decision-makers . . . Too close a link and policy begins to play back on estimates, producing the answers the policy makers would like, as happened with Soviet Intelligence. The analysts become courtiers, whereas their proper function is to report their findings, almost always unpalatable, without fear or favour. The best arrangement is intelligence and policy in separate but adjoining rooms, with communicating doors and thin partition walls, as in cheap hotels.[169]

An objective and advisory staff function is not only important to ensure objectivity in the analysis process, it is also important to reduce the colouring of the collection process, as a 'collector of intelligence [invests] far too much professional and personal energy into a source or a method to be able to evaluate the resulting intelligence in an unbiased manner'.[170] Intelligence would be invalid without high-quality and objective intelligence collection, and collection is therefore the substantial methodical activity of intelligence.

Collection as the Methodical Activity of Intelligence

Intelligence services would be invalid and insignificant without their own comprehensive collection capacities and capability. It is this character that makes them fundamentally different from other information producers, since intelligence services have the ability to balance their collection capacities in accordance with their constantly alternating analytical needs. They can focus laser-like on their targets, and can therefore constantly fill their analytical gaps, since 'dots must be collected before they can be connected'.[171]

Intelligence is all about finding and hunting for the dots, and constantly filling the gaps. However, the information gaps are endless, and intelligence services have a huge advantage since they can secretly hunt for the information that would otherwise be unobtainable if only open information channels were used. However, this does not mean that open-source intelligence is invalid. On the contrary, it actually means that open-source intelligence reflects the distinct character of intelligence, not because the source of information is open, but because the hunt is planned, focused and prioritised, and most importantly, because it is covert. Intelligence services must protect their methods, capacities, sources and intentions, because disclosure of the intelligence requirements may reveal the knowledge level in the intelligence service, as well as possibly revealing the political objectives of policymakers. That said, open-source intelligence must not be used separately. It is the balanced use of all the collection capacities, be they Humint, Sigint, Osint or Imint, that ultimately identifies high-performance intelligence gathering, and it is also this understanding and its relation to estimation through elucidation that identify and constitute objective, critical and intuitive intelligence.

Conclusion

Intelligence as an activity and practice is an extremely complex process. It is this complexity that needs to be understood if intelligence institutions are to hope to diminish the force of discourse failure. The essence of intelligence needs to be acknowledged, and intelligence operatives need proper education and training.[172] Intelligence is a highly demanding profession that is identified by the twelve images that have been described in this chapter. These images also serve as reminders of the challenges of intelligence.

Intelligence is method, it is a phenomenon and it is science and knowledge. It constantly deals with uncertainty, and its ultimate objective is to make uncertainty less uncertain through its estimation about the future. It is arguably tempting for many to close cognition, overlook the challenging and displace those factors that do not fit with orthodox beliefs and political assumptions. But it is in these very situations that intelligence is needed. Intelligence is meant to divide truth from deception, but sometimes fails to do so. In the next chapter, therefore, I will analyse whether the interplay between cognition, secrecy and intelligence tribal language influences discourse failure.

Part II

Complexity, Secrecy and Intelligence Tribal Language

3   Secrecy and Intelligence Tribal Language

> As living spies we must recruit men who are intelligent but appear to be stupid; who seem to be dull but are strong in heart; men who are agile, vigorous, hardy, and brave; well-versed in lowly matters and able to endure hunger, cold, filth and humiliation.[1]

Here, Sun Tzu captures the essence of the human character needed to do well as a secret agent. However, the quintessence of this philosophy is indeed transferable to the character needed for those intelligence officers who recruit these agents, and for those who process the information collected by the agents. By this, Sun Tzu's philosophy implicitly also captures the essence of modern intelligence: intelligence is science; it is method; it is also a social, cultural and political phenomenon, but intelligence is primarily power accumulated using secret methods. It exists in a hard and often mercilessly political landscape: it therefore requires operators who have sharp minds, intellectual bravery and mental endurance. Intelligence organisations exist because their masters need political excellence. They are on the dark edges of all societies, and some of their methods may easily be regarded as dirty and immoral. This book will not analyse the potentially immoral aspects of intelligence, but will for the record mention that some people may comprehend intelligence as a 'dirty' and unaccountable activity which is threatening to democracy.

Sun Tzu, though, emphasises that intelligence operators on all levels must be clever, wise and, most importantly, humble. These qualities, if embedded in intelligence operators in open societies, doubtless secure democracy. This implicitly suggests that the kind of intelligence existing in open societies contrasts with intelligence institutions in totalitarian and closed societies, since closed societies decrease cognition and discourse because such societies increase '"disciplinary groupthink" that either [ignores] or [discourages] alternative thinking'.[2]

Intelligence is therefore torn between secrets and distortion, and the search for truth. Accordingly, this chapter explores whether a negative interplay between secrecy, cognition and intelligence tribal language decreases imagination and creativity in intelligence operators, thereby increasing discourse failure.

The Analysis and its Structure

For analytical purposes, this chapter will be divided into four main parts. Part one presents and analyses secrecy and intelligence tribal language. Part two focuses its analysis on secrecy versus creativity, exploring whether secrecy threatens qualitative intelligence production. The investigation thereby addresses the paradox between the search for truth and knowledge, and secrecy and distortion. The study thus analyses the enormous challenge and paradox secrecy creates for intelligence institutions, and the scope of the analysis is to investigate whether human creativity may positively interplay with secrecy. Part three demonstrates how intelligence tribal language decreases creativity and discourse in intelligence institutions. The study also illustrates how the innate human fear of intellectual freedom, in interaction with a lust for power, fuel the development of intelligence tribal language. Part four concludes the chapter and addresses the interplay between human cognition, secrecy and intelligence tribal language, elucidating how the three factors contribute to discourse failure between intelligence institutions, their consumers, and consequently for society at large.

Secrecy and Intelligence Tribal Language

Secrecy

The challenge that the characteristic secret identity of intelligence creates can be summed up in the following question: how can intelligence institutions, using secret methods, and with due care and regard for their operators, gain and produce unique intelligence for the intelligence consumer without jeopardising the wellbeing of their operators and the open society they serve? Sun Tzu's philosophy is again instructive: it emphasises that 'he who is not sage and wise, humane and just, cannot use secret agents. And he who is not delicate and subtle cannot get the truth out of them.'[3] Hundreds of books and films about intelligence focus mainly on the dark, thrilling aspects of intelligence. This does not necessarily help intelligence organisations attract the kind of women and men needed. Sun Tzu's philosophy describes the recruitment and use of spies, but the philosophy is also illustrative for the personnel needed to conduct the daily work in intelligence services. Sun Tzu thus implicitly points out that intelligence institutions should strive to recruit those who do not want to work for such institutions. Intelligence institutions should thus recruit people who do not like secrecy, but who are social, and who have a deep social and political conscience. They should recruit those who love human beings, but who have no desire to become famous, popular or worshipped. Intelligence institutions should simply find and recruit people who are confident, who do not need confirmation from others and who comprehend and have the courage to embrace their own wholeness.

This is an ideal description of human beings, and probably impossible to achieve in all its perfection. Nevertheless, human perfection, if it is conceived of as something ideal and theoretical, serves an important role in a society. It is a human guide to morality and humanity. Intelligence organisations need such moral guides as a foundation for their mission and responsibilities. Intelligence operators on all levels must therefore always remember that actions which might undermine the constitution of the society they serve, or other actions which do not serve society, must never be permitted.

Intelligence institutions in free and open societies thus exist because they are protectors of the constitution of society, but they also exist in a parallel world of distortion and trickery, and this creates a duality in which intelligence institutions are torn between what they protect, and the methods that they have to employ. This world coexisting in parallel to the world which intelligence services protect is a realm of international obscurity and political distortion, where the political players on stage conceal their treasures in lies. Their counterparts attempt to reveal the truths swathed in lies, disorder and confusion. Intelligence services must hence institute their internal dialogue based on openness, clear and lucid language and healthy discourse, so that their secret methods do not negatively shape their organisational culture.

Secrets are secrets simply because they are too important to be publicly known. In other words, their power will diminish or dissolve if they are known by adversaries. Barton Whaley underlines this in stating that 'the ultimate goal of stratagem is to make the enemy quite certain, very decisive, and wrong'.[4] Secrets are therefore knowledge that gives an advantage to the possessor. This advantage disappears when the secret is disclosed by the adversary. An organisation that reveals such secrets will attain enormous power. It is therefore immensely important that the leaders and the operators in these organisations found their activities on free, open and libertarian principles, to ensure that this power is not misused.

Hegel clarifies that a state in itself expresses liberty and constitutes the human ability and possibility to convey liberty.[5] Intelligence institutions serve the state and must therefore, certainly in the confines of a liberal democratic polity, serve liberty. It may be contended therefore that institutions that are based on secrecy are in fact threatened by it, and that the unavoidable need for secrecy creates an enormous paradox for institutions that exist to protect liberty. This paradox inevitably threatens discourse.

However, this book does not consider that intelligence operations can be conducted within the realm of a gentlemen's agreement, since intelligence success presupposes failure of the adversary, and it is this nature that makes intelligence so dangerous and risky. It is also this nature that allows outsiders, often mistakenly, to understand the nature of intelligence as dirty and immoral. This misconception is often fuelled by the portrayal of intelligence in popular culture. However, intelligence collection is undoubtedly based on principles that by many are perceived as immoral, and it is for this very reason that intelligence services must be run, directed and controlled based on open and free discourse. That said, this does not imply that intelligence operations can ever be open; it only means that intelligence leadership and intelligence discourse inside intelligence institutions should avoid being shaped by the complexities offered by threats and the methods intelligence services use to collect on these threats. Intelligence services must use these techniques, which are usually considered immoral and dirty, simply because these are the sole methods that can potentially disclose the knowledge concealed in lies and disorder. Organisations permitted by the society they serve to use such tools against their counterparts must build their internal structures on free, healthy and open discourse. Intelligence services that do not manage to create a clear and distinct boundary between their external and internal life, communication and secret methods, will increase cognitive closure and thus increase discourse failure.

Sun Tzu's philosophy clarifies this apparent paradox in stating that intelligence is a dangerous, risky, mental and therefore deeply human activity.[6] It is humanly driven and seeks to obtain secrets from other humans. For this it uses Sigint, Humint, Osint and Imint, and an intelligence institution is not complete unless it has full horizontal and vertical capacity. The institution must have full capability and capacity on intelligence planning and direction, collection, analysis and dissemination[7] of its products to the intelligence consumer. Nevertheless, it is Humint that gives intelligence its specific secret identity and character.

MacGaffin notes that Humint is the 'indispensable element of national intelligence collection'.[8] It consists of the collection assets that best can collect information about deep intentions. MacGaffin captures the essential character of Humint and subsequently intelligence in stating that 'clandestine HUMINT has to focus, laser-like, on those crucial secrets we must have but cannot otherwise obtain'.[9] These words illustrate the quintessence of intelligence and explain why intelligence must be kept secret.

This chapter explores intelligence institutions' need for secrecy. It will also analyse whether and how the interplay of misused and misunderstood secrecy, human cognition and intelligence tribal language contributes to discourse failure. Intelligence tribal language will be described briefly in the following. Further analysis will be provided in part three.

Intelligence Tribal Language

> 'The serious threat to our democracy', [John Dewey] says, 'is not the existence of foreign totalitarian states. It is the existence within our own personal attitudes and within our own institutions of conditions which have given a victory to external authority, discipline, uniformity and dependence upon The Leader in foreign countries. The battlefield is also accordingly here – within ourselves and our institutions.'[10]

Fromm suggests in *The Fear of Freedom* that the greatest threat to positive human development and interaction must be comprehended through a conception of the human desire for submission and the lust for power.[11] Intelligence operatives, like everyone else, also fear freedom. Fromm is illustrative when highlighting that there is a psychological battlefield existing in the interaction between human minds and the institutions these minds collectively create. This is also where intelligence tribal language arises, as a negative psychological defence mechanism and counterweight to the often challenging, and holistic comprehension of threats. There is thus an unconscious human resistance to positive human development and comprehension of holistic phenomena, which is illustrated in Fromm asking whether 'freedom [can] become a burden, too heavy for man to bear, something he tries to escape from?'[12]

Intelligence tribal language offers an escape from positive discourse and freedom, and consequently an escape from integrity, wholeness and adequate comprehension of threats. Neither desire for submission nor lust for power is positive or developmental for discourse, and consequently destructive to qualitative intelligence production. Thus, it can be argued that they both decrease creativity and imagination, and that this reduction increases discourse failure in intelligence institutions and between these institutions and intelligence consumers.

These arguments illustrate once more that intelligence institutions are threatened by the activities they perform. Threat perception is therefore by definition threatened by threat perception itself. The complexity that discloses itself when trying to comprehend wholeness arguably threatens most humans' fragmented views of the world, and intelligence tribal language is a phenomenon that develops in intelligence institutions as an unconscious resistance to a comprehension of wholeness and complexity, and a mechanism that defends fragmented thinking. This also illustrates that imagination, creativity and discourse contrast with intelligence tribal language, secrecy, and power. It is therefore important to analyse the impact of secrecy on creativity.

The Impact of Secrecy on Creativity

Intelligence production's most important qualifying factor is integrity. This integrity must be understood as a kind of honest reliability that works as a counterweight to the politicising of intelligence production, given that integrity can be comprehended as cognitive and ethical wholeness.[13] Discourse therefore presupposes integrity and free and open dialogue. For analytical purposes, evaluating dialogue is thus imperative. Bohm emphasises that dialogue must be understood through a comprehension of the word itself. Dialogue derives from the Greek word *dialogos*, and *logos* should be comprehended as 'the meaning of the word', while *dia* means 'through'.[14] Dialogue is therefore an almost complete explanation and expression of discourse as such.

This implies that discourse presupposes dialogue, and that dialogue expresses the substance of discourse. Consequently, discourse is a form of communication that is characterised by a '*stream of meaning* flowing among and through us and between us'.[15] Bohm consequently emphasises that dialogue is creative, and that it creates a common new understanding for those who are involved in the dialogue.[16] Dialogue and discourse are hence creative processes that involve and presuppose cognitive stimulation. Cognitive stimulation is arguably more likely to be acquired from other humans, although Bohm argues that one person can have a dialogue with him or herself.[17]

The creative process that dialogues create arguably presupposes open and free environments, rather than secretive and closed environments. Secrecy undoubtedly does not provide such cognitive stimulation, inasmuch as secrecy in worst case implies veiling of information and knowledge.

Humans are social individuals and are cognitively, culturally and politically stimulated by other humans. Bohm elucidates this in noting that dialogue creates what holds societies together.[18] Misunderstood and misused secrecy decreases dialogue, and therefore threatens imagination, creativity and consequently the social structures of intelligence institutions. It is when this misunderstood secrecy mutates with intelligence tribal language that common understanding of meaning and context in threat discourse is seriously decreased.

Gill and Mark Phythian illustrate the relationship between reduced imagination and creativity on the one hand, and intelligence failure on the other, in emphasising that 'lack of imagination has been a notable contributory factor to intelligence failures'.[19] Whole imaginative and creative intelligence work branded by its integrity is what secures qualified and qualitative intelligence products expressed as a kind of knowledge providing power beyond the limits of formal reasoning to the intelligence consumer. It follows from this that intelligence is art, as is understanding in itself. Hans-Georg Gadamer elucidates this:

> The 'method' of understanding will be concerned equally with what is common, by comparison, and with what is unique, by intuition; it will be both comparative and divinatory. But in both respects it remains 'art,' because it cannot be turned into a mechanical application of rules. The divinatory remains indispensable.[20]

The laws that shape art also apply to intelligence production, and estimation, like art, cannot 'be turned into a mechanical application of rules'.[21] Intelligence products should thus seek to understand threats beyond the limits set by induction. It is when intelligence institutions achieve this, that they are identified by their unique potential intelligence power, an argument that implies that intelligence is similar to an intuitive art. This shapes intelligence's imaginary and creative distinctiveness, and illustrates that reduced imagination and creativity no doubt increase discourse failure.

Secrecy is no doubt immensely important for intelligence institutions, although it must be handled cautiously. This book contends that free and open imaginative and creative discourse decreases discourse failure, and thus increases the quality of intelligence products. However, it is important to emphasise that:

> it does not follow that all liberty, and specifically the freedom of speech, is necessarily helpful to the spread of the truth. We cannot take for granted Mill's optimistic conclusion that maximal freedom of speech must assist the emergence of truth in what has come to be called 'a marketplace of ideas.'[22]

Secrecy is therefore needed, but should nevertheless primarily protect the potential power of the intelligence product. The product needs to be protected against its enemies; those who will do anything to disclose the distortion. Secrecy's positive power should therefore always be characterised by its ability to protect without jeopardising the intelligence institution's capability to produce imaginary and creatively predictive intelligence for its consumers.

Secrecy that does not manage this balance is often extremely unconstructive to intelligence. That type of negative secrecy seriously destroys the possibility for necessary free and open internal intelligence dialogue. This kind of secrecy thus reduces the possibility for the necessary internal dissemination of information, and seriously hampers crucial dissemination of information between different agencies. More important than the reduction of dissemination is secrecy's negative impact on the creation and acceptance of new ideas, ideas that often threaten old worldviews. It is precisely this problem that probes to the heart of discourse failure. New threats are by their very nature so threatening that they are often simply too cognitively challenging to imagine, as elucidated in the 9/11 Commission Report. Numerous analytical papers were produced on Bin Laden and al Qaeda between 1998 and 2001, as well as classified briefings prepared for the government, with titles such as '"Bin Ladin Threatening to Attack US Aircraft [with antiaircraft missiles]" (June 1998), . . . "Bin Ladin Determined to Strike in the US" (August 2001)'.[23] Nevertheless, few took the threat really seriously. It may be contended that it was simply too threatening and challenging to imagine and comprehend that something like 9/11 could ever occur, simply because it had never occurred before. This not only threatened established worldviews; it also challenged the existing political language, a challenge that Popper has elucidated in implicitly reminding us that threats are infinite and in constant change, while the language humans have to understand these threats is finite.[24]

This implies that the language available to comprehend and describe a hypothetical threat is limited, and thus reduces imagination. Those analysts who actually believed there was a huge threat consequently faced an enormous challenge in attempting to win support for their views. This challenge was not made less problematic inasmuch as one of the few arenas for imaginary and speculative analysis, the National Intelligence Estimates on terrorism, were not produced between 1997 and 9/11. 'Such assessments, which provoke widespread thought and debate, have a major impact on their recipients, often in a wider circle of decisionmakers.'[25]

Important questions to address are therefore: why were there no National Intelligence Estimates on terrorism between 1997 and 9/11; why were there serious problems related to dissemination? The comprehension of these two questions may shed light on the following hypothesis: misunderstood secrecy hampered the dissemination process and reduced imagination and creativity in the intelligence community in the US. The interplay of this factor, and the enormous challenge it is to imagine anything new, made both production of estimates on 9/11 and the comprehension thereof enormously challenging.

The Lack of National Intelligence Estimates on Terrorism between 1997 and 9/11

The conclusion in the 9/11 Commission Report on dissemination culture in the intelligence community in the US is critical. It states that a human resistance existed to sharing,[26] and emphasises that security practices derived from the Cold War era seriously hampered the fruitful and effective dissemination of information to those who needed it. The report highlights that 'such a system implicitly assumes that the risk of inadvertent disclosure outweighs the benefits of wider sharing'.[27] The report also addresses the problems related to a culture embedded in an idea that it is the producing agency that owns the product.[28] If such notions fuse with misunderstood and misused secrecy, reduced discourse and eventually discourse failure may develop.

The reason why there were no National Intelligence Estimates on terrorism between 1997 and 9/11 is arguably to be found in an overburdened, fragmented and security-driven intelligence community whose members did not efficiently communicate with one another.[29] It was also a community primarily focusing on collection, given that most of the analysts in the CIA's Counterterrorist Center 'dealt with collection issues'.[30] These factors significantly diminished the effectiveness of the intelligence institutions and the quality of their products. The 9/11 Commission Report illustrates this: 'current security requirements nurture overclassification and excessive compartmentation of information among agencies.'[31]

National Intelligence Estimates that stimulate thought and debate[32] pose a threat to compartmentalisation and the 'need-to-know culture' since they facilitate a culture of integration and discourse that has a positive impact working across organisational borders. It is for this very reason that they should be produced and disseminated, and it was probably also for this reason that they were not produced between 1997 and 9/11, since 'imagination is not a gift usually associated with bureaucracies'.[33]

The National Intelligence Estimates have historically covered and often caused rapid action across departmental boundaries, and '[are] sometimes controversial for this very reason'.[34] Terrorism threats can therefore be countered only if imagination, creativity and discourse across departmental boundaries are encouraged and embraced. National Intelligence Estimates undoubtedly play such a positive role.

Why Serious Problems Were Related to Dissemination

This problem can be comprehended through an exploration of the fragmented character of the US intelligence community prior to 9/11. There were serious borders and information fences between the different agencies: these hampered the efficient and adequate exchange of vital information between different agencies.[35] This situation significantly reduced the important and necessary effect of information fusing, a crucial activity in intelligence information processing. There was a serious breakdown in communication, because there were 'differences in the agencies' missions, legal authorities and cultures'.[36] The result of such differences and fragmentations can be catastrophic. The apparent consequence is that there is no responsible authority ensuring that information covering the same intelligence requirement is fused, analysed and comprehended as a whole, and the result may be that 'leaders and their staffs [become] their own intelligence assessors'.[37] Such an inadequate, fragmented system may also lead to self-referring information products. This may occur when one source provides information to different agencies and the same information as a result appears as information from different sources. This implies that the same source verifies itself.

A fragmented system based on a misunderstood need-to-know principle, and in which there is little control over the origin of the information, can also mean that information shared between national agencies and bilateral partners is, at worst, circular, and consequently self-referential. Self-referring information arises and develops only when information sharing actually exists. There was no adequate and qualitative dissemination between the intelligence agencies in the US prior to 9/11, and 'analysis was [therefore] not pooled. Effective operations were not launched. Often the handoffs of information were lost across the divide separating the foreign and domestic agencies of the government.'[38]

There were hence serious problems related to information sharing because there existed a deep-rooted cultural resistance to it.[39] This culture was not a momentary phenomenon, but one rooted in 'the interplay of various ideological factors at work in the United States and other Western societies that influenced the political context in which the services operated'.[40] A hampered dissemination system inside agencies, between agencies and between agencies and the intelligence consumer developed into discourse failure, since the interplay between an old security 'need-to-know culture' and the resistance to imagination seriously decreased any valid comprehension of the threats against the US. This culture was identified by its 'constriction of the language and vocabulary to identify, analyze, and accept that a significant threat existed'.[41]

The consequence of the discourse failure related to 9/11 was that the obvious threat did not exist in the minds of intelligence operators, and if there is no conception of a threat, dissemination is probably deemed 'unnecessary'. The effect of this discourse failure manifested itself when 'the FBI [did] not recognize the significance of the information regarding Mihdhar and Hazmi's possible arrival in the United States and thus [did] not take adequate action to share information'.[42]

The Impact of Intelligence Tribal Language on Creativity and Discourse

Intelligence institutions' secret character is identified 'with its secret knowledge and special rituals and obligations. [The intelligence operator] joins a world of special "indoctrinations" and codewords, and knowledge compartments within compartments.'[43] Thereby Herman highlights the strongly secretive nature of intelligence institutions, and elucidates typical intelligence tribal language in his reference to indoctrination and codewords. Indoctrination and codewords (although codewords are extremely important) undoubtedly do not stimulate or increase imagination and creativity, as they decrease the binding effect of dialogue on humans and organisations. Herman also sheds light on intelligence tribal language in emphasising that intelligence has 'institutionalized barriers between the secret society and what it sometimes calls the "outside world"'.[44]

This 'outside world' is also the world intelligence institutions are meant to understand, and it is worth addressing how the secret intelligence identity and the intelligence tribal language Herman illustrates may decrease the comprehension of this 'outside world' through a reduction of discourse. Secrecy is no doubt important and necessary for intelligence institutions, although secrecy by its innate reductive effect on discourse stimulates an intelligence tribal language that may alienate intelligence operators from the world they strive to comprehend. Herman echoes this when he emphasises that 'secrecy's mystique is a source of influence for intelligence as a whole'.[45]

These words illustrate secrecy both as necessary for intelligence, and its reductive effect on discourse. The superiority of intelligence products depends on the ability of secrecy to protect the uniqueness of the product, a uniqueness that gains its identity from the fact that it is kept secret. The same secrecy can, however, also serve secrecy and mystique, and this can easily create a culture in which secrecy and intelligence exist for their own sake.

Secrecy creates a strong identity within intelligence institutions, one characterised through its intelligence tribal language. This culture can be defensive and introvert, and intelligence operators often 'develop habits of social reticence'.[46] A defensive, introvert and reticent social character does not necessarily entail a lack of imagination or creativity. Nevertheless, imagination and creativity are arguably stimulated by other humans, and can consequently be decreased by other humans. As noted earlier, there undoubtedly existed a deep resistance to imagination and sharing information in the intelligence community in the US, and Clarke told the 9/11 Commission that:

> . . . a lot of people said, behind my back and some of them to my face, why are you so obsessed with this organisation? It's only killed 35 Americans over the course of eight years. Why are you making such a big deal over this organization?[47]

Clarke thereby suggests that new threats are challenging to comprehend and accept. He also illustrates that new threats are by their very nature threatening to traditions, orthodoxies and political assumptions. Those who believe in them are consequently also a threat to conservative traditions. This implies that imagination and creativity, and consequently healthy discourse, substantially threaten traditional bureaucracy. The 9/11 Commission recognised this problem, as well as acknowledging that the lack of imagination seriously decreased the quality of intelligence production prior to 9/11:

... crucial to find a way of routinizing, even bureaucratizing, the exercise of imagination. Doing so requires more than finding an expert who can imagine that aircraft could be used as weapons. Indeed, since al Qaeda and other groups had already used suicide vehicles, namely truck bombs, the leap to the use of other vehicles such as boats (the *Cole* attack) or planes is not far-fetched.[48]

This quote is paragraphed under 'Institutionalizing Imagination' in the 9/11 Commission Report, and the statement and the heading illustrate that the essence of imagination and creativity is actually not fully understood by the 9/11 Commission. Imagination and creativity can hardly be institutionalised or bureaucratised. Systems, methods and routines are important and necessary for intelligence production, though they also pose a huge threat to imagination and creativity. It is easy to imagine and comprehend civilian airplanes as suicide weapons since 9/11, though it would have been harder to imagine the same scenario before 9/11, simply because it had never happened before. It would have been just an idea, hardly a theory.

There is a considerable cognitive distance from ideas to hypotheses compellingly convincing to the human brain. This challenge is increased by the distance that constantly exists between the infinite character of threats and the finite character of the language we have available to understand these threats. Prediction of complex threats no doubt presupposes operators capable of both understanding and decreasing this distance. To achieve this, they need imagination, creativity and consequently cognitive freedom. But intelligence operators, as well as everyone else, fear freedom.[49] The complexities of constantly changing threat structures arguably increases this fear, and it is, therefore, in this interplay between complex threats and the fear of freedom that intelligence tribal language is fuelled and starts to develop.

The Development of Intelligence Tribal Language

Herman emphasises that 'when intelligence influences governments' views on major matters it should be all source and authoritative'.[50] Qualitative and authoritative intelligence should therefore be focused and taken from different sources using diverse collection sensors. The collection process should be based on openness, curiosity, imagination and creativity. The collected data should be sanitised and fused into information of potential intelligence value. Fused information from different sources must then be critically and rationally analysed. Intelligence institutions should therefore strive and constantly feel obliged to search for and comprehend the wholeness of threats. They should ideally try to understand the as yet not experienced.[51] Qualitative intelligence work is consequently the search for a holistic insight[52] into the nature of prospective threats, and an explicit insight that gives the intelligence consumers foreknowledge.[53]

Intelligence is thus an authoritative and highly sophisticated activity requiring humility, intellectuality, political comprehension, cognitive consciousness and integrity. The significance of the service role must therefore be cultivated and endorsed. Intelligence operators should never forget that they serve a constitution, and that their activities and the quality of their products must always reflect this fact.

It is, therefore, through a deep understanding of what intelligence essentially is that a comprehension of intelligence tribal language can also be found. Practical and realistic intelligence is often far from the description given above, and this asymmetry between idealism and reality is in itself illustrative of discourse failure. It sheds light on the reasons for intelligence tribal language. Clarke's statement on the culture in the CIA is illustrative:

> Now, if you're in the CIA and you're growing up as a CIA manager over this period of time [where the CIA were routinely criticized by Congress] and that's what you see going on and you see one boss after another, one deputy director of operations after another being fired or threatened with indictment, I think the thing you learn from that is that covert action is a very dangerous thing that can damage the CIA as much as it can damage the enemy.[54]

Clarke draws attention to a culture in the CIA and consequently a culture that is probably widespread beyond the CIA and exists within most agencies around the world, and it is not the culture he intentionally refers to that should be explored. It is another and more damaging culture Clarke unconsciously touches on that must be addressed: the challenge related to a deeply rooted fear of freedom and of the unforeseen. Clarke's statement sheds an informative light on the human fear of freedom and its negative effect on intelligence. The statement also highlights that intelligence is a very demanding activity, not only for the intellect, but perhaps more so for intellectual courage and integrity. Intelligence requires psychological coherence and wholeness, as well as honesty and openness towards colleagues. It is perhaps only when such psychological traits are in place that real offensive intelligence operations may be conducted with success. Arguably, psychological coherence, wholeness, honesty and openness are the factors that can oppose the fear of freedom. Intelligence no doubt requires intellectual freedom. Clarke suggests that the CIA's reluctance to conduct successful covert operations resided in a fear of the political consequences. The findings in the 9/11 Commission Report and the Joint Inquiry presented and analysed earlier in this chapter suggest something else, however. The assumption that can be drawn from these findings is that there existed a resistance to and fear of the unforeseen and the unthinkable in the US intelligence community and that this fear accumulated and developed in an environment characterised by its bureaucratic traditions and secret image. Threats can only be sufficiently countered when this orthodox thinking is rejected, and intelligence must therefore be renewed and modernised. Clarke suggests that covert operations and Humint could be effective if there were less fear of the consequences if something went wrong. This is a traditional view and one that echoes those who claim that if there were more Humint, everything would be much better.

However, the only solution to the problem of discourse failure is an all-source intelligence community, with a deep-rooted sense of being a service existing to serve society. This service must have the best resources: human, technological and economic. This does not exclude covert action or Humint. On the contrary, it essentially implies covert action and Humint. An all-source intelligence community must be robust, and it must therefore have horizontal breadth and vertical depth. This means that the institutions must have full horizontal collection and analysis capacity, as well as full vertical depth from the consumer's intelligence requirements, through intelligence management, practical intelligence production, and consequently, the consumer's comprehension of the provided intelligence product.

In other words, the intelligence cycle must include all its necessary functions: collection, analysis, dissemination and action/decision by the intelligence consumer.[55] All these four constituting functions for intelligence activity must be based on sound intelligence direction on all levels. Intelligence is therefore a phenomenon that presupposes leaders, operators and consumers that have a common comprehension of its theory, definitions and capabilities.

The case of 9/11 illustrates that this common comprehension was fragmented and could have been better. Turner demonstrates how this fragmentation emerged when disagreement about the nature and principles of Humint resulted in an unwillingness in the CIA to change and modernise:

> HUMINT methodologies must be continually modified to produce a new type of agent who can penetrate terrorist cells or drug cartels and come out alive to tell his story. While this may be an obvious solution, bureaucratically entrenched entities like the CIA's NCS [(National Clandestine Service)] are resisting significant change in this direction.[56]

The premise in Turner's illustration supports the essence of Clarke's statement, though the conclusions are different. Clarke emphasises that some parts of the CIA did not act when they needed to because they feared the political consequences if something went wrong. Turner, on the other hand, argues that the explanations can be found in a resistance to change.

Turner emphasises that the CIA still adheres to the classic 'case officer recruits spy scenario'. The scenario may, if the target accepts the pitch, 'result in important information for the US government'.[57] However, Turner states that the scenario does not work very well when the target is a terrorist cell,[58] and one needs to ask why intelligence communities still adhere to this traditional and not particularly effective approach. It can be argued that the answer is the fear of change and of the unforeseen, and consequently a rooted fear of freedom. Traditions, systems, methods and well-known techniques provide security and comfort, while modernisation and change, as contrasts, provide freedom and uncertainty.

It has now been demonstrated that it is when complex threats interact with isolated cultures, identified by their misunderstood secrecy and fear of change and the unforeseen, that the problem of induction increases – and hence fuels the development of a distinct and restrictive intelligence tribal language. These factors decrease an intelligence institution's capability to detect and comprehend new threats.

Conclusion

Psychological phenomena, and thus intelligence tribal language, are difficult and challenging to comprehend. Intelligence tribal language is a phenomenon that arises and develops in closed and often self-referring cultures. This fuels the language as a communication form that can only be fully understood by those who belong to these specific cultures. The language creates a sense of pride and fellow feeling, but it also, and more importantly, develops intellectual isolation and consequently discourse failure between different agencies and their consumers. Each agency probably has its own specific language that increases simultaneously with a changing and increasingly complex threat, since intelligence tribal language develops in the battlefield that arises between the human fear of freedom and the complexities offered by prediction.

The communication between the intelligence communities prior to 9/11 was thus significantly hampered, and this is vividly exemplified in that 'the CIA [did] not inform the FBI that a source had identified Khallad, or Tawfiq bin Attash, a major figure in the October 2000 bombing of the USS *Cole*, as having attended the meeting in Kuala Lumpur with Khalid al Mihdhar'.[59] This is one of many examples illustrating that there were serious problems related to information sharing between the different agencies, and this book argues that these were not systemic failures, but rather failures caused by a negative interplay between limitations in human cognition, excessive secrecy and intelligence tribal language.

There were no doubt vast cognitive challenges prior to 9/11, given that the threat, in all its complicated simplicity, was challenging to comprehend holistically. This means that the nature of the threat, its changing character, its simple plan, and the fact that it appeared in new variations of old threats, together created a threat complexity that was hard to understand and communicate and acknowledge.

A complex threat that fused with 'product protection' and a 'need-to-know'[60] culture, and a rooted self-referring intelligence tribal language, seriously decreased discourse between intelligence operators and between intelligence institutions – but most importantly, and consequently most devastatingly, between the intelligence institutions and the intelligence consumer.

The fragmented intelligence community was not able to mobilise a joint effort against al Qaeda, resulting in a fragmented, unfocused product. They therefore realised too late that the 'enemy [was] sophisticated, patient, disciplined, and lethal'.[61]

Part III

The Case of 9/11: A Theoretical and Reflective Analysis

4 On Collection

In this chapter and the next three chapters, the analysis will explore whether and how human cognition, secrecy and intelligence tribal language increase discourse failure in the intelligence process. The following analysis will explicitly be assessed against specific factors in the collection process,[1] while the other components in the intelligence process will be analysed in the next chapters. The assessment will be weighed against findings in the 9/11 Commission Report and the Joint Inquiry.

The intelligence process is also known as the intelligence cycle and involves collection, analysis, dissemination and action/decision by the intelligence consumer. This seems straightforward, but it is important to engage somewhat more with the workings of the cycle and the misconceptions of what the terms 'intelligence cycle' or 'process' have traditionally referred to, and whether and how these conceptions have increased misunderstanding of intelligence and thereby intelligence failure. The intelligence cycle has traditionally explained and illustrated the processes that intelligence institutions conduct to transform decision-makers' intelligence needs into knowledge through focused and planned collection, analysis, dissemination, and into the political or operational decisions based on the intelligence consumer's comprehension of the finished intelligence product. Omand illustrates this in highlighting that the cycle traditionally:

> . . . started with the setting of requirements for collection and ended with the dissemination of finished product to the intelligence staffs of the NATO military commanders. Essentially it was a linear process, with a final stage of seeking user comments on the value of the intelligence reporting at the end to curl it round into a cycle of continuous activity.[2]

Omand by this highlights that the understanding has been strictly organisational, technical and linear, and his explanation of the classic intelligence cycle also demonstrates that the traditional understanding of the cycle is limited; he thus emphasises that the reality of intelligence work as it is conducted today is not properly reflected in the classic intelligence cycle.[3] The intelligence process has for too long been understood as organisation, and should in future be understood as functions[4] and network.[5]

The misconception and consequent miscommunication of the intelligence processes as technical and organisational have created an understanding of intelligence work as linear and bureaucratic. To some degree, this is a precise description of how intelligence has traditionally been conducted. However, it does not describe how it *should* work, and it is not a precise description of communication between humans in general. Organisational charts do not accurately communicate the real workings of any organisation. The classic technical and organisational understanding of the intelligence process has arguably made it challenging to understand the connection between the underlying cognitive processes in the cycle and intelligence failure.

The following analysis will therefore contest the strict technical boundaries that frequently inform organisational comprehension of the intelligence process, and its subsequent evaluation of collection is based on an understanding of the intelligence process as a narrative image of the dynamic functions that must be performed and interplay with each other in an interactive and dynamic intelligence network.[6]

Intelligence failure and discourse failure should therefore be understood as a cognitive and functional failure that operates beyond the organisational boundaries that have traditionally informed the understanding of the intelligence process.

Collection

Intelligence organisations are collection-driven, and this is one of the main reasons for intelligence failure. Herman illustrates the imbalance between collection and analysis in intelligence institutions in the following:

> In sheer quantity the single-source reports from collectors to all-source agencies inside the intelligence system are much more voluminous than the all-source reports going to the users outside it, in the same way as reporters and news agencies produce much more raw news than newspapers subsequently carry.[7]

The amount of data collected by intelligence organisations is enormous, though relatively little of it is analysed and disseminated to the intelligence consumer.[8] For example, 'Senate investigators noted critically that, as of fiscal year 1975, the US intelligence community still allocated 72 per cent of its budget for collection of information, 19 per cent for processing technical data, and less than 9 per cent for production of finished analyses.'[9] Although these numbers describe the situation in 1975, few changes took place before 2001, and the 9/11 Commission Report illustrates this with one finding: the intelligence community could only translate 30 per cent of material that was collected from sources from the 'most critical terrorism-related languages'.[10] This problem would not be diminished as long as the NSA continued to invest 'most of its budget in improved collection systems with dazzling capacities'[11] without simultaneously increasing the organisation's analytical capacity. Based on the above, intelligence organisations are arguably heavily focused on collection, and 'many who are familiar with the US intelligence community believe that the relationship between these two phases [collection and processing and exploitation] is badly out of balance'.[12] The intelligence ethos is hence based on a collection culture in which methods, more than information outputs and information sharing, shape and identify the institutions. This is illustrated by the fact that 'The United States has been obsessed with data, and that has come at the expense of judgement',[13] and the NSA does therefore not have adequate recourses, be they technical or human, to 'translate or read even a fraction of the ever increasing volume of communications traffic that it intercepts'.[14] Gill and Phythian illustrate this problem: 'a final problem is that the volume of information generated by SIGINT can create an information glut whereby a significant volume of information is never analysed'.[15] This situation is not improved by the fact that 'an estimated 80–90 per cent of intelligence information about al Qaeda still comes in as *sigint*'.[16]

These examples demonstrate that the organisational structure and manning in the US intelligence community are collection-driven, and that analysis focus is often downgraded. The 9/11 Commission Report is again illustrative in that one finding has disclosed that most of the thirty to forty operators at the Counterterrorist Center (CTC), which was meant to analyse, in reality focused on collection.[17] Intelligence institutions must therefore balance the relationship between collection and analysis.

However, collection should always be the backbone of any intelligence organisation, and 'collection advocates argue, usually successfully, that collection is the bedrock of intelligence, that without it the entire enterprise has little meaning'.[18] Collected single-source information is obviously the foundation and a necessity for qualitative intelligence analysis, since 'even the most comprehensive all-source analysis effort refers only to all *available* sources and not all *possible* sources'.[19] Nonetheless, 'the image or signal that is not processed and not exploited is identical to the one that is not collected – it has no effect at all',[20] and unexploited data is therefore useless.

Although it is now clear that comprehensive intelligence is based on a balance between collection and analysis, this alone is not enough. Qualitative intelligence also demands a fine balance between different collection sensors, the exploitation of their relative output and the production of highly qualitative intelligence analysis based on the fusion of the collected information. This quality parameter was elucidated by former British Foreign Secretary Robin Cook. He suggested that 'the collection of signals intelligence and of human intelligence often bears its greatest fruit and best results when the two are put together'.[21] Lowenthal echoes Cook: 'having a collection system that is strong and flexible and can be modulated to the intelligence requirement at hand is better than one that swings between apparently opposed fashions of technical and human collection.'[22]

The 9/11 Commission Report demonstrates the strength and wisdom of Cook's and Lowenthal's views in that the report recommends that the analytical and human intelligence collection capital should be rebuilt, and it emphasises the importance of a 'seamless relationship between human source collection and signals collection at the operational level'.[23] Israel has managed to exploit the relative effect of an integration of Sigint and Humint, and its 'national SIGINT organization, Unit 8200, has developed highly sophisticated techniques for monitoring Palestinian terrorist activities in the Gaza Strip and on the West Bank, using both conventional and unconventional SIGINT collection systems fused together with HUMINT'.[24] The force of this integrated system is illustrated by the fact that Israeli intelligence tracked down the Hamas bomb maker, Yeahia Ayyash, and eventually killed him 'in Gaza in January 1996 by an exploding cell phone planted on him by Israeli intelligence'.[25]

The examples presented illustrate that the US intelligence community was collection-focused prior to 9/11, and accordingly downgraded all-source analysis and assessment.[26] Though the 9/11 Commission Report identified that the intelligence institutions had to strengthen their analysis capacities, the debate after 9/11 was predominately focused on whether Humint was undervalued before 9/11, and that 'this neglect was a contributory factor in the events of 9/11'.[27] This illustrates that the intelligence discourse, whether in intelligence institutions, among decision-makers or in the media, was and probably remains collection-driven. It is therefore crucial to analyse whether and why so many intelligence institutions are collection-driven, and why they consequently focus less on all-source analysis. The following analysis will focus on the US intelligence community and explore whether and how a collection-driven culture facilitated discourse failure prior to 9/11.

The Analysis and its Structure

This chapter will for analytical purposes be divided into two main parts. Part one explores why intelligence discourse is collection-driven, and whether and how the interplay of human cognition, complexity, uncertainty and unpredictability shapes a collection-driven discourse in the intelligence community. Part two uses findings from the 9/11 Commission Report and the Joint Inquiry, and illustrates how a collection-driven culture in the US intelligence community shaped threat perception.

Why Intelligence Discourse Is Collection-Driven

Intelligence is surrounded by myths, many of which are self-imposed by intelligence institutions.[28] Some of the myths are clearly true, while others are false, but they are all 'characterized by mutually inconsistent extremes – intelligence agencies are imagined to be both omnipresent and incompetent'.[29] This dual identity of intelligence, torn between truth and falsehood and between wisdom and incompetence, shapes the popular understanding of intelligence, the public and political debate, as well as the internal intelligence discourse itself.

Most people think of spying when they hear the word 'intelligence', and most people understand spying to be the use of a human operator who collects information of possible information value from human sources (Humint).[30] Numerous books and films have been made about intelligence. They illustrate the classic spy, and a mystical, limited and often romantic comprehension of intelligence has consequently evolved in the public and political debate. This limited and narrow conception of intelligence hence identifies the public intelligence discourse. Undoubtedly, this image has damaged not only the public and political debate about intelligence, but also weakened the internal intelligence discourse, as important focus has been directed away from what makes intelligence important. It is the relevance, reliability and timeliness of intelligence that identify its quality. This demands high-quality intelligence operators on all levels, as well as wise and clever planning and direction. High-quality intelligence planning and direction hence ensure balance between intelligence requirements and the use of intelligence resources. The important dynamic between different collection sensors ensures this balance,[31] and all available sources must therefore be exploited. Herman highlights this necessary dynamic: 'the results of good collection can be lost if it is not properly interpreted on a multi-source basis. If there is any single guide to making sense of an intelligence system it is to be clear whether the output from any point is intended to be single-source or all-source.'[32]

Qualitative intelligence is hence by its nature holistic, and only all-source intelligence can comprehend the infinite nature of threat structures, since all-source intelligence is 'based on as many collection sources as possible to compensate for the shortcomings of each and to profit from their combined strength'.[33] 'All-source analysis evaluates [the different sources] critically against each other and produces a composite picture'[34] that may, if it is done well, help to understand the wholeness of a threat structure, and this sort of analysis hence manages to comprehend and reflect the complex structure of threats much better than single-source analysis: accordingly, it has elucidative power.[35] Regardless of the elucidative power of all-source intelligence, however, the infinite and complex nature of intelligence will continue to shape the internal and public intelligence discourse. This limited discourse does not make it easier to comprehend the complex nature of intelligence, and it becomes increasingly demanding for human cognition to understand a complexity that constantly tests and challenges human creativity and imagination.

Most humans arguably prefer certainty, predictability and all that is well-known to human cognition. The nature of intelligence is characterised by its uncertainty and unpredictability, and it is therefore everything but recognisable to human cognition. This shapes an intelligence discourse that is already identified by its limitations. The dual and challenging nature of intelligence and its relation to discourse failure therefore constitute a cognitive challenge, and this increases the need for cognitive closure. The intelligence discourse, as a result, becomes plain, one-dimensional and static. Qualitative all-source analysis that is identified by its creativity and imagination is arguably extremely difficult to achieve under such conditions and circumstances.

A collection-driven culture, however, offers a solution to and a cognitive escape from the complex challenge posed by the holistic nature that ideal and holistic intelligence provides, and it is probably for this reason that collection prevails at the expenses of analysis. Even so, collection is not at all easy. It demands discipline, precision, creativity and endurance, but it is not as complex and intellectually demanding as all-source analysis. A collection-driven culture therefore offers cognitive escape from the confusion and ambiguity that high-quality intelligence demands. Arguably, therefore, intelligence is collection-driven because it offers an escape from the demanding and highly challenging nature of high-quality intelligence.

Intelligence is hence not only data and information; it is wisdom derived from this data and information. Such wisdom is a result of high-quality intelligence analysis, and enormous amounts of information shape the analysis and can burden analysts as well as the analysis department. The Joint Inquiry illustrates this huge challenge:

> Prior to September 11, the Intelligence Community was not prepared to handle the challenge it faced in translating the volumes of foreign language counterterrorism intelligence it collected. Agencies within the Intelligence Community experienced backlogs in material awaiting translation, a shortage of language specialists and language-qualified field officers, and a readiness level of only 30% in the most critical terrorism-related languages used by terrorists.[36]

This finding demonstrates that collection alone is not enough. The collected data also need to be processed, analysed, disseminated and comprehended by the intelligence consumer. The finding serves as an ideal example of the consequences of an overly collection-driven organisation, and one might even argue that the effect of collection is seriously decreased if 70 per cent of the collected data remains unanalysed.

The finding also demonstrates that collection is far easier and not as cognitively demanding and boring as analysis can be, and anyone who has picked strawberries will quickly understand the following metaphoric comparison: picking strawberries is not much fun, not particularly demanding, but does require discipline and endurance. Washing and cleaning the strawberries, however, is extremely boring. It demands precision and extreme endurance. Picking the strawberries is consequently much more fun, although it was initially boring. Many people therefore prefer to pick strawberries instead of cleaning them.

Nonetheless, strawberries should not be eaten if they are not washed and cleaned, and someone needs to do that job. Picking more strawberries does not solve the problem. There needs to be a balance between picking and cleaning, and a balance between collection and analysis, and between requirements and capacity. Analysts and consumers must therefore acknowledge the notion 'that all sources of intelligence fused together into an "all source" intelligence product will be the only way to effectively combat terrorism'.[37]

This suggests that intelligence is collection-focused because the complexity and challenges that high-quality intelligence and all-source analysis provide and demand make many organisations focus on the relatively easy. They simply pick more strawberries and displace the necessary and demanding washing of the strawberries.

A collection-driven intelligence culture is therefore in practice cognitive closure characterised by its one-dimensional focus on collection at the expense of high-quality intelligence analysis. The intelligence culture becomes collection-driven given that the complexity provided by threats and its consequential necessary high performance analysis creates a cognitive challenge so great that many intelligence institutions choose to overlook the difficult, focusing instead on that which is not easy, but relatively easier than analysis. Many intelligence services will therefore tend to 'match capabilities to mission by defining away the hardest part of their job'.[38]

How a Collection-Driven Culture Shaped Threat Perception Prior to 9/11

The threat perception of and the countermeasures against al Qaeda prior to 9/11 were seriously flawed, although both the Bush and the Clinton administrations to a certain degree dealt with the threat. Indeed, 'each president considered or authorized covert actions, a process that consumed considerable time – especially in the Clinton administration – and achieved little success beyond the collection of intelligence'.[39]

This finding demonstrates that both the Clinton and the Bush administrations predominantly focused on collection. Collection is certainly necessary, but collected data and information do not produce a picture that mirrors or manages to reflect the wholeness of the threat, and the Joint Inquiry illustrates this:

> While the Intelligence Community had amassed a great deal of valuable intelligence regarding Usama Bin Ladin and his terrorist activities, none of it identified the time, place, and specific nature of the attacks that were planned for September 11, 2001. Nonetheless, the Community did have information that was clearly relevant to the September 11 attacks, particularly when considered for its collective significance.[40]

The US intelligence community had, as illustrated, amassed significant amounts of information but failed to bring it together to see its wholeness. They were looking at a mosaic at close range and could therefore not see the whole picture: consequently, they were unable to capitalise on the perceptible value of the collected information.

The finding in the Joint Inquiry elucidates that collection alone is not enough, and brings into focus the importance of high-quality collection management and intelligence direction. Collected information must not only be processed and analysed; collection also needs to be managed and directed sufficiently and effectively. Intelligence leaders must therefore focus on 'what is really important instead of what might be nice to do'.[41]

Intelligence collection leadership and management therefore require leaders who understand the complexities of threat structures constantly appearing in new variations, and must thus be able to manage the relative capacities of their collection capacities accordingly. Collection management and leadership hence entail both technical and human skills, and leaders possessing that combination understand that 'collectors should be encouraged to exceed expectations, demonstrate creativity, invest in long-term collection efforts, and work hard problems'.[42] However, consumers also need to comprehend the complexity of the enemy. They must know what they need so they can increase their knowledge about the enemy, and 'artful intelligence, including the capacity to distinguish friends from enemies and to design appropriate intelligence programs, has arguably proved stabilizing'.[43]

Intelligence institutions therefore need focused intelligence requirements and priorities. Collection units thus need prioritised, focused and balanced collection plans, and 'someone in the intelligence community should [therefore] be formally charged with the task of advancing cross-disciplinary collection strategies, identifying gaps, and proposing ways to close them'.[44]

Collection cannot be unfocused and random. The amount of information that can be collected in the world is infinite, and unfocused and incidental intelligence collection will only lead to confusion, overload the analysis departments and easily overburden an intelligence culture that is already characterised by its 'time pressure, concrete deadline, and the need for action'.[45] High-quality collection management and leadership is therefore identified by 'a high-quality intelligence process [that] balances investment and direction from decision makers with unbiased collection and analysis.' This is recognised through 'the timeliness, efficiency, and accuracy with which it supports national security decision making'.[46]

A collection-driven culture, however, increases and additionally accelerates unfocused collection in intelligence institutions which are already hampered and pressured. The time pressure, concrete deadlines and the need for action in intelligence communities can easily develop its own circular dynamic, and requirements and priorities can at worst be adjusted to fit the collection.

The collected information can thus confirm that which is pre-required, and contribute to new intelligence requirements and priorities that further fuel the intelligence institutions' collection focus, thereby leading the consumer in the wrong direction. This mirrors a situation in which 'precautionary escalation or procurement may act as self-fulfilling prophecies'.[47] It illustrates that a collection-driven intelligence culture easily creates a situation where collected data does not contribute to wisdom, but only confirms a self-imposed circularity, which ultimately creates intelligence that is self-referential and self-affirming. The situation is exacerbated when intelligence institutions '[bow] to pressures to tell the policy-makers what they [want] to hear'.[48]

The US intelligence community's collection-driven identity did arguably decrease threat perception before 9/11, because they 'failed to capitalize on both the individual and collective significance of available information that appears relevant to the events of September 11'.[49] It was therefore challenging for the community to create new intelligence requirements and priorities that could have led them in the right direction. This lack of direction made it difficult for the community to conduct high-quality analysis, and it was hence difficult to see connections between seemingly unconnected situations and information. They, as such, failed to connect the dots:

> No one will ever know what might have happened had more connections been drawn between these disparate pieces of information ... The important point is that the Intelligence Community, for a variety of reasons, did not bring together and fully appreciate a range of information that could have greatly enhanced its chances of uncovering and preventing Usama Bin Ladin's plan to attack these United States on September 11, 2001.[50]

The elucidation of these findings demonstrates that the community failed to capitalise on what they had, and that their classic Cold War-oriented collection culture did not manage to adapt to a new world order because 'long-entrenched civilian NSA employees [were] still fighting the Cold War and [were] more worried about maintaining security than improving tactical warfighting capabilities'.[51] Matthew Aid elucidates the damaging effect of such cultures: 'these restrictions have placed extreme burdens on the counterterrorist action agencies and effectively prevented them from using the intelligence gathered by NSA to go after terrorist organizations'.[52]

This example demonstrates a heavily collection-driven culture, and one can argue that a culture that values sources more than the political, strategic and tactical advantage that could have been exploited from them increases the dangers posed by cognitive closure and discourse failure. They did collect, and they did collect on the enemy. Even so, it was not a collection culture at the expense of analysis, which was the only problem. Their collection priorities focused abroad, and the intelligence community therefore failed to identify and 'meet the challenge posed by global terrorists focused on targets within the domestic United States'.[53] The result was that, 'serious gaps existed between the collection coverage provided by US foreign and US domestic intelligence capabilities'.[54]

This illustrates that a classic Cold War-oriented collection culture among domestic intelligence agencies focused on a typically 'case-oriented, law enforcement approach' and 'did not encourage the broader collection and analysis efforts that are critical to the intelligence mission'.[55] The domestic agencies had their focus at home while the US foreign communities continued to look abroad. The result was unfocused and divergent requirements, and intelligence agencies did therefore:

> Sometimes [fail] to coordinate their relationship with foreign services adequately, either within the Intelligence Community or with broader US Government liaison and foreign policy efforts. This reliance on foreign liaison services also resulted in a lack of focus on the development of unilateral sources.[56]

The enemy could as a result continue with preparations in a fairly safe translational window, and 'the FBI was unable to identify and monitor effectively the extent of activity by al-Qa'ida and other international terrorist groups operating in the United States'.[57] The terrorists were foreigners who had not yet committed any criminal acts. They did not therefore fit FBI collection requirements and law enforcement priorities. This shaped FBI requirements, as well as decreasing the FBI's focus on collection and thus its ability to analyse and understand the threat.

The foreign services, on the other hand, 'paid inadequate attention to the potential for a domestic attack'.[58] Accordingly, they did not focus on terrorists living and studying in America, and the US foreign services thus did not sufficiently 'watchlist suspected terrorists aggressively [and it] reflected a lack of emphasis on a process designed to protect the homeland from the terrorist threat'.[59]

The result of these two factors was damaging for adequate intelligence production and threat perception. Arguably, it went wrong because a classic, conservative, operationally collection-driven culture interplayed with a culture that did not manage to coordinate between foreign and domestic intelligence capabilities. The negative effects of this interaction were exacerbated when collection and operational operatives were regarded as better than analysts. It created a situation where analysts were downgraded as second-rate intelligence operatives. The ultimate and damaging result of this situation was that 'analysis and analysts were not always used effectively because of the perception in some quarters of the Intelligence Community that they were less important to agency counterterrorism mission than were operations personnel'.[60]

The consequences of not using analysis capabilities effectively enough are apparent, and patronising analysts' intellectual abilities and importance did not improve the situation. These circumstances therefore serve as an ideal example of how a collection-driven culture shaped the US intelligence community prior to 9/11. It also encapsulates how a closed culture can influence social structures and develop subcultures and as such decrease healthy discourse. Secrecy, security and a closed culture characterised by a distinct tribal language no doubt decrease constructive criticism and healthy dialogue. Herman emphasises that intelligence organisations cultivate their specialness and secrecy.[61] He is also right in emphasising that intelligence institutions provide social acceptance, and can give a strong feeling of belonging.[62]

This book, however, would argue that this feeling can be short-lived, and that it is often weak and artificial, especially because it '[distances] its members from the rest of society'.[63] Charles G. Cogan illustrates this: 'a lifetime of manipulation can be corrosive. There also is a boomerang effect. You can end up asking yourself, "Who are my real friends?" or "Do I have any?"'[64] Cogan is referring to the possible personal consequences of a long career as a Humint operator. Analysts do not feel the same pressure as do field operators, nor do they often experience mortal danger, and they do not live a professional life of manipulation. Nonetheless, they do work for an organisation that is shaped by secrecy, and parts of their lives are therefore concealed from relatives and friends. This can create a distance from society, which is not positive, and can become negative if it is fuelled by a secrecy-driven culture. It can increase blind loyalty, and also increases the fear of being expelled from the group. Intelligence institutions do not need operatives who fear exclusion – they need operatives who feel personally safe and intellectually free. Only then may wisdom prevail.

The collection-driven culture in the US intelligence community did shape the threat perception inasmuch as it decreased the focus and emphasis on high-quality analysis. The collection-driven culture arguably derived from institutionalised practices that focused on secrecy and operational matters. It decreased focus on analysis, and as such also limited the prioritising of holistic threat perception.

This book argues that the collection-driven culture was partly shaped by secrecy and its interplay with the problem of induction and intelligence tribal language.

Collection-Driven Surprise

The inquiries after the 9/11 terrorist attacks conclude that the US intelligence community did not acknowledge the nature of the al Qaeda threat that faced the US.[65] Only all-source analysis can give decision-makers such acknowledgement, since it synthesises available single-source intelligence and thereby produces an overall picture that more effectively elucidates and communicates the quintessential nature of threats. Nonetheless, authoritative all-source intelligence estimates can be produced only if there is high-quality single-source intelligence information. The US intelligence community had collected on al Qaeda, and they had, as illustrated previously, collected information that could have shed light on the true nature of the threat – if it had been capitalised on. However, findings in the 9/11 Commission Report also demonstrate that there were serious gaps in collection focus and priorities:

> The CTC did not propose, and the intelligence community collection management process did not set, requirements to monitor such telltale indicators. Therefore the warning system was not looking for information such as the July 2001 FBI report of potential terrorist interest in various kinds of aircraft training in Arizona, or the August

2001 arrest of Zacarias Moussaoui because of his suspicious behaviour in a Minnesota flight school. In late August, the Moussaoui arrest was briefed to the DCI and other top CIA officials under the heading 'Islamic Extremist Learns to Fly.' Because the system was not tuned to comprehend the potential significance of this information, the news had no effect on warning.[66]

This finding illustrates that details are immensely important in intelligence production. It also demonstrates that there need to be systems and methods that help intelligence operatives to observe the significance of the details and put them together to form a pattern corresponding to reality. There is, though, one important, highly challenging factor. Intelligence deals with the future, and only assesses history against trends. Historic events are possible to analyse, and analysts can therefore put episodes in order to form the reality as it took place. Yet historic analysis is also known to be capricious, and historians can accidentally perform poor analyses if they '[overlook] the only really important social laws–the laws of development'.[67] But they do have factors that are observable. Intelligence deals with the future, and collected information can therefore never provide anything but indications. This is the greatest challenge for intelligence. The reality of the significance of the collected information therefore discloses its true nature only after events, and it illustrates that connections are hard or even impossible to foresee before they have in fact become connections. Even so, it is hard to see connections if one does not even try, or have systems or methods to capitalise on the available information; and the US intelligence community had not, as illustrated in Chapter 3, produced any national all-source estimates on terrorism since 1997.[68]

There was therefore no one in the intelligence community who connected the dots, and important single-source data passed through the intelligence cycle unprocessed. Whether production and dissemination of national all-source estimates would have increased intelligence operatives' interest in Moussaoui and aircraft training is impossible to say. All we can be fully certain of is that the system today would have blinked red if a report named

'Islamic Extremist Learns to Fly' had been disseminated, and this introduces an even more important question: will the warning system blink red if terrorists again challenge our imagination? Or, and even more challenging: will the warning system blink red if orthodoxies and political assumptions are challenged again? The answer to these two questions is probably no, thereby suggesting that high-quality intelligence ultimately depends on a mix of sound judgement and imagination, and not on automatic warning systems. The 9/11 Commission Report elucidates this:

> Richard Clarke told us that he was concerned about the danger posed by aircraft in the context of protecting the Atlanta Olympics of 1996, the White House complex, and the 2001 G-8 summit in Genova. But he attributed his awareness more to Tom Clancy novels than to warnings from the intelligence community.[69]

Clarke had the ability to combine imagination and sound judgement, but he did not, and could not possibly convince the wider community that his theory represented a real danger. The community's requirements, priorities and collection focus therefore did not reflect a possible danger from airplanes used as suicide weapons on domestic US targets, and the community's warning system therefore did not blink red when they actually received such information.

All this demonstrates that high-quality intelligence needs to involve the courage to take intellectual chances, and certainly the courage to believe the unbelievable and consequently act on it. This does not mean, though, that future intelligence should consist of well-equipped, well-paid fortune-tellers, trying to outdo one another in their warnings. It means that modern intelligence needs to cultivate imagination and creativity, and it needs to have the courage to challenge its own orthodoxies and political assumptions, so that 'new way[s] of thinking about a problem or the world situation in general'[70] can be introduced. Only then can one hope to foresee new threats.

New threats can arguably be foreseen if sound judgement interplays with imagination and if details are synthesised and disseminated to everyone who may need the information in the wider intelligence community. The secrecy culture must therefore be modernised, and only secrets that need to be secret should be kept secret. More emphasis should hence be given to dissemination, dialogue and constructive criticism. This description of the way in which intelligence should change to diminish discourse failure also illustrates how limited cognition, secrecy and intelligence tribal language may decrease discourse, since their three-dimensional interaction may decrease sound judgement and imagination.

The attack on Pearl Harbor elucidates the immense danger of surprise attack, and surprises are essentially such simply because humans are cognitively reluctant to accept the factors that facilitate the surprise. This marshals a situation in which 'the victim, sure of his own position, is more likely to be taken by surprise'.[71] The nature of surprise attacks therefore elucidates the essence of discourse failures, and the understanding and acknowledgement of this relation may raise awareness of cognitive limitations, since, 'if leaders were made self-conscious and self-critical about their own psychologies, they might be less vulnerable to cognitive pathologies'.[72] Whether intelligence institutions are aware of this connection is difficult to evaluate, but doubtless, the Americans after Pearl Harbor did definitely understand the huge dangers that surprise attacks constituted, and the US intelligence community therefore devoted generations to understanding the nature of threats and particularly surprise attacks, and developed methods to safeguard US against future threats. The 9/11 Commission Report emphasises that the methods have:

> ... four elements in common: (1) think about how surprise attacks might be launched; (2) identify telltale indicators connected to the most dangerous possibilities; (3) where feasible, collect intelligence on these indicators; and (4) adopt defences to deflect the most dangerous possibilities or at least trigger an earlier warning.[73]

These methods reflect the community's trust in systems and methods. However, another factor is more serious: all these questions are by their nature inductive, and therefore cannot answer speculations about the future. The questions therefore fail to challenge orthodoxies and political assumptions. Kuhns emphasises the weakness of an inductive approach in intelligence estimation: the 'central problem is that the method by which analysts make their forecasts has traditionally been one of *induction*'.[74] This thesis therefore holds that surprise is only possible to foresee if orthodoxies and political assumptions are challenged. This would facilitate healthy, constructive discourse, and hence stimulate creativity.

The following analysis will therefore explore the four elements in the classic US forecasting tradition that shaped US threat perception prior to 9/11, and evaluate them against the challenges represented by the problem of induction. The findings will be weighed up against the three-dimensional force of cognition, secrecy and intelligence tribal language, and the study aims to illustrate how this force interacted with the limits of induction and caused discourse failure in the collection process.

The Nature of US Threat Perception Tradition Prior to 9/11, and the Problem of Induction

Popper devoted his academic career to solving the problem of induction because he believed that the world is undergoing constant change, and classic formal inductive logic can thus not capitalise on or foresee this change: 'it almost looks as if historicists were trying to compensate themselves for the loss of an unchanging world by clinging to the faith that change can be foreseen because it is ruled by an unchanging law.'[75]

The reality of the 9/11 terrorist attacks demonstrates the enormous weakness of an inductive approach. The attacks undoubtedly constituted change that appeared as threats that arose in new variations. The inductive approach does not lend itself to change, and threats that represent change can therefore not be foreseen inductively, since they cannot be reflected in empirical premises. It is therefore worthwhile evaluating how an inductive approach, in its interaction with secrecy and intelligence tribal language, did shape the nature of threat perception in the US intelligence community.

The Nature of US Threat Perception Prior to 9/11

1. Think about how a surprise attack might be launched

This first element does actually lend itself to imagination and creativity, and could in isolation counteract the negative influence of a classic inductive approach. However, the four elements interact, and the sum of their interaction increases the problem of induction. The characteristic and identity of the question in element one propose that one should think about how a surprise attack might be launched. It therefore presupposes the possibility of change and works against the general empirical premises; it thus involves speculation that gives change a chance, and as such implies a contrast to inductive reasoning. Nonetheless, the element does not fit with element two, which suggests a quantitative and inductive approach to threat perception. Any positive results derived from speculating about the question in element one will therefore be shaped and outweighed by the characteristic inductive tell-tale identity of element two. However, there is another and more serious problem with the question in element one.

The question focuses on how attacks might be launched, not by whom or why. US intelligence was as such unable to focus effectively on one prioritised enemy. The result of this weakness in the threat approach is that one focuses solely on the nature of the attack itself, neglecting the motivation, willingness and capability of the enemy. Clausewitz elucidates this: 'inversely, the weaker the motive for conflict, the longer the intervals between actions. For the stronger motive increases willpower, and willpower, as we know, is always both an element in and the product of strength.'[76]

Whether one likes it or not, terrorism must also be seen as politics, though in an extreme form. The dialectics in classic terrorism threat perception seriously decrease its effectiveness and precision, as it creates a distinct and often limiting discourse that at worst may reduce understanding of modern enemies. Al Qaeda was prior to 9/11 a modern enemy. The organisation constituted change, it existed outside classic political and strategic discourse, and as such posed a bigger threat to the United States than the US intelligence community managed to perceive, and one can therefore ask whether a deeper appreciation of Clause-witz would have been helpful:

> The more powerful and inspiring the motives for war, the more they affect the belligerent nations and the fiercer the tensions that precede the outbreak, the closer will war approach its abstract concept, the more important will be the destruction of the enemy, the more closely will the military aims and the political objects of war coincide, and the more military and less political will war appear to be.[77]

The US 'war on terror' has changed its identity and its name. It is now the called the Long War,[78] an identity that is indeed characteristic of the motives that shape al Qaeda and the threat from Salafi jihadists, and reflects a deeper understanding of Clausewitz's theory. The war is political, although it is a different form of politics from that seen in classic warfare. The motives are extreme, and there is no willingness to stop or limit the terror, and the war will therefore be long. The political objectives of al Qaeda and other Salafi jihadists are hence almost absolute, and they therefore constitute themselves in motives so strong that the war itself becomes apolitical on the battlefield. The Long War is therefore almost total, since it is shaped by extreme political ideologies that constitute themselves on an unlimited and apolitical battlefield.

The question in element one was created to foresee classic threats from nation states, and did not stimulate a discourse that embraced the possibility of the reality of war without political limitations. It was therefore severely challenging for the US intelligence community to think that someone could have the motives, motivation, willingness and resources to attack civilians and high-value targets on American soil. The practical consequence for collection was that 'there was no coordinated US Government-wide strategy to track terrorist funding and close down their financial support network'.[79]

Element one could have counteracted the limits of induction on threat perception had it not been shaped by the three other elements. Still, the question is by its nature limiting and reductive to constructive threat discourse, since it does not value the true nature of threats that may appear in new variations. It is limited to how, without asking who and why, and the question indeed illustrates the limiting threat discourse that existed prior to 9/11. This restrictive discourse was shaped by classic threat cognition, and a restrictive and secrecy-driven intelligence tribal language that led to the following situation:

> The September 11 attacks fell into the void between the foreign and domestic threats. The foreign intelligence agencies were watching overseas, alert to foreign threats to US interests there. The domestic agencies were waiting for evidence of a domestic threat from sleeper cells within the United States. No one was looking for a foreign threat to domestic targets. The threat that was coming was not from sleeper cells. It was foreign – but from foreigners who had infiltrated into the United States.[80]

This finding illustrates how cognition and intelligence tribal language may have shaped the threat perception and consequently collection prior to 9/11. The words 'domestic' and 'foreign' are by their nature forceful, and influence as demonstrated above the comprehension of intelligence focus and priorities, as well as organisational discourse expressed in a distinct intelligence tribal language. The finding not only illustrates the force of organisational identity and belonging, it also implicitly suggests that intelligence tribal language can shape intelligence personnel's identity as either domestic or foreign intelligence officers, and it is when this strong identity interacts with a complex transnational threat that it creates a circularity where organisational identity influences the discourse that creates the identity.

Threats become challenging to comprehend and communicate for analysts operating in this sort of cognitive climate, even in situations where analysts understand the challenges they face. Daniel Byman is illustrative here: 'cognitive disjuncture between the knowledge of individuals and the logical actions that should flow from that knowledge is the limited attention given to defensive measures against terrorism, particularly in the United States itself.'[81] This example illustrates that it is challenging for analysts who comprehend transnational threats to communicate this in a climate and in organisations that are heavily shaped by either their foreign or domestic intelligence discourse. The question is whether it is possible to claim that the earth is round in a world that appears to be flat. History shows that this has been challenging, and even life-threatening, and intelligence should hence be conscious of orthodoxies and strong belief systems.

The threat from al Qaeda was neither foreign nor domestic, and the US intelligence community thus 'faced a target that operated in the shadows of nation-states but wasn't one'.[82] There was therefore neither a language nor a threat discourse that could communicate the threat, and it is unlikely that intelligence institutions will ever develop discourses that manage to fully communicate threats that appear in new variations, 'because the issues keep changing, even perfection – if it were achievable, which it is not – in procedures and organization to tackle this year's issues will be outdated next year'.[83] This relation, between a threat that appeared in new variations and guise, and a limited discourse to communicate this change, created a complex situation that was challenging to comprehend. The situation was further made more difficult to understand since the threat existed in a realm where 'a division between domestic and international spheres of terrorism no longer existed'.[84]

Even so, the design of the US intelligence bureaucracy still had a distinct border between domestic and foreign intelligence focus, responsibility and resources, causing ineffective 'management of transnational operations',[85] and 'under outmoded conditions it was impossible to adequately cope with, and respond to, these new asymmetric attacks'.[86] Speculation and critical thinking about how a surprise attack might have been launched were hence shaped by this distinct border, and the situation was not made better by 'mature bureaucracies without much initiative, imagination or creativity'.[87] The intelligence community's ability to capitalise on the important interactive questions – who, why, where, when and how – were hence decreased. These questions are crucial in threat perception because they focus on motives, motivation, willingness, resources and capability. Yet asking these questions and taking them seriously presuppose one comprehending and taking seriously the enemy.

The threat from al Qaeda was indeed highly challenging to comprehend and constituted confusion and ambiguity, fuelling the human tendency to close cognitive understanding. It was when cognitive closure interacted with a secrecy-driven discourse where 'culture and policy issues also limited the extent to which CIA shared counterterrorism information within the Intelligence Community'[88] that discourse failure increased. It was further fuelled as it interacted with a distinct domestic/foreign intelligence tribal language that failed to communicate the reality of a translational threat, illustrated by the fact that 'the CIA [did] not develop a transnational plan for tracking Mihdhar and his associates so that they could be followed to Bangkok and onward, including the United States'.[89] It ultimately resulted in a collection focus that failed to capitalise on the lethal translational threat from al Qaeda, and the situation where 'it was NSA policy not to target terrorists in the United States'[90] is illustrative.

2. Identify tell-tale indicators connected to the most dangerous possibilities

Induction is problematic since it implies that understanding is strictly shaped by historical premises.[91] This is probably also why humans so easily develop orthodoxies and political assumptions, and the philosophical description of induction as such supports Neumann and Smith, who highlight that another 9/11 can only be avoided if humans question their orthodoxies and political assumptions.[92] This study hence suggests that intelligence institutions should ask themselves whether their orthodoxies and political assumptions are shaped by inductive cognitive closure, since the problem of induction primarily '[reflects] a habit or custom of the mind.'[93]

The question above therefore does not essentially decrease threat perception. It is the habits and customs it may create, and the inferences that intelligence institutions may derive from it, that may be damaging. This implies that intelligence institutions indeed need to collect information. However, they must be careful about dealing with the collected information. The question presupposes that the intelligence institutions actually know the most dangerous possibilities, but this is a misleading notion, since one can argue that the most dangerous threats are those which are not yet perceived and those existing outside the limits of induction. The most dangerous possibilities are therefore challenging to imagine and foresee.

The arguments presented suggest that the question in element two is problematic since its character implies that it is only able to foresee those threats which correspond to empirical premises, and therefore are inductively knowable to the intelligence institutions that try to foresee them. The question's tell-tale inductive identity limits adequate and qualitative threat perception, and this analysis will in the following investigate how its limiting character shaped intelligence collection prior to 9/11. It is again important to look at the nature of the threat. Madeleine Albright's illustration of the threat from al Qaeda demonstrates that she understood something profound:

> We are dealing with a brand-new threat in a way that spreads through these variety of groups where people are given sanctuary and where, in fact, I think there is a question in the long term how we deal with it in terms of educational issues.[94]

Albright captures the true nature of the threat in many ways, and demonstrates its multiple character. She illustrates that Al Qaeda was not, and is not, only an organisation. It was and is still primarily a Salafi jihadism ideology that is spread through various groups around the world. It is therefore a global ideological threat. This was new prior to 9/11. Global transnational terrorism was challenging for the terrorists before the internet revolution. The internet changed all that, and direction, management and ideological leadership beyond nation state borders have become easier, making it possible to create and develop Salafi jihadism as 'a network of networks of networks, in which terrorists from various organizations and cells pool their resources and share their expertise'.[95] Salafi jihadists' capacity to communicate their ideology has therefore increased accordingly, arguably creating many associated supporters who get their instructions 'through Arabic websites on the internet, which intelligence services worldwide are not yet recovering or translating in a comprehensive or timely fashion'.[96] This factor makes it more challenging to understand the ideology of Salafi jihadism, and to identify the different terrorist groups that develop from this ideology. The structure of the threat becomes multiple, and it becomes harder and harder to perceive it; and the fact that, 'for example, neither the Internet nor the end of the Cold War have been fully integrated into the thinking and practice of many of the traditional intelligence organizations'[97] has made it increasingly challenging for intelligence institutions to monitor and understand global terrorism.

Albright, a former US Secretary of State, demonstrates that she understood this complexity; however, it is important to ask whether this complexity was sufficiently understood prior to 9/11. It is therefore also important to ask how the tell-tale identity of the question in element two provided a methodical opportunity to shape an understanding of this complexity, and if the collection focus prior to 9/11 identified adequate threat perception.

The perception of bin Laden and the threat from al Qaeda were characterised prior to 9/11 by the Clinton administration's focus. Bin Laden was indeed taken seriously by the administration, but it was unknown whether he was only a financer of terrorism, or whether he had a more central role:

> Osama bin Laden did not become a viable target entity as far as the US intelligence community was concerned until sometime in 1994, when intelligence reports began to circulate indicating that bin Laden's organization, al Qaeda (which in Arabic means 'The Base'), was providing financial support to a number of Muslim extremist organizations in the Middle East and elsewhere around the world.[98]

But he was taken so seriously that 'in 1996, as an organizational experiment undertaken with seed money, the CTC created a special "Issue Station" devoted exclusively to bin Laden'.[99] The establishment of the 'Bin Laden station' illustrates that the CIA took him so seriously that they spent time and money on him, and 'by 1998 DCI Tenet was giving considerable personal attention to the OBL threat'.[100] However, the CIA did not capture bin Laden, nor did his power decrease. On the contrary, he became stronger and stronger. President Clinton therefore ordered a new strategy in

1999 and it resulted in 'The Plan', implying a much more comprehensive and aggressive tactic against bin Laden.[101]

The 1999 evaluation of the strategy against bin Laden, and the subsequent revision and refocus, introduced a prioritised and much stronger approach than previously. But it was too late, and the strategic revisions in intelligence focus implied operational changes that, due to the complexities, would have taken too long to implement. Intelligence collection focus before 1999 had been on 'Afghan proxies alone',[102] that is, 'particular indigenous groups . . . who might be able to operate in different parts of Afghanistan'.[103] However, the CIA wanted better intelligence and accordingly decided to 'create the CIA's own sources'.[104] Officers with counterterrorism experience had to be recruited and trained, and the CIA intended to fill important gaps in intelligence collection on Afghanistan by improving coordination between Sigint and Humint priorities and outputs. This indeed illustrates a radical shift in the approach against al Qaeda, and the CIA consequently planned to 'penetrate Al Qaeda directly'.[105]

The US intelligence requirements did not, however, communicate focus and priority on al Qaeda, and 'Intelligence Community officials [suggested] that many felt that the prioritization process was so broad as to be meaningless'.[106] It can be argued that the priority system demonstrated confusion, and as such cognitive closure. An inductive approach does not suppress the human willingness to submit to cognitive closure. On the contrary, it stimulates cognitive closure, since it increases the forces of habits and customs. As such it facilitates orthodoxies and political assumptions, and intelligence institutions can hence easily confirm their preconceived assumptions. This can contribute to a priority and collection process that creates and develops its own self-referential spiral, where questions and answers only verify those empirical premises that originally shaped the collection priorities. The Plan intended to increase intelligence collection and focus on bin Laden. The strategy was aggressive and would have, if it had been fully implemented, fundamentally refocused US intelligence collection priorities. Nonetheless, the reality of the priority process was different. It was unfocused, broad and inflexible,[107] and as such illustrates that inductive habit and routines reduce focus, imagination and flexibility. Habit and custom can easily be misunderstood as focus.

However, this book argues that proper intellectual focus, and hence also intelligence focus, are fundamentally different from habits and routines. Habits and routines identify orthodoxies and political assumptions, and thus contrast with qualitative intelligence priorities.

The inductive tell-tale question in element two and the findings illustrating an unchanged focus on bin Laden demonstrate that the intelligence requirements and intelligence collection priorities prior to 9/11 were shaped by habit and custom. The findings and the analysis hence also illustrate that inductive reasoning fuels cognitive closure and stimulates a cognitive circular process, where induction facilitates habitual and conventional thinking, which further stimulates inductive and self-referential thinking. The question in element two therefore facilitated an inflexible inductive system that did not identify the change represented by the al Qaeda threat.

It has now been demonstrated that the inductive approach to threat perception and collection priority did fuel habitual and conventional perception of the enemy. The substantial nature of the threat was therefore not acknowledged. The inductive approach reduced cognitive awareness, and effective defence against cognitive closure was further decreased by a secrecy-focused discourse that greatly decreased coordination and cooperation between different agencies.[108] The result was 'bureaucratic confusion about responsibility for counterterrorism'.[109] Lack of cooperation and coordination refuelled a secrecy discourse that gave imaginative thinking few chances against cognitive closure. Habits and custom therefore prevailed, and creativity and imagination in the collection process decreased. The aggressive collection strategy in 'The Plan' was thus not conducted as intended, and the intelligence community:

> . . . did not effectively develop and use human sources to penetrate the al-Qa'ida inner circle. This lack of reliable and knowledgeable human sources significantly limited the Community's ability to acquire intelligence that could be acted upon before the September 11 attacks.[110]

The above analysis illustrates that collection and analysis of 'tell-tale' indicators connected to the most dangerous possibilities are misleading, since the process is unable to capitalise on indicators that appear beyond the evidence provided by experience. This consequently leads intelligence institutions into habitual and conventional thinking. This reductive thinking is further influenced by a distinct secrecy culture that decreases critical rationalism, which contributes to an intelligence tribal language refuelling itself and further increasing inductive thinking. The result is a limiting discourse that leads to discourse failure. This illustrates that the relation between habitual and conventional cognition, secrecy and intelligence tribal language both fuels and is fuelled by the problem of induction, and intelligence institutions can hence easily believe that there is a habitual and customary inference between inductive conclusions and their empirical premises.

Imagination and creativity have few chances in an inductively driven collection system, since innovation and alternative intelligence requirements and collection priorities reflect change. Inductive reasoning does not identify threat actions occurring beyond our experiences, and changes in threat structures may therefore represent confusion and ambiguity and increase cognitive closure.[111] Identification of tell-tale indicators that are connected to the most dangerous possibilities is therefore a question that greatly increases the possibility of cognitive closure, and the question as such fuels discourse failure.

3. Where feasible, collect intelligence on these indicators

'The Plan' reflected a shift in the strategy against bin Laden. It did not work as intended, and the most radical collection priorities were not implemented. However, the plan contributed to increased collection on al Qaeda, but 'still, going into the year 2000, the CIA had never laid American eyes on bin Ladin in Afghanistan'.[112] President Clinton was not satisfied, and urged his administration to increase their efforts against bin Laden.

Sixteen Predator surveillance flights were therefore conducted over Afghanistan in the autumn of 2000, and findings indicate that someone who could have been bin Laden was spotted twice.[113] The Predator operations in 2000 were regarded as a relative success, and optimistic tests demonstrated that the Predator could be armed with missiles. Clarke and Assistant DCI Allen therefore suggested that the reconnaissance Predator operations should continue in the spring, and that the armed Predator should be used against bin Laden as soon as it was ready. However, Tenet and officers in the Joint Staff were reluctant and temporarily stopped the plan, arguing that using the reconnaissance version before the armed Predator was finished would 'forfeit the element of surprise for the armed Predator'.[114] Tenet prevailed, and 'Clarke believed that these arguments were stalling tactics by CIA's risk averse Directorate of Operations'.[115]

Reconnaissance Predator missions were therefore set on hold, while the armed Predator was prepared. The work on finishing the armed Predator accelerated, though it was not finished before 9/11. However, Tenet did finally agree on further reconnaissance operations after 'a meeting of NSC principals on September 4, [where] National Security Advisor Rice summarized a consensus that the armed Predator was not ready, but that the capability was needed'.[116]

These findings demonstrate that new intelligence requirements and priorities are difficult to implement. Nevertheless, the findings also illustrate that the US intelligence community did conduct collection operations against al Qaeda that were relatively successful, though they did not capitalise on the collected information obtained from these operations. However, the successful Predator missions did constitute change, and they were therefore challenging to implement in 'cultures that had moulded agencies like CIA, NSA and the FBI for years'[117] and, 'Assistant DCI Allen said that the CIA's senior management was originally reluctant to go ahead with the Predator program, adding that "it was a bloody struggle".'[118]

Allen's statement reflects the fact that new ideas, operational concepts and doctrines are challenging to implement – even more so when they originate from threats that appear in new variations. Traditional threats are easier to deal with; they facilitate habit and custom, and as such represent relative safety. Threats appearing in new variations, however, represent ambiguity and challenge the human willingness to accept change. But the reality of the Predator programme reflects a willingness to think innovatively, though only to a certain degree. Armed Predators challenged the orthodoxy, and it therefore proved much more difficult to obtain approval to carry out armed missions. Consequently, even reconnaissance missions were put on hold.

Whether the Predator missions were a result of adequate knowledge about al Qaeda, or foresighted innovative and creative thinking by Clarke, is difficult to evaluate, though it is clear that the threat from bin Laden had started to disclose some of its character. However, the presented evidence suggests that the missions first of all were conducted because Clarke, Allen and Vice Admiral Scott Fry from the Joint Staff jointly urged that reconnaissance operations should be conducted.[119] The operations were thus the result of wise thinking by men who had understood the threat before it had become compelling to the rest of the US intelligence community. This fact also made it easier to put the operations on hold, since the operations did not originate from a threat perception about al Qaeda that was institutionally implemented in the Armed Forces and in the intelligence community. The Joint Inquiry demonstrates this:

> Prior to September 11, the Intelligence Community's understanding of al-Qa'ida was hampered by insufficient analytic focus and quality, particularly in terms of strategic analysis.[120]

Qualitative intelligence collection requires adequate threat perception that originates from and is implemented throughout the intelligence community. The Predator's missions did actually originate from tell-tale indicators.[121] Nonetheless, the perception of the enemy was fragmented and unfocused. The Predator missions targeted bin Laden, and those responsible for the missions knew 'that killing bin Laden would have an impact but not stop the threat'.[122] This fact illustrates that bin Laden was not seen as the prime target. Even before 9/11 al Qaeda was acknowledged as the prime threat, and the CIA told President-elect George W. Bush 'that the only long-term way to deal with the threat was to end al Qaeda's ability to use Afghanistan as a sanctuary for its operations'.[123] Thus, al Qaeda was seen as the threat, and the US intelligence community and the decision-makers made an adequate distinction between the man and the organisation. Even so, the threat was perceived in a classic manner, and the CIA and the US Armed Forces hence planned to attack al Qaeda in Afghanistan. But the 9/11 attackers were already in the US, and they did not need guns or explosives to carry out their deeds. The threats were identified, but their true and full nature was not acknowledged.

The US intelligence community did, as illustrated, collect telltale indicators, and the indicators pertaining to al Qaeda that they collected were true and valid. But the indicators and consequent collection had an inductive approach, and collection therefore reflected a classic collection strategy that targeted bin Laden and al Qaeda in Afghanistan, and consequently not the danger emerging on US soil.

The threat from al Qaeda did not follow geographical borders; it was global and ideological; it challenged classic threat structures and was therefore difficult to comprehend for the US intelligence community, whose traditional focus was on nation states, a task at which it was largely successful. As Friedman emphasises:

> The greatest capability of the CIA – and the intelligence community in general – is covert operations that gather information from a nation's leadership. The CIA is not perfect at this, but it is outstanding. However, an event that involves non-nation-state actors (such as Castro, prior to the Cuban revolution) or more important, in which the leaders of the nation-state are themselves unaware, leaves the CIA helpless.[124]

The threat from al Qaeda, however, did not fit traditional threat structures. It did not emerge from a state, and appeared in new variations that confused an intelligence community which possessed:

> . . . a long history of defining internal threats as either foreign or domestic and assigning responsibility to the intelligence and law enforcement agencies accordingly. This division reflects a fundamental policy choice

and is codified in law. For example, the National Security Act of 1947 precludes CIA from exercising any internal security or law enforcement powers.[125]

The threat from al Qaeda indeed challenged this traditional intelligence system that was conservatively divided into a foreign and domestic domain, and therefore confused the US intelligence community. The system was bureaucratic, and was designed to comprehend and counter threats that were either foreign or domestic, and it was therefore unfit to detect and counter the danger posed by al Qaeda. The new variations the threat appeared in were therefore not fully comprehended or acknowledged by the US intelligence community. It hence became challenging for the community to coordinate its effort against the threat, and the intelligence community did not manage to produce a compiled product that could have increased their holistic perception of the threat. This led to a situation where al Qaeda was on the map, but caused more confusion and internal turmoil than focus. One illustration of this is that James Pavitt, the head of CIA's Directorate of Operations, told Clarke that 'while the CIA's Bin Ladin unit did extraordinary and commendable work', his chief of station in London 'was just as much part of the al Qaeda struggle as an officer sitting in [the Bin Ladin unit]'.[126] Pavitt's statement may demonstrate that he understood the transnational character of the threat from al Qaeda. However, the statement may also suggest that Pavitt only saw the 'Bin Ladin unit' as internal competition, and that he only wanted the funding, priority and resources to go to the Directorate of Operations. Pavitt's statement may therefore indicate internal friction between what Pavitt refers to as 'the Bin Ladin unit' and his own Directorate of Operations, and that this friction led to a counterterrorism strategy that was unfocused and organisationally fragmented.

Clarke illustrates this friction, as he was sceptical towards the Directorate of Operations and argued that 'CIA spending on counterterrorism from its baseline budget had shown almost no increase'.[127] This demonstrates the dissent that existed in the intelligence community, and Clarke elucidates this in telling the Commission that 'my view was that he [Pavitt] had a lot of money to do it and a long time to do it, and I didn't want to put more good money after bad'.[128] Clarke's position was based on figures from the Office of Management and Budget (OMB).[129] However, Clarke's view contrasted with Pavitt's standpoint, as the 'CIA still believed that it remained underfunded for counter-terrorism',[130] and this division made it challenging to implement a profound counterterrorism strategy.

Although Pavitt's statement illustrates dissent in the intelligence community, it also communicates that he understood the danger needed to be confronted on all fronts. Furthermore, it indicates another important factor: it is the need for knowledge, and where it geographically can be found that must shape intelligence require-ments and priorities. Intelligence institutions must therefore avoid being method-driven, and become knowledge-driven. They should operate where there is valuable information. Arguably, there was more information about al Qaeda in London prior to 9/11 than in Afghanistan. This illustrates that the real fight against Salafi jihadism is not in Syria, Afghanistan and Iraq, but in the midst of the free and democratic societies: in London, New York, Madrid, Mumbai and Paris.

An inductive approach to intelligence collection failed to iden-tify transnational terrorism, and al Qaeda's essential nature as a global ideology was accordingly not properly comprehended. It was, prior to 9/11, challenging to identify the threat from al Qaeda, since there did not exist any empirical validation pertain-ing to global transnational terrorism. The problem of induction, however, increases with empirical reasoning, since it increases the force of habits and custom. This implies that threats will con-stantly be in front of the intelligence institutions that are sup-posed to foresee them. Induction was therefore useless prior to 9/11, and remains useless. This is illustrated as the aftermath of 9/11 and the problem of induction have created a new orthodox threat discourse that has replaced the old one. There are few signs demonstrating that intelligence institutions have managed to free themselves from the chains of tradition and custom, and the result is too much focus on threats from terrorists who may hijack air-liners and use them in suicide attacks against domestic targets, or terrorist cells conducting deadly attacks against random civilians in European cities.

The terrorist attack in Oslo on 22 July 2011 is illustrative, and demonstrates that the most unthinkable attacks, and those that exist beyond the limits of our morality and induction, are the most dangerous. High qualitative intelligence must therefore constantly challenge existing threat discourses, since such attacks not only influence the society that is affected, but also shape national discourse, as well as shaping the discourse in intelligence collectors and analysts. The 9/11 attacks therefore created a discourse that does not necessarily develop a deeper comprehension of transnational threats. 9/11 could on the contrary have created a new discourse that led to only a cosmetic shift in conventional thinking, just as the bombing and shooting attack in Oslo on 22 July 2011 may have led to a new threat discourse that may have reduced the Norwegian intelligence community's ability to detect and acknowledge future threats that appear beyond the threat discourse that 22/7 created.

Tell-tale indicators and consequent collection would hence probably only lead intelligence institutions to focus on targets and react to threat indicators that confirm a discourse shaped by the 9/11 attacks and the 22/7 attacks. Future terrorist threats that appear in new forms will therefore become as difficult to identify and accept as the al Qaeda threat was before 9/11. Threats are therefore by their nature not only highly challenging to identify and comprehend using an inductive approach, they also constantly shape new threat discourses that potentially further increase the problem of induction. Creativity and imagination are therefore called for. Friedman illustrates that unconventionality should identify creative intelligence work, and further demonstrates how the CIA's orthodox management techniques actually increased the problem of induction, thus decreasing the institution's ability to comprehend threats that appeared in new variations:

> These techniques are designed to create orderly processes. But the world isn't orderly, and neither should the intelligence process be. It should celebrate the unconventional, the iconoclastic, the brilliant.

These are not orderly values. Tenet's slow grinding system of committees and reviews had failure built into it. People learned that in order to get along, they had to go along – so everyone did.[131]

Friedman illustrates a distinct intelligence tribal language that is arguably universal. Intelligence institutions deal with confusion and ambiguity, and these factors increase the possibility of cognitive closure and hence discourse failure. Confusion and ambiguity cannot be understood automatically. Systems, methods and routines are indeed needed. The amount of information is enormous and it is impossible for the human mind to remember or capitalise on it. Imagination and creativity on the one side, and systems, methods and routines on the other, are not easily compatible, but intelligence institutions need them all. The technology experts, the system engineers, the courageous field operators, and the brilliant analysts that can see signals through noise are all needed. Threats that appear in new variations, the complicated systems that intelligence institutions need to capitalise on the information they collect, and the tension a complex threat may cause between personalities in intelligence institutions, all contribute to a distinct intelligence tribal language. The problem of induction does not make it any better. The inductive approach not only leads intelligence institutions astray; it also facilitates cognitive closure and discourse failure, because it provides a cognitive harbour that stimulates cognitive safety and leads to tranquillity (though a very negative tranquillity, and one that certainly does not stimulate imagination and creativity).

Collection pertaining to potential threats that are detected by indicators such as those in the US tell-tale indicator system will not increase imagination and creativity, nor will it increase intelligence institutions' comprehension of the threat from al Qaeda or any other danger in the future. The system of indicators only confirms history, and leads intelligence analysts into the problem of induction. The problem of induction, habitual thinking and custom reduce intelligence institutions to information managers. Intelligence services should instead seek to be critical of induction, and produce knowledge that probes beyond formal reasoning.

This presupposes imagination and creativity. A misunderstood secrecy culture and a limiting, restrictive and bureaucratic intelligence tribal language can fuel orthodox bureaucracy and thus decrease imagination and creativity:

> That's what happened at the CIA: A culture of process destroyed a culture of excellence. There are many outstanding people at the agency, in both the Directorate of Intelligence and Operations. The agency's obsession with intelligence process crushes these people daily. Those who flourish in this environment are those who can sit through long meetings without falling asleep. The people who can peer through the darkness and see the truth are either sucked into the surreal world of modern management or shunted aside.[132]

Systems, methods and processes are indeed important in intelligence production, and intelligence would certainly be seriously handicapped without them. However, systems and processes can also, as Friedman describes, be damaging to excellent intelligence, and intelligence tribal language is arguably both fuelled by and fuels limiting and bureaucratic processes. The need-to-know culture is an illustrative example. It identifies the almost principal focus of secrecy in intelligence organisations. Secrecy is important. But secrecy for its own sake does not stimulate debate and dialogue. It may, on the contrary, develop suspicion and cognitive insecurity, causing a diminished 'sharing of information and collaboration between different'[133] intelligence services.

It is when this culture mixes with the problem of induction that threat perception is seriously hampered, and leads intelligence institutions to collect data on indicators that are a result of habitual and conventional thinking. The result demonstrates itself: 'NSA adopted a policy that avoided intercepting the communications between individuals in the United States and foreign countries.'[134] This finding illustrates that inductive thinking led the US intelligence community to overlook the importance of the transnational space, and as such demonstrates that tell-tale indicators and consequent collection on these indicators easily lead to discourse failure. The next part of this chapter will therefore investigate whether the interaction between the problem of induction, cognition, secrecy and intelligence tribal language shaped collection and thus influenced adaptation of threat defences, and whether and how these adaptations reflected the restricted inductive approach to threat perception.

4. Adopt defences to deflect the most dangerous possibilities or at least trigger an earlier warning

The CTC was at the forefront in the war against bin Laden, though it suffered from the lack of resources given to it, and the CIA's reluctance to use money on terrorism from its baseline budget[135] indicates that the threat from al Qaeda had not sufficiently become a priority that was institutionalised in the CIA. The following analysis is illustrative:

> The record of this Joint Inquiry indicates that the DCI *did not* marshal resources effectively even within CIA against the threat posed by al Qaeda. Despite the DCI's declaration to CIA officials that the Agency was at war with bin Laden, there is substantial evidence that the DCI's Counterterrorist Center needed additional personnel prior to September 11, and that the lack of resources had a substantial impact on its ability to detect and monitor al Qaeda's activities.[136]

The following analysis will therefore evaluate whether inductively driven intelligence priorities, focus and collection made it challenging to identify and accept the essence of the threat from al Qaeda, and thus contributed to discourse failure.

The decision-makers' needs and requirements shape the priorities, the collection plans, the analysis and the dissemination in an intelligence organisation. A threat such as that from al Qaeda challenges this system, as it does not lend itself to inductive inquiry, to traditional threat perception or to current collection thresholds. Threats that appear in new variations will easily fall between two chairs in such a system, and the damaging result may be that important data go uncollected or are not disseminated. The NSA had collected signals on:

suspected terrorist facility in the Middle East that had previously been linked to al-Qa'ida activities directed against US Interests . . . [but] the information was not published because the individuals mentioned in the communications were unknown to NSA, and, according to NSA, the information did not meet NSA's reporting thresholds.[137]

This example illustrates that requirements shape not only collection but also dissemination, and it demonstrates that an orthodox requirement system may prevent crucial information from being disseminated to other agencies and to decision-makers. The threat from al Qaeda thus existed and developed outside existing discourse and the threat could therefore evolve undisturbed. However, the Clinton administration did observe the threat. It also understood some aspects of its nature, although it did not manage to capitalise on possible intelligence value in the information collected. It was consequently unable to effectively counter the threat.

Clarke's working group did propose actionable countermeasures that could have proved effective against the threat, and they included establishing 'an interagency center to target illegal entry and human traffickers'.[138] Clarke and his group also proposed measures that in short would have tightened immigration, heightened the control of immigration, increased effective legal authorities against people suspected of terrorism and increased the international standard of travel documents.[139] All these proposals were foresighted and innovative, and could have hampered the terrorists. Nonetheless, none of the measures focused on domestic travellers, and the measures would thus have proved ineffective against the 9/11 terrorists.

Such proposals, however, were always likely to be difficult to implement, since their effectiveness depended on cooperation and coordination between underfunded agencies. The proposals also needed support from 'powerful congressional committees, which were more responsive to well-organised interest groups than to executive branch interagency committees. The changes sought by the principals in March 2000 were only beginning to occur before 9/11.'[140] This indicates that tightened control of domestic immigration would probably have been difficult to implement, if not impossible.

This example demonstrates that there existed a threat discourse that limited innovation and creativity. Clarke and his group certainly looked beyond classic threat perception. Nonetheless, even they did not have the imagination to foresee the quintessential reality of the threat, and few if any could have seen it. It was not helpful when this classic threat discourse interacted with a bureaucratic and slow working system that gave innovation few chances.

The focus of the collection is illustrative. The Americans cooperated with the leader of the Northern Alliance, Massoud, and gave him technical support that helped him to collect intelligence on al Qaeda in Afghanistan. Massoud's motivation was shaped by his political objectives, and he accordingly sought more commitment from the Americans. He therefore 'wanted the United States both to become his ally in trying to overthrow the Taliban and to recognize that they were fighting common enemies'.[141] His willingness to help the Americans was hence driven by his objective to overthrow the Taliban and take power. Clarke and the head of the CTC, Cofer Black, wanted to become more effective and direct against al Qaeda and bin Laden, and proposed that the Americans should seek an alliance with Massoud and overthrow both the Taliban and bin Laden. Even more direct actions were discussed, such as the use of American Humint agents on the ground in Afghanistan. However, the proposal was deemed too risky and never carried out.[142]

The cooperation with Massoud, the potential use of American Humint agents in Afghanistan, and the use of the Predator illustrate that the Americans focused predominantly on bin Laden and Afghanistan when it came to collection. The consequence was that the threat that evolved on US soil continued to develop undisturbed. Nonetheless, the general threat from al Qaeda and the domestic threat from the organisation had grown too strong, and it would have been severely challenging if not impossible to counter the threat's centre of gravity 'that possessed one unassailable attribute: many of its adherents were willing to commit suicide for the cause, and would strap on a bomb just to take civilian bystanders with them'.[143] Understanding this would certainly have been helpful; it would have given the US intelligence community a better comprehension of the enemy, and they could have prioritised their collection efforts differently. A better acknowledgement of the enemy would have helped them to see that the temporary fight against the threat had to be on American soil and was against tactical terrorist operatives who were already in the country. The US intelligence community hence failed to capitalise on collected information which indicated:

> . . . the possibility of terrorist attacks within the United States. Nonetheless, testimony and interviews confirm that it was the general view of the Intelligence Community, in the spring and the summer of 2001, that the threatened Bin Ladin attacks would most likely occur against US interests overseas, despite indications of plans and intentions to attack in the domestic United States.[144]

Conclusion

This analysis demonstrates an intelligence community that was collection-driven at the expense of analysis, uncoordinated and that did not comprehend the essence of the threat. Some parts of the US intelligence community did, however, capitalise on the available intelligence. It led them to al Qaeda, although it can be argued that the problem of induction increased the force of a classic threat perception that led them to focus too much on Afghanistan and bin Laden. It was clear that bin Laden was the leader of al Qaeda. It is less clear to what extent al Qaeda's strength depended on bin Laden's leadership. Arguably, the threat from al Qaeda and Salafi jihadism will continue to exist although bin Laden is dead.

Nevertheless, the US intelligence community's focus on Afghanistan and bin Laden indicates that bin Laden in practice operated as his own diversion and scapegoat, since he managed to have the US intelligence community focusing more on him than on his organisation and on the threat evolving on American soil. Whether it was intentional or not is unknown, but the focus of US intelligence on bin Laden and al Qaeda in Afghanistan led them away from the terrorists in the US. It led the focus of US intelligence away from al Qaeda's real target; New York and Washington.

Blind belief in the force of history made intelligence operatives think that history repeats itself. But history, of course, never repeats itself, although it 'will be in part like the past and in part not at all like the past'.[145] Nor do threats repeat themselves. However, they do appear in new forms and varieties, and these may easily be misjudged as historical echoes. This may lead to orthodox beliefs that fuel a classic threat discourse that easily misleads. The US intelligence community thus failed to capitalise on the collected material they already had, and they were therefore not able to identify the change that had occurred on their threat radar. It was therefore highly challenging, if not impossible to adopt defences that could have deflected the most dangerous possibilities, simply because the most dangerous possibilities lay in the changes of the threat that were so challenging to identify, comprehend and accept.

5   On Analysis

Bertrand Russell suggests that philosophy, and thus scientific inquiry, should start with doubt. High-quality intelligence should also be shaped by doubt, and should thereby probe into deeper questions than those answerable by classic intelligence methods, since intelligence analysis based on induction is only able to draw conclusions entailed by the premises in the argument. As a result, classic intelligence analysis cannot predict the future. High-quality intelligence analysis must therefore be based on doubt; institutions should constantly ask whether there is:

> . . . any knowledge in the world which is so certain that no reasonable man could doubt it? This question, which at first sight might not seem difficult, is really one of the most difficult that can be asked. When we have realized the obstacles in the way of a straightforward and confident answer, we shall be well launched on the study of [intelligence analysis] – for [intelligence analysis] is merely the attempt to answer such ultimate questions, not carelessly and dogmatically, as we do in ordinary life and even in the sciences, but critically, after exploring all that makes such questions puzzling, and after realizing all the vagueness and confusion that underlie our ordinary ideas.[1]

Intelligence analysis exists in the realm between science on the one hand, and philosophy and art on the other, and one should thus evaluate why established and classic inductive intelligence analyses cannot answer intelligence requirements that probe beyond inductive logic. Former UK security and intelligence coordinator Sir David Omand warns of 'the risk that intelligence analysts fall into an inductive fallacy, regarding fresh intelligence that is consistent with a judgement they have reached as strengthening their belief in it'.[2] He presents elucidation[3] as a better tool with which to reach intelligence organisations' ultimate goal: the production of estimates about the future that support the intelligence consumer in conducting their extremely demanding task.

The Analysis and its Structure

This chapter will focus on the problem of induction, and the analysis will evaluate whether, how and to what extent the problem of induction and cognitive closure shape and limit discourse in intelligence institutions. Furthermore, the analysis will evaluate and demonstrate how this limited and restrictive discourse, in its interplay with secrecy and intelligence tribal language, greatly decreases the quality of intelligence analysis.

The chapter will be divided into three main parts. Part one analyses the problem of induction. Part two evaluates the problem of induction against classic intelligence analysis, and seeks to demonstrate the limits of classic intelligence analysis. Part three evaluates the problem of induction and the limits of intelligence analysis against findings in the 9/11 Commission Report and the Joint Inquiry.

The Problem of Induction

The problem of induction is not linked merely to the logical process itself, but to the mental perception thereof. Induction takes the observer from empirical experiences to empirical conclusions derived from these experiences,[4] and it presupposes that those who believe in induction must believe that 'conclusion [involves] the same properties or relations as the premises'.[5] Heuer is illustrative in emphasising the following:

> Of the diverse problems that impede accurate intelligence analysis, those inherent in human mental processes are surely among the most important and most difficult to deal with. Intelligence analysis is

fundamentally a mental process, but understanding this process is hindered by the lack of conscious awareness of the workings of our own minds.[6]

The practical result of a belief in induction is the implication that history shapes the future, and may hence be helpful as intelligence indicators. David Hume would have contradicted this, as he emphasised that 'induction presupposed belief in the uniformity of nature, but that this belief had no defence in reason, and merely reflected a habit or custom of the mind'.[7] The problem of induction therefore lies in the belief that there 'is something rationally compelling about the inference'[8] between premises and conclusions.

Intelligence institutions in general and the US intelligence community in particular have traditionally conducted their analyses based on an inductive method,[9] and hence facilitated and nurtured a strong belief in the uniformity of nature. The detection of threats appearing in new variations has few chances in such a system. The problem of induction is simply 'whether the future will be like the past'.[10] The answer to this question, and to this problem, is that it will not. However, the problem needs more in-depth analysis. Popper did not believe in induction, suggesting that the problem of induction can be solved because the future never copies the past, although it sometimes seems to.[11] This implies that history sometimes seems to replicate itself, but it will nevertheless always appear in new variations and in new contexts.[12] There are evident consequences for intelligence institutions, which approach threats inductively: they will create a circular, destructive threat logic that is self-evidential and proves itself.[13] Threat perception can easily become self-evidential in such a system, and leads to 'frequent practical mistakes in inductive behaviour'.[14]

Discourse failure can thus be seen as a failure arising from a limiting language evolving in a restrictive inductive atmosphere, and discourse failure is as such a mental and philosophical phenomenon that probes beyond the strict, technical boundaries of the intelligence cycle.

Hume argued that humans are no more than irrational animals because:
1) We reason, and must reason, inductively.
2) Inductive reasoning is logically invalid.
3) To reason in a logically invalid way is irrational.

Therefore, we are, and must be, irrational.

The human thought process, Hume argued, could therefore be understood as follows:

> *Inductive scepticism:* since induction is invalid, no evidence-transcending belief can be justified (shown to be true, or probable)
>
> *Justificationism:* it is only reasonable to believe what has been justified (shown to be true, or probable)
>
> *Therefore irrationalism:* no evidence-transcending belief is reasonable.[15]

Arguably, humans are inherently entrenched in an inductive trap, which moulds a limiting and restrictive language facilitating discourse failure. However, that would imply that history is worthless for intelligence analysis, and that intelligence, accordingly, is impossible. That is not the case, and Popper illustrates this in disputing that humans *must* reason inductively. This implies that the inductive problem can be diminished because humans can choose to understand it, and hence reduce its negative effects by using falsification and critical rationalism. Uncritical inductive behaviour thus facilitates discourse failure, while Popper's falsification and critical rationalism provide a guide beyond the limitations and problems of induction.

Popper neither rejects history, nor argues that humans cannot argue from experience; one of his books is therefore entitled *Poverty of Historicism*, not *Poverty of History*. Accordingly, it is 'Hume's assumption that we *must* reason inductively that is Popper's real target'.[16] Popper rejects the idea that an inference between history and future exists that creates a uniform belief in nature. This is because 'the point is that there is no rule of inductive inference – inference leading to theories or universal laws – ever proposed which can be taken seriously for even a minute'.[17]

Popper did try to understand whether there was such a thing as inductive inference, concluding that 'sensible rules of inductive inference do not exist'.[18] He searched the inductivist literature and rhetorically stated the following: 'the best rule I can extract from all my reading of the inductivist literature would be something like this: *'The future is likely to be not so very different from the past.'*[19]

Popper demonstrates that inductive inference is invalid: classic intelligence analysis and threat perception must thus be also invalid, since they are built on the notion of a formal logical inference between empirical premises and empirical conclusions supported by the empirical premises. All this seems very theoretical, as indeed it is. Best practice cannot be understood without theories, 'since there can be no theory-free observation, and no theory-free language, there can of course be no theory-free rule or principle of induction; no rule or principle on which all theories should be based'.[20] Popper therefore holds that the assumption that the future is likely to be not so very different from the past is a rule that most would accept. Nonetheless, he also argues that the rule is too vague, and that 'the rule assumes too much, and certainly much more than we (and thus any inductive rule) should assume *prior* to all theory formation; for it assumes a *theory of time*'.[21] Inductive logic is therefore invalid, since it is built on a theoretical framework constantly seeking its justification in the future, and Popper argues as follows:

> Thus induction is a myth. No 'inductive logic' exists. And although there exists a 'logical' interpretation of the probability calculus, there is no good reason to assume that this 'generalized logic' (as it *may* be called) is a system of 'inductive logic'.[22]

Clearly, Popper believed that induction is a myth, since inductive logic presupposes a theoretical approach that exists prior to its own justification, and therefore lends itself only to this justification. Popper is illustrative in emphasising the way in which the problem of induction can be diminished:

> Nor is it to be regretted that induction does not exist: we seem to do quite well without it – with theories which are bold guesses, and which we criticize and test as severely as we can, and with as much ingenuity as we possess.[23]

The challenges related to classic intelligence analysis and discourse failure can hence also be diminished, since the negative impact of discourse failure on intelligence is diminished when the problem of induction is acknowledged and reduced, since Popper's theory demonstrates that scientific inquiry should not be based on a blind and habitual belief in inference between empirical premises and empirical conclusions. Popper therefore believes in *inductive scepticism*, but he differs from Hume and rejects his irrationalism. He must hence reject justificationism, and 'he must think that it may be reasonable to believe what has not been justified, established as true or probable'.[24] But this does not imply that Popper believed in belief without critical rationalism, and Popper emphasised that, 'like E. M. Forster he "[did] not believe in belief"'.[25] Popper thus believed in beliefs that had withstood the test of falsification, since: 'A conjecturally knows that P if and only if (a) A believes that P, (b) P is true, and (c) A reasonably believes (is justified in believing) that P, in the sense of CR [critical rationalism].'[26]

Intelligence estimation must thus not be based on inductive logic, or on belief based on verification. It must be based on qualified estimates that have withstood the test of falsification and critical rationalism. This can be explained as follows:

> Faced with an evidence-transcending hypothesis H, there are two ways we can proceed. We can try to justify H, give reasons for it, show that it is true or probable. Or we can try to criticize H, give reasons against it, show that it is false. Hume's inductive scepticism means that the former will not work. We should forsake the way of justification in favour of the way of criticism. No invalid inductive reasoning is involved in rejecting an evidence-transcending hypothesis H as false because it contradicts some perceptual or evidential belief. But suppose our critical endeavours fail, and H stands up to our efforts to criticise it. Then this fact is a good reason to believe H, tentatively and for the time being, *though it is not a reason for the hypothesis H itself.*[27]

Popper demonstrates his rejection of 'the view that a reason for believing something must be a reason for what is believed',[28] as well as rejecting '*logomania*, the view that only reason or reasoning provides a good reason for believing anything'.[29]

It has now been illustrated that inductive logic is challenging as a tool for intelligence estimation, and that induction cannot describe holistic phenomena since these phenomena gain their identity from their place in a greater context beyond the limitations of syntax and formal analysis.[30] The ultimate and damaging result of the limits of induction is that it makes it impossible for intelligence institutions to detect new threat variations. Foreseeing 9/11 thus became highly challenging, since the threat appeared in new variations, and as such facilitated a threat discourse that impeded threat comprehension beyond the strict syntax of the inductive approach. This strict syntactical approach implies that if one believes P, another P needs to be true. Or because one knows that one P is not true, this consequently entails that another similar P is not true. The damaging result of such an inductive approach on adequate threat perception is evident: new variations of threats would be impossible to foresee and comprehend because most people believe what they believe (P) because they believe R, 'and infer P from R'.[31]

An inductive approach to intelligence perception is therefore problematic since it presupposes a belief in inference between the empirical premises and the conclusion derived therefrom. A conventional belief in such an inference would imply that the future is always a repetition of history. New variations of threats have demonstrated repeatedly the invalidity of this notion, and it captures the problem of induction and the consequential problem for intelligence estimation. Intelligence institutions are meant to look into the future and foresee new and possible threat variations. Inductive logic in this context is both unhelpful and counterproductive, since it is unable to embrace the complex context of new threat variations. The next section of this chapter will therefore analyse the problem of induction against classic intelligence analysis, and explore and demonstrate how the validity of classic intelligence analysis is reduced by the negative impact stemming from the problem of induction. It will be argued that the problem of induction reduces the scope of intelligence method and terminology: this creates a distinct intelligence tribal language and an intelligence discourse incapable of probing beyond the limits of induction, and therefore incapable of embracing the kind of creativity and imagination needed by intelligence institutions to estimate the future. It will also be illustrated that this problem is increased because no proper intelligence theory exists. The absence of intelligence theory makes it challenging to characterise success and failure,[32] and it will be contended that the deficiency of theory hence makes it inherently difficult to understand intelligence failure, since it is challenging to detect and understand failure if one is not able to define theoretically success and failure in the first place. It is challenging to understand what is wrong if one does not understand what is right.

Intelligence Analysis and the Problem of Induction

Analysis is 'the process of breaking a concept down into more simple parts, so that its logical structure is displayed'.[33] Intelligence institutions, however, should seek to foresee the future. The future can never exist at present as a logical concept, and intelligence analysis in its classic form is therefore a fallacy, since it seeks to predict the future by using a formal process which offers only comprehension of the past and present. Intelligence analysis also involves prediction and estimation, although arguably even these approaches to intelligence analysis have been influenced by a classic inductive analytical approach, since humans, as Hume argued, approach their surroundings inductively.[34] Nonetheless, this study echoes Popper, and argues that humans do not need to do that.[35] Humans can therefore reduce the inductive problem. The inductive problem in intelligence analysis thus needs to be understood, and the analysis will evaluate how the problem of induction has shaped intelligence methods, terminology, intelligence tribal language, intelligence discourse, and thus classic intelligence analysis.

Lowenthal emphasises that estimates '[assess] the relative likelihood of one or more outcomes'.[36] He highlights that intelligence estimation would be unnecessary if predicting the future were possible.[37] Even so, as the future is impossible to predict with certainty, estimation is the key to skilful and successful intelligence production, since intelligence consists of uncertain estimates that are made less uncertain through the estimation process. Nonetheless, an investigation is required into whether intelligence estimation has traditionally been as it has been described, or if it has been merely classic inductive intelligence analysis in disguise. General Brent Scowcroft makes it clear that estimation provides information about three key areas: the forces at work in the world, what the trends are, and what kinds of possibilities intelligence should consider.[38] This is a very precise description of skilful and highly qualitative intelligence production.

It has been demonstrated and established that classic intelligence analysis is invalid as a tool with which to estimate the future, since it is based on an inductive approach that is only able to break down concepts that already exist, and futuristic concepts that do not exist cannot hence be analysed. Classic intelligence analysis therefore only provides intelligence institutions and their consumers with knowledge about the past and present. It tells them nothing about the future. The theoretical description of estimation, however, provides something more, and brings intelligence from science to art, because the process frees the empirical premises from their strict, inductive boundaries, inasmuch as the three-stage estimation is identified by its capability to capture the context.[39] Estimation is therefore not classic intelligence analysis in disguise, and provides something to intelligence analysis that probes beyond the limits of induction.

Estimation seeks to comprehend the forces at work in any given situation and in any subjects. The process is therefore intuitively perceptive to the complex order of constantly changing threats, and the method hence aims to perceive both mental and physical forces at work in variable, changing threat structures; not strictly their inductive history, but also their existing and estimated prospective structures in the future. Estimation is hence a method that potentially frees the intelligence analyst from the problem of induction, since it makes it mentally possible for the analyst to perceive and estimate observed mental and physical forces beyond their strict, inductive boundaries. Estimation may thus facilitate the perception of threats in their complex context, a context that exists outside the strict, syntactical boundaries of inductive logic, while a classic inductive analytical approach is only capable of assessing threats strictly syntactically. However, it remains to be seen whether estimation has worked as intended, or whether it has only worked well in theory.

It seems that estimation has in many cases been nothing more than theory, and that a classic inductive approach has prevailed. Findings from the Joint Inquiry are illustrative:

> The Intelligence Community's focus was also far more oriented toward tactical analysis of al Qaeda in support of operations than on the strategic analysis needed to develop a broader understanding of the threat and the organization. For example, as mentioned earlier, the DCI's National Intelligence Council never produced a National Intelligence Estimate (NIE) on the threat to the United States posed by al Qaeda and Osama bin Laden.[40]

This finding indicates that the DCI's National Intelligence Council did not holistically estimate the threat; they analysed it only inductively, and did not aim to comprehend it in its context. They therefore did not give themselves a chance to develop a deeper comprehension of the complexity and nature of the enemy, thereby indicating that estimation prior to 9/11 was only a theoretical model which was not fully incorporated as a comprehensive analytical tool in the intelligence community. The problem presented is not unique to the US intelligence community, and Agrell is illustrative in arguing thus:

> The fundamental problem is the implicit model for knowledge production in intelligence systems that have been in place for more than a half-century. If the problem is the intellectual output, transformation has to address it – that is, with the way intelligence *thinks*.[41]

Agrell's contention implicitly demonstrates that the problems outlined in the Joint Inquiry reflect the idea that the factors causing intelligence failures are complex and inherited in intelligence discourse and culture, since 'intelligence is not a science but rather something that could be called a protoscience: a field of intellectual problem-solving but thus far lacking a comprehensive set of theories, a scientific discourse, and self-reflection'.[42] There is, as demonstrated, something fundamentally wrong with the way intelligence is conducted today, and with its theoretical base. Collectors and analysts may do their best, but it is the lack of a robust theoretical framework for intelligence activity identified as adequate intelligence discourse that causes the problems and, which, at worst, may lead to intelligence failure. Intelligence institutions should hence strive to 'step from protoscience to an applied science with an open culture in which competing interpretations are the norm, not the (barely tolerated) exception'.[43] To do this, intelligence institutions need a theoretical framework, and one should ask why none exists. Julian Richards is demonstrative in maintaining that:

> On the one hand, academics and theorists can think about and try to develop theories of intelligence, but practitioners have to get on and to it; often without time to consider its philosophical underpinnings. The answer is that intelligence is more than just a theoretical construct – it is also a practical activity with very real consequences.[44]

Does this imply that theories exist beyond the realities they describe, or that intelligence practice per definition can be theory-free? Nothing is theory-free and activities seeking to free themselves from their inherent ideas and theories will fail, 'since there can be no theory-free observation, and no theory-free language'.[45] This implies that intelligence, like all concepts, is based on an idea. It is created because someone wants to understand something about something or someone else. It exists for a purpose, and it is therefore not theory-free. However, clearly it can be conducted in isolation from its original ideas, as illustrated by Richards, and it is also for that reason that it can go so disastrously wrong. One may thus conclude that intelligence is not theory-free, but that the importance of theory, as illustrates, often loses out to time constraints, the need for action and the subsequent importance of the reality of intelligence as a practical activity. Nonetheless, this does not imply that theory is less important than practice, nor that a solid intelligence theory exists. It means only that intelligence is not theory-free, and that it accordingly can and should be understood and defined theoretically. Intelligence should be based on solid theory, since it does not do very well without it. This by no means implies that this study does not acknowledge the seriousness of intelligence as a practical activity, or the deadly consequences if intelligence makes mistakes. It is for this very reason that intelligence needs a solid theoretical framework: accordingly, in the following I will analyse how a lack of intelligence theory increases the problem of induction and discourse failure, and how these factors, in their interaction with intelligence tribal language and secrecy, develop an inductive analytical culture that reduces threat perception. The Joint Inquiry is demonstrative in stating that 'active analytic efforts to identify the scope and nature of the threat, particularly in the domestic United States, were clearly inadequate'.[46]

The inadequacy of the analytical efforts reflects an intelligence culture and an approach to intelligence that were fragmented, and that failed to understand intelligence as a whole. The institutions did clearly collect data on the enemy and analyse them. However, they did not sufficiently estimate the enemy's threat structure, and the analysis was therefore unable to perceive the enemy's characteristics and complex nature. Such an understanding is arguably only possible if one seeks to perceive the enemy beyond the strict boundaries of an inductive approach, a possibility offered by estimation. Yet estimation presupposes coordination and cooperation between both intelligence operators and intelligence institutions, as well as between these institutions and their intelligence consumers, and unfortunately, a lack of cooperation and coordination was arguably one of the greatest hindrances prior to 9/11. The National Intelligence Strategy of the United States of America (2005) stated that:

> The Director of the National Counterterrorism Center will develop a comprehensive national intelligence plan for supporting the nation's war on terror. The plan will identify the roles and responsibilities of each number of the Intelligence Community involved in supporting

our national counterterrorism efforts, including their relationships with law enforcement and homeland security authorities. The Program Manager, Information Sharing Environment, will ensure the information needs of federal, state, local and tribal governments and the private sector are identified and satisfied.[47]

Such a strategy may have been fine up to a point, but it is challenging to implement coordination and cooperation if there is no commonly understood intelligence discourse, or a general perception of what intelligence is, and one should evaluate whether such an understanding presupposes intelligence theory. Davies argues that intelligence can exist without intelligence theory, and states the following:

> . . . theory in a more ambitious sense is all too easily a slippery slope into metaphorical speculation, woolly reasoning and disingenuously-packaged dogma. Indeed, I would argue that an axiom of any properly valid and validated social sciences effort should be that all of the most important questions about society are empirical ones, as are the most important answers. This is as true of the study of intelligence as of any less esoteric sphere of inquiry.[48]

Based on the above, should one conclude that intelligence does not need theory, since theory, according to Davies, easily becomes woolly and dogmatic? The consequences of such a conclusion would have been interesting, not only for intelligence, but for science in general and for the human understanding of life as such. Davies holds that theory easily becomes dogmatic, and he is right, but that is not a problem only for intelligence: this problem applies to all scientific inquiry, and to thinking in general. It is easy to become dogmatic and orthodox, and it is easy to seek comforting and easy solutions, but it is for this very reason that theory is important, since it constantly ensures that the scientist challenges his or her own theories and, consequently, his or her ideas. Theory is not static. It undergoes constant change, and for this very reason good theory moves science towards new discoveries. Good theory reflects ideas. Ideas undergo constant change, and a theory of intelligence is therefore a structured model mirroring and elucidating the idea of the way in which intelligence is understood and perceived through the mind.[49]

Davies also argues that the most important questions about life are empirical ones, and that the most important answers are provided by empirical reasoning. He is partly right in that, but it does not follow from this that theory is less important than empirical reasoning, and one should ask what empirical studies would have been if they had not been based on solid theory. Excellent empirical reasoning is based on qualitative theory and good ideas because 'fundamentally new ways of looking at the whole world, such as those arising in the work of Newton and of Einstein, depend very strongly on the perception of the relevance of certain key questions, which help point to some contradictory or confused features of previously accepted general ways of thinking'.[50] Empirical questions without theory are therefore poor, unfocused and unhelpful, since qualitative empirical reasoning presupposes a hypothesis that presupposes theories that are based on ideas.[51] Davies is right in claiming that the most important questions about society are empirical, but he forgets to mention that good empirical questions need a theoretical origin. But his contention is more problematic for another reason: his statement seems to imply that empirical reasoning alone produces good intelligence, and he is wrong, simply because empirical reasoning with no theoretical framework facilitating and highlighting the importance of critical estimation probing beyond induction, will lead intelligence straight into the inductive problem. Davies's contention that empirical reasoning is the most important for intelligence is, therefore, incorrect since intelligence institutions which base their intelligence production on empirical reasoning alone would fail to imagine threats that appear in new variations, since these variations would exist beyond empirical premises. Intelligence institutions must hence free themselves from the chains of simple empirical reasoning and the consequential problem of induction, and learn how to 'be able to learn something new, even if this means that the ideas and notions that are comfortable or dear to [intelligence] may be overturned'.[52] This way of perceiving reality is the prerequisite for originality,[53] and it implies that original thinking and, as a consequence, good intelligence probe beyond induction and empirical reasoning, and 'are not justifiable by our immediate experiences, but are, from the logical point of view, accepted by an act, by a free decision'.[54]

The arguments presented demonstrate that classic intelligence analysis based on induction shapes intelligence negatively, since it creates a damaging belief in the uniformity of nature. Intelligence institutions basing their analysis on induction therefore incorporate the problem of induction into their assessment procedures, and it thus becomes highly challenging for these institutions to acknowledge threat structures appearing in new variations, and therefore existing outside the boundaries of the inductive approach. Richard J. Kerr illustrates this problem in emphasising that '*mindsets* that prevent analysts from asking the right questions often result when poor information forces them to rely on an adversary's past behaviour or on what they previously judged to be an intelligence target's most likely course of action'.[55] The next section of this chapter will therefore evaluate the problem of induction and the limits of intelligence analysis against findings in the 9/11 Commission Report and the Joint Inquiry. The analysis explores whether and how the problem of induction influenced the analysis process in the US intelligence community prior to 9/11. It is based on the hypothesis that the negative interaction between the problem of induction, discourse failure, unnecessary secrecy and intelligence tribal language arises from, and increases because of, the lack of a common understanding of what intelligence is. Accordingly, it becomes increasingly challenging to comprehend and accept threats appearing in new variations.

The Problem of Induction and 9/11

The former CIA analyst Richard L. Russell argues that a damaging culture existed in the CIA. He highlights that knowledge was not merely difficult to obtain because of its holistic character, but also because competing cultures existed in the CIA with highly different views of the meaning and role of intelligence, and more importantly, because different views existed on the meaning of thinking. He elucidates this:

> Because of the CIA's shallow analytic expertise, for technical exper-
> tise, policy makers dealing with WMD proliferation know to turn to
> the National Laboratories run by the Department of Energy, not to
> the CIA. The dirty little secret in the intelligence community is that
> the National Laboratories go out of their way to recruit and train
> highly qualified PhDs in a variety of disciplines, whereas CIA manage-
> ment culturally discriminates against PhDs. The CIA has even lost a
> few of its best analysts to the National Laboratories where the work-
> ing environment is much better than that of Langley.[56]

Russell's statement illustrates what the consequences for intelligence may be if intelligence institutions downgrade the importance
of education and training based on a solid theoretical foundation.
Classic analysis based on induction is complicated enough in itself,
and its complexity is not decreased by intelligence analysts' lack of
proper education and training, because:

> Analysis is likely to improve when we look beyond what is going on
> in our own heads – when we use any of several techniques designed
> to make explicit the underlying structures of our argument and when
> we encourage others to challenge our analogies and heuristics with
> their own.[57]

It is hardly a surprise if such a culture is regarded as challenging or even a burden against a culture shaped by the problem of
induction, given that knowledge and wisdom disclose ignorance.
This introduces one of the main problems and challenges of intelligence: the constant struggle between those who cultivate the methods and the terminology for the sake of the methods themselves,
and those who cultivate the outcome and the objective of intelligence; intelligence as wisdom that may increase the quality of
political decision-making.[58] High-quality intelligence on all levels
undoubtedly presupposes both camel drivers and chess players,[59]
and Russell demonstrates what the consequences are if these two
cultures cannot communicate and cooperate sufficiently.

Russell's statement also indicates that displeasure existed against academics and intelligence theory in the CIA. Arguably his statement indicates something more serious and much more damaging: there existed resistance against critical thinking in the CIA. Intelligence is doubtlessly about thinking, and more importantly about deep critical thinking. Resistance against it can be severely damaging. However, self-awareness may increase critical thinking, and James B. Bruce and Michael Bennett illustrate the importance of critical thinking and self-awareness:

> The *know yourself* principle emphasizes continuous awareness of the vulnerable mind's most exploitable weakness: its own preconceptions, expectations, and beliefs. Mitigating cognitive biases is vital to improving analysis; a key corrective technique is the use of hypothesis. The failure of analysts to generate alternative hypotheses is insufficiently recognized in the intelligence community. This failure can be attributed to the use of a suboptimal heuristic of choosing the first explanation that seems to be the closest fit to the evidence at hand ('satisficing' and jumping to conclusions). A major contribution of Alternative Analysis is that it shows the value of multiple hypotheses.[60]

Bruce and Bennett thereby demonstrate that a culture that rejects self-criticism and doubt increases the problem of induction and, consequently, discourse failure. Intelligence institutions seeking to improve the quality of their products must therefore employ operators who embrace critical thinking and doubt, because 'the rigorous challenging of conventional wisdom through the regular use of better and more transparent analytic tradecraft can reduce – if not totally eliminate – the hazards of unconscious mindsets'.[61] Critical thinking thus demands highly qualified operators on all levels, and analysts especially need to be intelligent and critical. This was also the kind of culture Kent dreamed of, and he accordingly described the perfect analysts as:

> . . . people to whom research and rigorous thought are the breath of life, and they must accordingly have tolerance for the queer bird and the eccentric with a unique talent. They must guarantee a sort of academic freedom of inquiry and must fight off those who derogate such

freedom by pointing to its occasional crackpot finding. They must be built around a deference to the enormous difficulties which the search for truth often involves.[62]

There are few findings in the 9/11 Commission Report and the Joint Inquiry to demonstrate that Kent's vision ever came into being, an assumption illustrated by Russell's observation. Arguably, therefore, the main problem for the CIA was that it was not a truly deep-thinking organisation possessing a philosophy based on high-quality intelligence theory, and it would be no surprise if this were also a challenge for intelligence organisations around the world. Nonetheless, this does not imply that there were no deep thinkers in the CIA or other intelligence organisations; it implies only that deep thinking probably did not characterise the identity of the organisational culture and the discourse. Russell's observation demonstrates that the CIA did not sufficiently cultivate imagination, creativity and the spirit of free thinking, an observation supported by findings in the 9/11 Commission Report.[63]

Russell might be understood as arguing that having a PhD is the answer to these problems. High-level academic qualifications certainly do help when an organisation and its employees seek to explore the problem of induction, as well as in attempting to comprehend complex threats. Nonetheless, high-level academic qualifications are not in themselves enough, since the problem pertains more to the culture and the mindset of these organisations, and to the way in which intelligence is understood. Doctorates in intelligence, war studies, security policy, political science or philosophy do not in themselves solve the problem, nor do academic degrees automatically create a spirit of doubt. The absence of doubt in itself is, therefore, much more serious than whether intelligence operators have a PhD or not, since 'an intelligence consensus is difficult to challenge with new data because people are reluctant to change their minds – to admit to having been mistaken and to being surprised, which could hurt their careers by giving them a reputation for being unsteady and unreliable'.[64]

Intelligence institutions hence require people with curiosity, creativity and doubt, and a PhD or a master's degree may help humans in general and intelligence operators to acknowledge the advantage of academic education and critical thinking when conducting systematic doubt, since academic training is substantially about engaging with methodical doubt.

The above seems to suggest that the problem of induction increases when intelligence operators are not critical enough of their observations, and of the conclusions they derive therefrom. The absence of intelligence theory, the existence of bureaucracy, secrecy and entrenched intelligence tribal language increase orthodoxies and political assumption, thereby fuelling a self-referential language decreasing discourse and which constitutes a culture that has a strong belief in the uniformity of nature. Clarke illustrates this in a personal note to Condoleezza Rice communicating his fear of the CIA's bureaucracy: he warned that the:

> ... bureaucracy, which was 'masterful at passive aggressive behaviour,' would resist funding the new national security presidential directive, leaving it a 'hollow shell of words without deeds.' The CIA would insist its other priorities were more important. Invoking President Bush's own language, Clarke wrote, '*You are left with a modest effort to swat flies*, to try to prevent specific al Qaida attacks by using [intelligence] to detect them and friendly governments' police and intelligence officers to stop them. *You are left waiting for the big attack*, with lots of casualties, after which some major US retaliation will be in order[.]'[65]

Clarke's note to Rice illustrates that orthodoxies, intelligence tribal language and a strong belief in existing worldviews shaped the CIA prior to 9/11, and arguably this culture was probably also representative of the US intelligence community as a whole. The fact that 'the FBI was struggling to build up its institutional capabilities to do more against terrorism'[66] demonstrates that it was not only the CIA that was struggling to comprehend the substance of the emerging threat and adapt to the new reality.

The CIA, the FBI and the other agencies were all in a cognitive mode, where a strong belief in the existing, and most importantly, a strong belief in the uniformity of nature, handicapped the intelligence community, creating an inductive thought process that shaped the intelligence process, and making it increasingly challenging to observe and, most importantly, accept the apparent and cognitively challenging. Amy B. Zegart is illustrative in describing how the entrenched structure, culture and incentive systems made it challenging for the CIA to 'disrupt the September 11 plot and limited its ability to capitalize on the few opportunities that it had . . . Failures of adaptation led to failures of performance.'[67] This does not imply that the community did not have information about the threat towards the US, nor does it imply that this was not reported to the White House. It was the nature of the threat that they found challenging to cognitively understand and accept; consequently, the US intelligence community focused on classic foreign threats. The result of this was as follows:

> Far less was done domestically – in part, surely, because to the extent that specifics did exist, they pertained to threats overseas. As noted earlier, a threat against the embassy in Yemen quickly resulted in its closing. Possible domestic threats were more vague. When reports did not specify where the attacks were to take place, officials presumed that they would again be overseas, though they did not rule out a target in the United States. Each of the FBI threat advisories made this point.[68]

It is easy to be wise after the event, and such evaluations are often shaped by hindsight. Still, the US had on its own soil been under violent attack from al Qaeda before. The threat was not entirely new, and American lives had already been lost during the attack on the USS *Cole*, on the American embassies in Kenya and Tanzania and on the military bases in Saudi Arabia.[69] So why did the US intelligence community, and much of the developed world, refuse to acknowledge the deadly threat from al Qaeda? In the following, it will be contended that the 9/11 attacks were not caused merely by systemic failures in the intelligence community, but by inherent psychological and cognitive weaknesses in all humans, regardless of their religious or cultural background. It will also be contended that these weaknesses were increased by no solid intelligence theory existing, and that the combination of these two factors increased the problem of induction, which consequently reduced the level of intelligence discourse and developed a limiting and restrictive language unable to reflect on and communicate the nature of the threat. These problems were additionally increased by a distinct culture identified by its secrecy and intelligence tribal language.

The Lack of Intelligence Theory, Culture and the Problem of Induction

It is illustrative that Bin Laden was only mentioned as a terrorist financer in the last 1997 national intelligence estimate,[70] and 'the CIA did not write any analytical assessments of possible hijacking scenarios'.[71] These findings demonstrate that, despite the fact that the community had substantial information that pointed to a profound threat to the US,[72] it was challenging to reflect on and communicate it because 'the methods for detecting and then warning of surprise attack . . . were not employed to analyze the enemy that, as the twentieth century closed, was most likely to launch a surprise attack directly against the United States.'[73] This finding at first sight seems to demonstrate that the failure was systemic. However, this can be contended, and May is illustrative in arguing that '[thought] scenarios were slow to work their way into the thinking of aviation security experts'.[74] This illustrates that threats appearing in new variations challenge human cognition. It is therefore hard to understand and accept threats that evolve outside of the existing intelligence discourse, and even harder if the imagination one needs to understand such threats must be conducted in a culture that is theory-free and identified by its secrecy and its distinct intelligence tribal language. Jack Davis illustrates the consequences of such a culture in describing how 'the public record indicates (1) strategic warning was given, (2) warning was received, (3) warning was believed, at least by some recipients. Yet commensurate protective measures were not taken.'[75] This finding implicitly supports the discourse failure theory, since if the information was disseminated, received and believed, but still not acted on, this indicates that it was not cognitively accepted.

Human Cognition, the Cold War and the Problem of Induction

The above demonstrates that threats appearing in new variations challenge the human mind. They create a cognitive room where humans must think without any guidance from history, or instructions from experience. Theodor Adorno is illustrative in highlighting that 'repressive intolerance toward a thought not immediately accompanied by instructions for action is founded in fear'.[76] Fromm, as described earlier, echoes this argument in clarifying that it is the fear of freedom that is the most devastating and serious threat to democracies.[77] Fromm can be understood as arguing that the fear of freedom is fuelled by the human desire for submission and the lust for power, and these two human emotions can arguably be understood as human tendencies that are constituted by fear[78] and at the same time contribute to, and accelerate, the development of more fear. The relationship between fear, submission and power is hence circular, and it creates a threat climate in which these three emotions make high-quality cognition severely challenging: it thus becomes difficult to think truly freely, since 'open thinking points beyond itself'.[79]

Threats emerging in new forms and variations therefore presuppose perception that goes beyond itself, and arguably these threats create a form of undefined and not easily understandable unrest and anxiety that may develop into fear and an unwillingness to think truly beyond the possibilities given by history, and the possibilities that are consequently provided by induction. The result is that empirical reasoning chains imagination and creativity and fuels orthodoxies.

The threat from al Qaida was such a threat. It existed beyond the boundaries and traditions provided by the classic nation-state thinking, and Kerr demonstrates how the Cold War shaped security policy in highlighting how 'many international crises and brushfire or proxy wars across the world had their roots in the cold war'.[80] Treverton echoes this and is illustrative in stating that 'traditional intelligence as practiced during the Cold War focused on nation-states; non states or "transnational" actors were secondary'.[81] The former enemy had been huge, well organised, well equipped and most importantly politically and ideologically dangerous, but communism lost against the free states of the West. Accordingly, it was not only difficult to comprehend, but also challenging to accept that the new blurred enemy emerging in the aftermath of the Cold War could be a threat to these well-organised democratic states that had crushed such a dangerous enemy as the Soviet Union. The new enemy emerging became challenging to perceive and accept since 'weaknesses in structure, culture, and incentives festered throughout the Cold War and became debilitating in the 1990s, when the Soviet Threat was replaced by an entirely new breed of terrorist enemy'.[82] This demonstrates that the Cold War shaped a threat perception culture that obstructed any adequate understanding of the new enemy emerging, and this weakness was additionally increased by the West's self-image as the democracies that had prevailed against a suppressive regime. It was hence challenging to identify the transnational non-state character of the threat. Arguably, the world in general, and intelligence communities as such, had been fooled by their inductive belief in and understanding of history that have shaped an intelligence culture and discourse in which the 'legacy of the past [has been] so powerful that innovations so far have been piecemeal'.[83]

The study of history is of course important, and qualitative thinking is moulded by sound historical appreciation, but it must ideally be conducted without direct interference from it, and conclusions in intelligence estimations must be taken without reference to a possible inference between history and future. Adorno is demonstrative in highlighting that 'as long as thinking is not interrupted, it has a firm grasp upon [possibilities]'.[84] Robert Jervis supports Adorno's viewpoint in metaphorically highlighting that while analysts 'should indeed think first of horses, they should not neglect zebras either'.[85]

However, the self-image that much of the West assumed for itself after the Cold War did interrupt thinking that pointed beyond itself, and consequently beyond induction and history, and the intelligence communities in these societies hence reduced their ability to comprehend the possibility of threats that could emerge in new forms and variations. 9/11 as such mirrors Pearl Harbor. Laqueur illuminates this point:

> Pearl Harbor was a case not of oversuspicion, but of overconfidence. The idea that a small and industrially backward country like Japan would dare to attack mighty America seemed so strange and outlandish that the president and the military leadership were disinclined to attribute much importance to information about an impending attack.[86]

Pearl Harbor and 9/11 are two intelligence failures illustrating the force of the problem of induction. Humans in general and intelligence analysts easily become entrenched in their traditional mindsets, orthodoxies and political assumptions, and this problem also came to light when the Israelis, prior to Yom Kippur, refused to accept the apparent since 'reluctance to anticipate a possible Egyptian attack was reinforced by the Israelis' preconceived mental pattern of Egyptian behaviour'.[87] These examples illustrate the force of preconceived threat perceptions shaped by the problem of induction, and the problem of induction is also increased by what Davis calls the 'paradox of expertise', which 'explains why the more analysts are invested in a well-developed mindset that helps them assess and anticipate normal developments, the more difficult it is for them to accept still inconclusive evidence of what they believe to be unlikely and exceptional developments'.[88] Davis thereby illustrates that the empirical experience of intelligence analysts can increase the problem of induction so that it becomes increasingly challenging to identify and accept threats that appear beyond the expertise provided by the inductive experience given by normal developments. But threat characteristics develop beyond normal developments, and it is therefore difficult to identify and accept them. Moreover, they arguably threaten the analyst's self-image as an expert, and Adorno implicitly sums up the damaging relationship between suppression, fear and thought when he makes it clear that 'the universal tendency toward suppression goes against thought as such'.[89] High-quality analysis seeking to detect and understand threats appearing in new variations must therefore embrace thinking that challenges traditional intelligence expertise. It can be concluded from this that humans who do not give themselves the opportunity to think freely and beyond the boundaries of induction and history have given in to their fear, thereby suppressing their own cognitive ability and the possibilities provided by free and deep thinking. Intelligence institutions are no more than the humans that form them, and the intelligence operator's fear and self-invoked cognitive suppression may become institutionalised and can easily appear as orthodox perceptions of threats.

Threats challenging these worldviews are not easy to accept. It not only presupposes the ability to think freely and beyond the boundaries of history: it also, and most importantly, presupposes humility, and the willingness to admit that one has erred. However, it is not easy for anyone to admit mistakes. Norman Dixon describes this unflattering human tendency precisely in explaining how the 'inability to admit one has been in the wrong will be greater the more wrong one has been, and the more wrong one has been the more bizarre will be subsequent attempts to justify the unjustifiable'.[90] The Joint Inquiry illustrates Dixon's argument:

> Despite intelligence information on the immediacy of the threat level in the spring and summer of 2001, the assumption prevailed in the US Government that attacks of the magnitude of September 11 could not happen here. As a result, there was insufficient effort to alert the American public to the reality and gravity of the threat.[91]

This finding demonstrates that a strong reluctance existed to accepting the apparent in the US intelligence community. Accordingly, in the following one will evaluate the direct impact of the problem of induction on the intelligence process, and how this problem was increased by a lack of intelligence theory.

The Problem of Induction and the Intelligence Process

First, it is interesting to look at how the evolving threat influenced the CIA's budgeting practices and priorities. Clearly, despite the fact that the CIA had gone to war against al Qaeda, Tenet regarded counterterrorism as a kind of additional work, since the CIA clearly distinguished between their classic priorities and their

Bin Laden unit, and they thus decided to '[preserve] what they had, restoring what they had lost since the beginning of the 1990s, and building from there – with across-the-board recruitment and training of new case officers, and the reopening of closed stations'.[92]

These priorities did not reflect a clear conception of the magnitude of the threat. Instead of creating a robust organisation capable of countering the new threat, they decided to build on an organisation created in 1947 and that had developed and been shaped by the Cold War. A classic 'spy hunt spy' paradigm is obviously ineffective when trying to penetrate or understand al Qaeda, and the reopening of old CIA stations around the world illustrates that the CIA's priorities originated in a uniform belief in an inference between history and future. The CIA had fought against communism, and their priorities reflected their intention to fight terrorism in the same way. Clarke elucidates this in stating to the 9/11 Commission that it 'seemed [evident] that the CIA's leadership did not give sufficient priority to the battle against bin Ladin and al Qaeda'.[93] Johnson demonstrates the problem related to a 'classic spy in embassy approach' in emphasising that 'collection failures occur, too, because of a tendency by some nations to place their operational officers inside the limited confines of their embassies overseas'.[94] Arguably, such a collection approach undoubtedly also shapes the analytical approach. And importantly, despite overall increased funding for counterterrorism prior to 9/11, 'overall Intelligence Community funding fell or remained even in constant dollars'.[95] It would not be strange if this imbalance between overall funding and funding of terrorism-related issues may have created an atmosphere where the community perceived counterterrorism as the stepchild of classic intelligence collection and analysis. Nonetheless, these findings do illustrate that entrenched beliefs and paradigms influenced the priorities in the intelligence community. Wohlstetter illustrates how preconceived assumptions about the enemy can shape intelligence production in highlighting the 'tendency to select whatever [is] in accord with one's expectations'.[96]

The problem of induction also influenced the way in which terrorism financing was understood. Financial systems mirror their societies, and these financial systems further influence how threats are understood. Mindsets developed as a result, and the damaging effect was that the 'tendency to evaluate newly acquired information through an existing hypothesis, rather than using new information to reassess the premises of the hypothesis'[97] shaped the understanding of al Qaeda's financial structure in the first place.

The result of this mindset was that states were classically understood as states, also financially, and individuals were understood as individuals, also financially. This initially led to the belief that bin Laden sponsored al Qaeda. Consequently, al Qaeda's financial structure was insufficiently understood. The comprehension of the financial systems in the West obstructed the intelligence institutions from understanding that bin Laden and al Qaeda were a structure of financial networks within networks. This system was thus challenging to follow and penetrate.[98] The financing of al Qaeda could continue almost undisturbed, but it could have been better understood had someone tried to comprehend its structure and complexity. However, there had been plans prior to 9/11 to 'create an all-source terrorist-financing intelligence analysis center . . . but neither Treasury nor the CIA was willing to commit resources'.[99] Consequently, al Qaeda's financial structure was not comprehended, and the planning of the 9/11 attacks could continue undisturbed.

These findings illustrate how a classic understanding, not only of threats, but also of financial systems, obstructed the intelligence community in adequately understanding al Qaeda's financial structure and funding. It was not only the community that did not prioritise the matter: 'before 9/11, [the] Treasury did not consider terrorist financing important enough to mention in its national strategy for money laundering'.[100]

These examples show how history shaped important priorities not only on a political level, but also in the CIA and the Treasury. It would hardly be strange or surprising if these priorities strongly influenced the analysis. Analysts cannot look at the world blindfolded. They need focus, priorities, guidance and leadership. They undoubtedly were given all of these, but the findings in the 9/11 Commission Report demonstrate that the problem of induction guided them in the wrong direction. However, the picture is not as simple as this.

The Bush administration did focus on terrorism, and an anonymous CIA official called 'Richard' told the 9/11 Commission that

'Rice "got it."'[101] The CIA had created a classic covert action plan against al Qaeda, and it is unknown whether this plan was based on a conventional perception of al Qaeda; but it is clear that the CIA and the Treasury, prior to 9/11, did not have adequate information on al Qaeda's financial structure, and the CIA's covert action plan against al Qaeda was probably based on a moderate understanding of the financial and organisational structure of al Qaeda. It is neither possible to fully understand such organisations as al Qaeda, nor is such knowledge necessarily needed to eliminate them. Possibly, therefore, the CIA and the Bush administration, despite their limited understanding of al Qaeda, could have been successful if they had carried out their covert action plan, and had they accepted the nature of the threat from al Qaeda. Nonetheless, complex enemies demand complex countermeasures, and such measures need to be based on solid intelligence. A successful operation based on a plan without sufficient intelligence about the enemy would arguably have come about thanks to fortune and luck, rather than to wisdom and knowledge.

These presented arguments and the 9/11 Commission Report findings demonstrate that both the Clinton and the Bush administrations did prioritise terrorism to a certain degree, but they did not base their different priorities on sufficient all-source analysis. It is therefore important to look at the level of information that was available prior to 9/11, and examine why the information was not properly understood.

The 9/11 Commission report writes characteristically that the drumbeat began in the spring of 2001.[102] The heat rose when the intelligence community warned in March of a heightened threat from Sunni extremists to US interests, including personnel and facilities. The threat discourse and proximity to Washington also rose when Clarke warned that terrorists could choose to use truck bombs on the White House, and he accordingly advised that Pennsylvania Avenue, which had been closed, should continue to be so, since the West Wing could be destroyed in such an attack. He continued his warning by telling Rice 'that he thought there were terrorist cells within the United States, including al Qaeda'.[103] The drumbeat continued to thunder, and many of these warnings were given to President Bush in Tenet's daily briefings.[104] The intelligence reports reached their climax as the headlines to top officials in June 30 stated:

> 'Bin-Ladin Planning High-Profile Attacks.' The report stated that Bin Ladin operatives expected near-term attacks to have dramatic consequences of catastrophic proportions. That same day, Saudi Arabia declared its highest level of terror alert. Despite evidence of delays possibly caused by heightened US security, the planning for attacks was continuing.[105]

These findings from the Commission Report clearly demonstrate that the intelligence community and decision-makers had access to information that indicated a threat from al Qaeda, but it is more important to analyse whether the information was good enough to be acted upon.

The plethora of information

It did not pinpoint exactly where and when the attack would be carried out, and it serves as a good example of how too much information, if not precise enough, can often make users blinder than they would have been without it. This is a radical statement, but arguably information that has not been contextualised, and that is perceived outside its connections, only creates more chaos and misconceptions. Wohlstetter is illustrative, and makes it clear that the US intelligence community 'failed to anticipate Pearl Harbor not for want of the relevant materials, but because of a plethora of irrelevant ones'.[106] John Hollister Hedley echoes Wohlstetter in stating that 'in the twenty-first century, a principal analytic challenge lies in the sheer volume of information available'.[107] One therefore needs to evaluate whether and how the intelligence community managed to connect the dots prior to 9/11, and how the problem of induction decreased their ability to carry out this very important task.

Connecting the dots

Connecting the dots traditionally sums up the meaning of intelligence analysis, but the phrase is also misleading, since it implicitly suggests that the outcome of intelligence work is solely the result of the fusion of available information of possible intelligence value, and as such it may create a comprehension of intelligence outcome as answers that are almost fully adequate descriptions of reality as it is. That is a confusing comprehension of intelligence analysis, since intelligence estimation is about something more profound, and 'analytic judgements [are] not akin to painting by the numbers. Ask any analyst how easy it is to connect the dots when you aren't sure you have two "dots," or verifiable dots, dots that correlate.'[108] The essence of intelligence estimation is hence not quantitative telling, but 'information plus insight, derived from subject matter knowledge'.[109] Martin Petersen elucidates this in highlighting that 'the key is our ability to put the political behaviour that policymakers see into a larger cultural and histori-cal context – that they do not see – with enough sophistication to demonstrate that the context matters'.[110]

Communicating the context, form and structure of the threat

Intelligence is therefore the ability of the organisation to commu-nicate to the policymaker the context, form and structure of the threat. However, this task is challenging, and intelligence hence has its weaknesses, one of which is that intelligence at any given point can only probe into and describe small and limited parts of huge social phenomena. But this weakness may also be a strength of intelligence if it is properly understood, and Omand supports Petersen in emphasising that in-depth, 'all-source assessments should therefore be prepared to tackle mysteries as well as shed light on secrets. Thus analysis is more than validation: it implies understanding of context'.[111]

It is when intelligence reports, although they are limited parts of a bigger threat structure, are placed in their context that the real-ity and limitations of intelligence can be understood and appre-ciated. The ultimate result will be that 'an analyzed intelligence report, placed in its context, with understanding of significance, is likely to be more powerful provided that its timeliness is pre-served'.[112] Intelligence thus becomes more accurate and powerful when one understands the context, and when one acknowledges that the context only reflects a limited and selected part of a threat structure that at any given point is unlimited in its relation to the analysts who try to understand it.

Understanding the context

One important question is whether it was possible to understand the context prior to 9/11, and whether it is generally possible to understand multiple possible context variations. It is probably not possible to understand these variations. The information available may be understood in its present context, and it will be contended that the transnational context was neither understood nor focused on prior to 9/11, since the intelligence community 'divided intelligence responsibilities by geography, leaving huge gaps in coverage . . . nobody, however, was clearly responsible for monitoring the communications or movements of suspected terrorists *between* the United States and foreign countries'.[113]

This illustrates that connecting the dots was challenging, since the transnational window was not covered. Yet it does not follow from this that integration would have been impossible. It would, of course, have been impossible if the goal had been to cover all the dots, and such an objective is ideal, since the future consists of unlimited variations of possibilities. But integration of collected data would have been possible had the transnational window been covered, and had the domestic services cooperated better with the foreign services, and vice versa.

The failure of integration

Richard A. Posner also contends that 9/11 was a failure of integration, since 'the best bits were not obtained until late in August 2001, and it is unlikely that they could have been integrated, understood, and acted on in time to foil the plot'.[114] He thereby also implicitly suggests that 9/11 was not a failure of integration, since integration, due to time constraints, would have been impossible anyway. But that is a constructed argument, since the inability to integrate the information in time was not necessarily a failure of integration, but arguably one of management, efficiency and coordination. Posner is much more convincing in arguing that 'the idea of such attacks was so bizarre that it would have taken unusual imagination to realize what the warning signs added up to'.[115] He thereby suggests that 9/11 was challenging to accept, supports the discourse failure theory and illustrates that intelligence failure is generally a problem caused by cognitive limitations.

The relation between threats and the institutions and analysts who try to understand them is like the relation between the variations of our world and the language that, at any given point, is available to describe it. Threats are infinite, while intelligence institutions' threat discourse is at any given point finite and limited. This does not mean that language and threat discourse is finite as such. It only means that the language that we use to comprehend and communicate threats does not develop simultaneously with threats, but will always come into being and develop in the aftermath and resulting from these threats. A language and a threat discourse which seek to communicate a threat that has not yet materialised will not only be hypothetical, but for most people severely challenging to understand, and even meaningless. This is obviously a huge challenge for intelligence institutions, but it also serves as a good example of the challenges related to intelligence as an art seeking to comprehend and describe the future.

The infinite character of threats

The relation between the infinite character of threats and a threat discourse that, at any point, is limited by its set language creates the dynamic and infinite character of intelligence. Every information phenomenon that intelligence institutions try to understand can be understood metaphorically as huge circles of unperceivable diameter. The focus, priorities and collection assets exist as smaller circles somewhere in this circle, but the challenge is that intelligence institutions are unable to know exactly where their focus and priorities exist in relation to the parameters of the phenomenon they attempt to comprehend. Their focus, priorities and collection assets increase the amount of collected information of possible intelligence value, and consequently increase the radius of the circle: this can be termed the intelligence production circle. But more knowledge does not decrease the radius of the circle that intelligence institutions try to understand: it increases it. Intelligence production, as knowledge, is essentially endless, and the intelligence process is therefore 'a never ending cycle'.[116]

More information therefore increases the need for more information, and does not necessarily lead to more insight and wisdom. The practical result is that more intelligence collection and analysis do not necessarily provide a greater understanding of threat phenomena. The possible negative effect may be that thousands of reports on al Qaeda do not necessarily create a deeper perception of what al Qaeda is as a phenomenon, and at worst can decrease such an understanding. Popper demonstrates this infinite character of knowledge, and hence for intelligence, in stating:

> Every solution of a problem raises new unsolved problems; the more so the deeper the original problem and the bolder its solution. The more we learn about the world, and the deeper our learning, the more conscious, specific, and articulate will be our knowledge of what we do not know, our knowledge of our ignorance. For this, indeed, is the main source of our ignorance – the fact that our knowledge can be only finite, while our ignorance must necessarily be infinite.[117]

This means that wisdom is the awareness of ignorance. However, thinking without doubt may only lead to more ignorance. Unfocused intelligence analysis can therefore contribute to ignorance, and a more critical and holistic approach is called for. Davis elucidates the strengths of focused intelligence, or what he calls 'organised information', contending that 'research findings or organized information on subjects of importance to policymakers will over time become the analysts' most important and appreciated contribution to the policymaking process'.[118]

The holistic approach

Prospective intelligence estimation must therefore perceive and communicate the context of the threat structure, and it must add value to intelligence through its ability and willingness to evaluate what might happen in the future under specific, possible prospective contexts. High-quality intelligence estimation should therefore 'provide added value to policymakers who probably already have both a good sense of what is going on in their area of concern and a good feel for the significance and consequences of events that take place'.[119] Davis illustrates the importance of this possible strength of intelligence in recounting the story of a US governmental official who had spent 60-plus hours a week on an important negotiation. He was insulted when the agency sent him a *National Intelligence Daily* feature telling the 'story' of the week's events: 'I am the story. Please tell me what you know that I don't know.'[120]

Intelligence services must hence strive to elucidate to the policymaker the wholeness of the threat, and the information must therefore be understood in its context. The objective must be that the threat in its context is properly perceived by the policymaker, an approach demanding a much more holistic approach to threats than intelligence institutions have usually shown, or than a conservative intelligence tribal language immediately offers.

Mindsets and preconceptions

Unfocused and restricted intelligence collection and analysis which are shaped by a strong belief in the uniformity of nature where induction rules may cause an intelligence outcome that does not necessarily increase the institution's knowledge of the wholeness of the threat. The damaging result can be that 'as new events occur, data consistent with earlier patterns of beliefs are more likely to be accepted as valid, while data that conflict with an analyst's expectations are discounted or set aside'.[121] The challenging character of threat phenomena is that they are, like other social phenomena, infinite and in constant change. Intelligence focus, priorities and collection are therefore in practice often blinded, since intelligence work is not only influenced by the action and reaction of the counterpart, but also by the holistic and constantly changing dynamic of the threat phenomenon and the level of threat perception itself.

Peter Jackson suggests that the 'levels of uncertainty are liable to increase in direct relation to the importance of the issues at stake'.[122] This illustrates that the dynamics of threat structures may develop simultaneously with the seriousness of the threat perception, since action always creates some kind of reaction. Intelligence institutions can therefore become victims of the threats they try to perceive, as well as of the mindsets and discourses developed by earlier threats: these mindsets and discourses that previously were helpful can easily 'become an Achilles' heel to professional strategists or intelligence analysts when they become out of touch with new international dynamics'.[123] Jackson further elucidates this in illustrating the 'tendency to filter out evidence that challenges preconceptions and predispositions'.[124] Intelligence institutions must therefore manage their resources carefully, and direct their collection and analytical focus wisely.

The infinity of the threat and unfocused collection

Hyped and intensified collection pertaining to a specific threat gives the intelligence institution more information, but it does not necessarily give the institution more knowledge: the amount of collected data about the threat does not necessarily increase the understanding of the threat, but may decrease it, since unfocused and quantitative intelligence collection easily creates information overload on all levels of the intelligence cycle. Kent's thoughts are illustrative here:

> In our business we are as likely to be faced by the problem of a plethora of raw intelligence as by one of its paucity. In many of our tasks we have so large a volume of data that no single person can read, evaluate, and mentally file it all.[125]

More information than the institution can handle can therefore increase ignorance rather than decreasing it. Intelligence institutions should hence be aware that collection pertaining to threats creates a reaction in which the circle that illustrates the threat will increase and develop simultaneously with the quantum of information collected by the intelligence institution. One therefore rhetorically has to ask whether the US intelligence community, prior to 9/11, knew the nature of the threat circle, where they were heading and whether they adequately acknowledged the content of the information in its context. Nonetheless, this study does not contend that intelligence institutions should collect less, or that threats are theoretical phenomena that are impossible to comprehend. But the circle metaphor presented serves as a reminder that threats develop constantly, and mostly ahead of the institutions that try to understand them. This creates a huge challenge for intelligence. Intelligence institutions should therefore try to think differently if they want to win, and they should understand the intelligence cycle functionally and not organisationally.[126]

The modern intelligence cycle

The functional approach may reduce the negative impact from a divided and fragmented understanding of the intelligence cycle, and help intelligence institutions, as Omand illustrates, to understand that perceiving 'targets such as terrorists, proliferation networks and criminal gangs, seems to be rather different from what the categories associated with the traditional intelligence cycle might suggest'.[127] Omand suggests that the intelligence cycle should be modernised, and proposes a new theory focusing on user integration between all the classic disciplines in the old cycle. He highlights that collection and analysis especially should be integrated closely and be renamed 'access' and 'elucidation'. Omand's intelligence cycle is an interactive network and reflects the complexities of the constantly changing nature of threat structures.[128] His interactive intelligence network thus reflects the problem of induction, and its interactive form, across departments and bureaucratic borders, may decrease the problem of intelligence tribal language and secrecy, and hence the problem of induction and discourse failure.

All-source intelligence

Omand's emphasis on the problems of the old intelligence cycle and its strictly compartmentalised structure implicitly illustrates that single-source information or intelligence that is taken out of its context, and that has not been produced in an interactive network, is seriously damaging to present to decision-makers. Qualitative intelligence production is therefore based on the principle that 'sources need to be supplemented and complemented to be as complete as possible and to be verified to the greatest extent possible'.[129] But this does not imply that single-source information should not be used at all. Some of this information is actionable, and may in some cases serve a good case: 'there is an increasing emphasis in post-Cold War intelligence work on dealing with 'action this day' intelligence material, particularly in the areas of proliferation, terrorism, narcotics and serious crime.'[130]

However, it is important that single-source information is understood and acted upon in isolation, without trying to use this information to understand the wholeness of the threat, and the potential danger of circular reporting and corroborating evidence should be diminished by informing the policymaker 'of the secret intelligence being reported, as closely as possible to the terms in which it was accessed'.[131] The case of 9/11 illustrates that it was the lack of all-source intelligence assessments that decreased an understanding and acknowledgement of the gravity of the threat. President Bush did receive information that indicated a threat from al Qaeda against the US, and he understood that 'al Qaeda was dangerous, which he said he had known since he had become President'.[132] Nonetheless, this information did not give the president a holistic understanding of the enemy, nor did it offer an opportunity for action. The president simply lacked fused, all-source intelligence covering the sum of the knowledge throughout the US intelligence community.[133]

This example illustrates that high-quality information of intelligence value is not in itself enough as a tool if politicians are seeking to comprehend complex threats: it also demonstrates that the information must be presented and understood in its context. That is only achievable when the information is fused with other relevant information, processed, understood and presented to the consumer in a manner that communicates the wholeness of the threat. But intelligence institutions should remember that this is difficult, since '[having] multiple sources to corroborate each other is ideal; [but] it is by no means the rule'.[134] All-source intelligence assessment must therefore include and be a result of all available and relevant information. This means that all intelligence agencies involved in a specific case provide all available information of possible intelligence value to someone who coordinates the production of a fused product. Omand illustrates the important of all-source intelligence assessment in emphasising the following: 'such assessments, if done well, have genuine explanatory power. Crucially, they will be forward-looking and often predictive, based on understanding of the past.'[135]

Good all-source intelligence assessments could have elucidated the threat from al Qaeda, giving the President the understanding and acknowledgement he needed to accept the threat and react against it. However, no such picture was given to him, as National Intelligence Estimates in the USA were not produced between 1997 and 9/11.[136] This not only blinded the intelligence community but also made the President helpless, since he was unable to fully see the wholeness of the threat. He was given briefs every day by the CIA. These briefs became more and more serious and probably gave him a great deal more new information, but, as demonstrated, few of them gave him insight into or a deep understanding of an enemy that was imminently threatening to the USA.

The positive force of pooled intelligence reflected in National Intelligence Estimates is evident, since all-source information 'allows the accomplished analyst to make an estimative judgement about a looming danger with high confidence'.[137] Its strengths are also vividly demonstrated in the statement of the Commission Report: 'a National Intelligence Estimate distributed in July 1995 predicted future terrorist attacks against the United States – and *in* the United States'.[138] The estimate warned that symbols of capitalism, infrastructure, the capital and even the White House were possible targets, and concluded that the attack against the World Trade Center in 1993 had not only been a pure act of political terrorism; it had also been conducted with the intention of killing many people.[139] The content of the estimate was that the US was facing a threat that was more imminent and much more dangerous than the type of terrorism faced by the world thus far. The nation was threatened by an enemy willing to go to war with America on its own soil. This example shows that pooled intelligence from all available relevant sources strengthens the quality of the intelligence product. However, as there were no Intelligence Estimates between 1997 and 9/11, the coordination, sharing and pooling of information became challenging.[140] The consequence of such division and fragmentation between intelligence institutions is evident, and it is important to evaluate why this occurred.

Uncertainty and the reciprocal nature of intelligence

Estimating the future is certainly not easy, and the reciprocal nature of powerful nations competing on the world stage does not make it any easier. The nature of intelligence, identified by its secrecy and intelligence tribal language, which conducts its mission amid power struggles between nation states, arguably increases the complex nature of estimation. This nature is further intensified by new players and enemies that enter the stage, a factor which additionally increases the complexity of the threats that intelligence institutions seek to understand. Intelligence is thus one of the most challenging trades that exists. Its necessarily secret character, the pressure on many field operators, and the fact that these institutions constantly deal with uncertainty (an uncertainty that is not minimised by the production of knowledge, but rather is intensified by it) fuel the complex and challenging nature of intelligence. The psychological pressure is therefore enormous for dedicated intelligence operators whose aim is to attempt to conduct their work with dignity, integrity and humility. This kind of uncertain and mentally tough environment easily lends itself to mental displacement and redirection; and secrecy and intelligence tribal language can arguably provide an escape from the uncertainty that characterises highly qualified intelligence work.

Uncertainty, and its negative force on a hyped secrecy culture in which a distinct intelligence tribal language can develop, can also make pooling intelligence between different intelligence institutions challenging – and if dissemination is challenging, highly qualitative analysis is almost prohibitive. The consequence of this prior to 9/11 was that the intelligence community insufficiently managed to conduct qualitative strategic analysis.[141] The Joint Inquiry also highlights that differences in culture and policy hampered sharing between the agencies.[142] Differences in culture and policy also decrease the community's ability to cooperate enough analytically.

National Intelligence Estimates

It has been demonstrated that National Intelligence Estimates could have decreased the problem of induction and provided the president with intelligence that increased his understanding of the enemy. But National Intelligence Estimates can also make a situation worse, especially when they are not critically produced or properly questioned.

National Intelligence Estimates should reflect and communicate different views, since this better secures and capitalises on the nature of threats appearing in new orders and variations, and because 'analysts may seek consensus rather than appraising alternative explanations. This problem, often particularly acute in small groups, has been labelled "groupthink".'[143] All-source assessment should therefore principally present competing hypotheses in order to reduce the problem of groupthink, thereby reducing the negative effects of the problem of induction and consequent discourse failure. But this presupposes that the consumer understands the nature of intelligence and the problem of induction, and that a good and productive relationship exists between the intelligence producer and the intelligence consumer. National Intelligence Estimates should therefore never be based on consensus, since this increases the risk of groupthink and induction. The following description of how the problems of consensus and groupthink can negatively shape National Intelligence Estimates illustrates that these estimates do not necessarily reflect or communicate an adequate comprehension of the wholeness of a threat.

The US intelligence community recommenced producing National Intelligence Estimates after 9/11, and Clarke's description of the quality of these estimates, both prior to 9/11 and after, implicitly suggests one reason why the community did not produce any estimates between 1997 and 2001, and why they should be seriously questioned after 9/11. Clarke argues that the National Intelligence Estimates warning that Iraq had Weapons of Mass Destruction were a result of groupthink, and his description of his experience of working on the production of National Intelligence Estimates during the Reagan administration illustrates how consensus and culture decreased proper discourse and shaped the outcome.

Clarke has described being sent by his superior to what his superior referred to as 'dreadful' meetings. He also claims that fifteen of the sixteen agencies would repeatedly answer 'We support the NIE,'[144] whenever CIA Director William Casey asked them for their opinions. Clarke usually communicated his agency's dissenting view, but the estimate would still pass by a 15–1 vote.[145] Clarke was at that time Deputy Assistant Secretary for Intelligence in the State Department, and his description of the production process in the National Intelligence Estimates Committee illustrates that the estimates that were produced during the Reagan administration did not reflect the views of the State Department. It is evident that estimates that have been subject to a vote do not necessarily increase a holistic understanding of threats appearing in new orders and variations. Voting and a majority do not consolidate a proper understanding of the complexity of such threats, but may arguably decrease it. Thoughts that challenge the existing narrative are difficult to accept[146] because 'analysts naturally favour information that fits their well-formed mental models and often dismiss other information that might support an alternative hypothesis'.[147] Heuer elucidates this in highlighting how mindsets and, consequently, discourse 'can color and control our perception to the extent that an experienced specialist may be among the last to see what is really happening when events take a new and unexpected turn'.[148] Voting and consensus certainly do not decrease the negative force of discourse failure.

The threat, society and discourse failure

Clarke's description of the production of National Intelligence Estimates during the Reagan administration, and his account of the National Intelligence Estimates on Iraq as a result of groupthink, suggest that National Intelligence Estimates in themselves do not represent a solution to the challenges that 9/11 disclosed. It is therefore important to evaluate and describe the way in which a national threat discourse that interacts with a secrecy-driven intelligence threat discourse is shaped not only by the problem of induction. It also influences and intensifies further negative inductive reasoning in a circular synergy that is intensified by its own limited discourse, and consequently negatively shapes the national threat discourse in a synergy where discourse failure shapes further discourse failure. A strong, orthodox belief in the uniformity of nature and a fear of uncertainty intensify this negative circular synergy, and arguably the problem of induction fused with fear is the source of orthodoxies and political assumptions. The problem of induction and fear therefore shape social, cultural and political discourse, and may also contribute to discourse failure. But it was not only the intelligence community and the political leadership that failed to comprehend the threat that faced the United States of America, since 'there was very little in newspapers or on television to heighten anyone's concern about terrorism'.[149] This reflects the fact that terrorism was not on the national agenda. It was a topic for specialists, and ordinary Americans had little interest in it. Ultimately the evolving threat shaped society, and intelligence institutions reflect the societies they serve. Intelligence operatives are also citizens of a society, are members of communities and families, and are formed and influenced by the debates they have with their families around the dinner table. It would thus hardly be strange or surprising if they found it difficult to comprehend a futuristic threat existing outside the borders provided by the existing and prevailing societal discourse.

This example illustrates that the societal discourse in America prior to 9/11 was not characterised by its focus on terrorism in general, or the threat from al Qaeda as such. It was simply not on the national agenda, and therefore received neither the focus nor the necessary interest from the intelligence community.

It would therefore not be strange if this societal situation stimulated an intelligence culture in which the problem of induction and discourse failure could develop. It was additionally intensified by the human tendency to discourage and displace observations that challenged a strong belief in the uniformity of nature. The complexity of the threat, the human tendency to redirect and displace cognitive challenges and the problem of induction were a deadly trinity that was additionally intensified by its interaction with misused and misunderstood secrecy. It concealed constructive and creative communication and intensified and developed an intelligence tribal language that already existed, characterised by its limiting effect on cognition and intelligence analysis.

Intelligence theory and high-quality analysis characterised by creativity, imagination and openness have few chances in such environments, and the outcome was analysis that failed to capitalise on the real magnitude of the threat posed by al Qaeda. The USA consequently 'learned that the institutions charged with protecting [their] borders, civil aviation, and national security did not

216

understand how grave this threat could be, and did not adjust their policies, plans and practices to deter or defeat it'.[150]

Conclusion

This chapter will now conclude by arguing that the understanding and acknowledgement of the problem of induction and its negative force on discourse failure bring intelligence studies towards a new theory of intelligence failure, and thus towards a new theory of intelligence. The understanding of discourse failure opens a window to intelligence failure as a circular problem that intensifies itself by the human tendency to displace and redirect new knowledge that threatens orthodoxies, political assumptions and a uniform belief in nature. The result is that threats appearing in new variations will not easily be acknowledged or accepted, since they exist outside the normative threat paradigms and outside the existing language available to communicate threats that exist outside the possibilities of induction.

The acknowledgement of this phenomenon discloses the problems that arise because intelligence has lacked a proper intelligence theory. It illustrates that if intelligence institutions want to reduce the damaging effect of the problem of induction and discourse failure, and produce qualitative intelligence, they must probe beyond the limits of induction. A deep acknowledgement of the discourse failure theory therefore explains the reciprocal nature of intelligence, as well as capturing and identifying the circular dynamic between threats, threat perception and intelligence failure, since the theory elucidates that identified and acknowledged threats do not increase our conception of threats – they merely redirect our attention, consequently creating a breeding ground for new discourse failures.

The discourse failure theory as such identifies that the human acknowledgement of threats is the source of discourse failure. The practical result of this comprehension is that 9/11 created new threat paradigms that inevitably led to new intelligence failures. The main focus prior to 9/11 was the threat from long-range missiles and nation states. 9/11 reshaped all this, and led Western intelligence institutions to focus on the threat from al Qaeda and other asymmetric threats. This creates a window of opportunity for adversaries wanting to misuse the prospect created by the problem of induction, and as such facilitates new discourse failures.

The discourse failure theory therefore accepts that intelligence failure and surprise are not only inevitable,[151] but natural.[152] It accepts that human language at any given point is too limited to communicate the complexity and uncertainty of futuristic threats, and the theory acknowledges and embraces the problem of induction. The theory simply embraces Socratic ignorance, and suggests that intelligence failure can only be diminished when intelligence communities are ready to allow for more openness, imagination, creativity, attentiveness, alertness, awareness, sensitivity and critical rationalism.

6   On Dissemination

Herman captures the importance of intelligence dissemination as well as its challenges in stating that it tends to be the Achilles heel of intelligence.[1] Even if intelligence organisations have the best technical resources available, the best collectors and the best analysts, all these factors are futile unless the product is disseminated to the decision-makers and the intelligence consumers intelligibly and in a timely manner. Intelligence dissemination is therefore 'the most critical [phase] in the entire intelligence process'.[2] Friedman illustrates this in highlighting that the intelligence product is useless if it is not provided to the intelligence consumer.[3] Laqueur seems to concur: 'even excellent intelligence is of little consequence unless its most senior consumers, the president and secretaries of state and defense, take cognizance of it and believe in its accuracy'.[4] Dissemination is therefore the effective 'delivery of useful, user-friendly product at the right time, especially when timeliness is of the essence for decision-taking',[5] and 'there is [therefore] an obligation on the part of the Intelligence Community to make sure that policymakers understand the context and limitations of the data provided. So, ideally, no information provided to policymakers goes to them completely unexplained.'[6] Dissemination is thus the most important function of an intelligence institution as a '[provider of] intelligence analysis to policymakers'[7] that can contribute to wisdom that makes uncertainty less uncertain. Intelligence is therefore not intelligence before it is disseminated to, and understood by, the intelligence consumer. The Joint Inquiry indicated that there were serious problems with dissemination prior to 9/11:

> Serious problems in information sharing also persisted, prior to September 11, between the Intelligence Community and relevant

non-Intelligence Community agencies. This included other federal agencies as well as state and local authorities. This lack of communication and collaboration deprived those other entities, as well as the Intelligence Community, of access to potentially valuable information in the 'war' against bin Laden.[8]

This finding demonstrates that information that could have increased understanding of al Qaeda was not disseminated to those that needed it, and the following finding illustrates why this could occur:

> The perception that collecting agencies have 'ownership' of the intelligence they acquire impedes the free flow of information. In a Joint Inquiry interview, one DIA official complained that analysts were often denied access to critical intelligence held in other Intelligence Community agencies.[9]

Gill and Phythian echo this: 'for example, all agencies jealously guard their sources and methods, not just because they are short-sighted but also because they fear their compromise if information they provide is used unwisely'.[10] These two findings indicate how a collection-focused intelligence community, shaped by a secretive culture identified by its distinct intelligence tribal language, may have hindered adequate dissemination of information to those that needed it prior to 9/11, and 'bureaucratic politics and institutional culture and policies, undoubtedly play a role in limiting the dissemination of classified information'.[11] It can of course be contended that these findings illustrate an intelligence community that was just shaped by bureaucracy, and this argument is valid to a certain degree. It is more likely, though, that the damaging bureaucracy was shaped by an 'ownership' culture rather than a culture of openness and dissemination. This culture of secrecy and protectionism shaped an intelligence community that failed to perform its duty to 'report to policymakers its conclusions about the information that [had] been collected and analyzed'.[12] The damaging result was that the community and the decision-makers underestimated the enemy and the threat to the US. The Joint Inquiry therefore proposed that there was a need to 'establish and sustain effective channels for the exchange of counterterrorism-related information with federal agencies outside the Intelligence Community as well as with state and local authorities'.[13]

It has now been demonstrated that there were serious flaws in the dissemination procedures prior to 9/11. We therefore need to analyse the workings of this system, and why it did not work as intended; and the 'ownership' culture described in the Joint Inquiry indicates that it is meaningful to start with the need-to-know culture.

The 9/11 Commission Report elucidates the problems related to an introvert need-to-know culture and highlights that the isolative need-to-know culture 'assumes it is possible to know, in advance, who will need to use the information'.[14] The 9/11 Terrorist attacks and other serious intelligence failures remind us that it is highly challenging to know in advance who needs information when the threat is not understood. Reality is a bit more difficult than the reality proposed by the 'ownership' culture, since 'the range of issues to which both policymakers and analysts must be attentive has grown in scope and complexity'.[15] Important information can easily drown in this complexity, and seemingly insignificant information can be overlooked and thus not disseminated to colleagues, other agencies or decision-makers who need it. Intelligence institutions must thus be attentive to the increasing complexities around them and make sure that decision-makers understand 'the degree and nature of uncertainty and, where possible, what steps might be taken to reduce that uncertainty'.[16] It is therefore important that intelligence institutions disseminate information that challenges preconceived assumptions given by induction, since 'policymakers themselves [and the intelligence producer] may suffer a form of self-inflicted delusion, in which they interpret intelligence that has been influenced by their own perceptions as confirmation of those perceptions'.[17] High-quality dissemination may, therefore, reduce politicisation and uncertainty, since it creates an information flow that reminds the decision-maker 'that it was his own interest in the topic that stimulated the flow'.[18] This consciousness helps the decision-maker to acknowledge that the complexity of the threat stimulated the self-inflicted delusion in the first place and created a negative circularity, making it increasingly difficult to return to the truth. Such delusions therefore need to be constantly challenged. Good intelligence dissemination must thus challenge orthodoxies and political assumptions, and intelligence operators should accordingly be intellectually courageous and disseminate information based on a courage-to-share principle, so those who may need information can access it. Intelligence institutions must therefore ensure that 'policymakers are immediately privileged to any subsequent information that casts doubt on earlier information that was provided to them'.[19] The 9/11 Commission Report accordingly states that 'information procedures should provide incentives for sharing, to restore a better balance between security and shared knowledge'.[20]

As a result, the US and Western intelligence communities transformed after 9/11 from a need-to-know culture into a need-to-share culture, and the National Intelligence Strategy of the United States of America (2005) decided to 'create an information sharing environment in which access to terrorism information is matched to the roles, responsibilities, and missions of all organizations engaged in countering terrorism, and is timely, accessible, and relevant to their needs.'[21] This strategy implicitly illustrates that the secret and introvert need-to-know culture was seen as problematic, and that the strategy reflected a cultural shift in the US intelligence community. The need-to-know culture prior to 9/11 is hence one factor that explains why vital information was not disseminated between agencies, and between agencies and decision-makers, and why the terrorist threat was consequently so difficult to understand and communicate. In the following, therefore, I will illustrate how this culture negatively interplayed with cognitive closure and secrecy and reduced adequate dissemination.

The Analysis and its Structure

For analytical purposes, this chapter will be divided into two main parts. The overall objective of the analysis is to illustrate how an introvert need-to-know culture seriously decreased adequate and effective information-sharing prior to 9/11. Part one explores whether and how the need-to-know principle shaped the dissemination culture in and between intelligence institutions in the US intelligence community, while part two explores how the need-to-know principle shaped the communication of intelligence between decision-makers, and how this relationship was influenced by political and strategic dispositions in the White House.

The Force of a Negative Need-to-Know Culture on 9/11

Open discourse between the intelligence producer and decision-makers is a prerequisite for effective communication and dissemination: 'the watchword [for the relationship should] be intelligence-sharing rather than compartmented intelligence access'.[22] Intelligence and dissemination are an ongoing process that is dynamic and infinite, and this presupposes open dialogue between the intelligence producer and the intelligence consumer. This dialogue needs to be constantly nurtured, since 'too much analytical detachment or too little interaction between analysts and policymakers, however, virtually guarantees that finished intelligence will fail to address the issues that fill policymakers' in-boxes'.[23] Clarke's statement to the 9/11 Commission illustrates the consequence if policymakers' in-boxes are not filled, and the possible positive consequence if a need-to-share culture had been in place before 9/11:

> Congressman, it is very easy in retrospect to say that I would have done this or I would have done that. And we'll never know. I would like to think that had I been informed by the FBI that two senior al Qaeda operatives who had been in a planning meeting earlier in Kuala Lumpur were now in the United States . . . I would like to think that I would have released . . . their names . . . and caused a successful nationwide manhunt . . . but I don't know because you're asking me a hypothetical and I have the benefit now of 20/20 hindsight.[24]

This finding highlights that dissemination in an environment without dialogue decreases the decision-maker's understanding of potential threats, and his or her ability to take appropriate action.

The need-to-know culture no doubt decreased this very important dialogue and contributed to the 9/11 intelligence failure that manifested itself as discourse failure, and the Joint Inquiry illustrates this:

> Growing concern about the terrorist threat did not noticeably increase the amount of information shared between the Intelligence Community and the State Department before September 11, which, in contrast, advised the Joint Inquiry that it received at least 1,500 CIA Central Intelligence Reports containing terrorist names shortly after September 11. State Department officials also spoke about the difficulty in obtaining data for watchlisting purposes from the FBI National Crime Information Center, in spite of ten years of negotiations with the Bureau for access.[25]

This finding reflects a secretive culture that for a generation had 'learned that sensitive information should be disclosed only to those with a demonstrable "need to know" the information within the rigidities of a national security classification system',[26] and this also indicates a system based on orthodox threat perception shaped by induction. The consequence of this inductively shaped threat perception resulted in a belief that 'the CIA should not play an internal security role'.[27] These entrenched and orthodox understandings of threats and bureaucratic roles made a coordinated effort against the threat highly challenging. Although the DCI had been given this responsibility, he did not have the authority or resources needed to coordinate a focused and harmonised process that attempted to comprehend the wholeness of the threat, and 'the Intelligence Community continued to be fragmented without a comprehensive strategy for combating Bin Laden'.[28] This handicapped the US intelligence community and made it challenging to comprehend the wholeness of the threat. It is difficult enough to comprehend, describe, communicate and disseminate a threat that is known and experienced; but it is even more difficult to do so with the unknown and unexperienced. The illustrative irony is that the intelligence community failed to coordinate the threat from al Qaeda because the distribution of DCI Tenet's declaration of war against bin Laden was limited.[29] This demonstrates that the war that Tenet declared against bin Laden and al Qaeda was not properly known in the intelligence community because it was not properly disseminated, and a community identified by its secret and often reductive culture and limiting discourse discloses itself. The Joint Inquiry seems to concur with this in the following description: 'The Joint Inquiry was told repeatedly that host agencies restrict access to information and limit databases detailees can query on security and policy grounds. Detailees often learn about intelligence only after host agency employees make ad hoc judgments to share information.'[30] It is when vague threats interact with this kind of culture that human cognition is challenged. The consequence is often cognitive closure, and it is likely that the information that has caused the closure will be deliberately or unconsciously overlooked, and consequently not disseminated to those who may need it. Such information is also difficult to disseminate, simply because it is challenging to understand or foresee who needs it. It is also likely that the kind of information that exists outside the limits of induction and that challenges cognition is the very information which could have taught intelligence institutions more about threats. This suggests that the information that was not disseminated by the US intelligence community could have been the vital information that could have given decision-makers what they needed to understand the threat from al Qaeda. The result of the negative interplay between the problem of induction, intelligence tribal language and secrecy was that critical information 'was not sufficiently shared, not only between different Intelligence Community agencies, but also within individual agencies, and between the intelligence and the law enforcement agencies'.[31]

The presented Joint Inquiry findings echo the essence of the discourse failure theory since they illustrate how discourse and language, and consequently decreased communication and dissemination, shaped the US intelligence community's comprehension of the threat from al Qaeda. However, it is more challenging to demonstrate how culture negatively influenced the community's decreased ability to disseminate its intelligence product. It is here that the importance of intellectual courage is evident, since a lack of individual and institutional courage seems to be one plausible factor that shaped the restrictive and limiting culture in the US intelligence community. Clarke illustrates this:

> If analysts do not feel that they can count on their supervisors to protect them from policy makers' trying to slant their work, the interaction becomes poisonous. Sadly, it appears that in the case of intelligence about Iraq before the US invasion, some intelligence community analysts did not think they had 'top cover' to tell the truth as they saw it.[32]

It is likely that this finding is qualitatively precise and descriptive of the overall culture in the US intelligence community prior to 9/11, although it refers to Iraq in 2002/03.

The courage to be critical, humble, and most importantly, the courage to have sufficient integrity to stand up to the majority and the existing beliefs are essential when humans are confronted by uncertainty and the unforeseen. These human notions are vital to humans who seek to develop their personalities, as well as to organisations that search for wisdom, and especially if these institutions exist in a realm of distortion and trickery. It is when the world and culture of trickery interact with the problem of induction and secrecy that a limited and restricted intelligence tribal language evolves. These factors and their interaction slowly fuel and develop a characteristic, damaging culture that decreases an institution's capability to detect and comprehend new threats. The intelligence tribal language that evolves is further influenced and shaped by the secret collection methods used by intelligence institutions, and the result is decreased dissemination. Decreased dissemination reduces the decision-maker's ability to reduce uncertainty: 'without knowledge one cannot act skilfully. Knowledge must come from every available source and extend to all aspects of the enemy.'[33] Sun Tzu helps intelligence institutions remember that information alone is not enough. It is the holistic insight of the enemy that assures victory, and such victory can only be achieved if all this information is brought together, measured, compared, analysed and checked. Only then can one hope to catch glimpses of the wholeness of the threat. This is what separates excellent intelligence from good intelligence, and the US intelligence community prior to 9/11 did not have this capability, inasmuch as they did not manage to adequately disseminate vital information to the decision-makers who needed it. Nonetheless, some decision-makers did receive the information, but their ability to react to the threat depended on their ability to disseminate their knowledge up the chain of power, since 'it is dissemination outside of the community that establishes the credibility and utility of intelligence'.[34] One will therefore in the following evaluate the dissemination culture between the decision-makers prior to 9/11. The terms 'producer' and 'consumer'/'decision-maker' will be used in the following to illustrate that decision-makers exist who also perform the role of disseminators of intelligence.

The Dissemination Culture between Decision-Makers Prior to 9/11

Communication and dissemination between intelligence producers and intelligence consumers/decision-makers are worthless without proper dialogue, since 'intelligence agencies need to know what information to collect and when it is needed'.[35] The dialogue must be based on understanding and respect, and more importantly, the intelligence producer must understand the consumer's needs, as well as the consumer having to understand the essence of intelligence. 'Thus intelligence is at the mercy of users' unpredictable attitudes towards it; but it tries to make its own luck with them through persuasion, personal relations and marketing.'[36] This illustrates that a consumer's comprehension of the intelligence product depends on the quality of the dialogue between the producer and the consumer. However, an atmosphere of open dialogue, mutual respect and understanding has been hard to develop, since the relationship between intelligence organisations and decision-makers has often been shaped by distrust. President Truman had an ambivalent and almost complex view of intelligence. He knew he needed it – indeed, he established the CIA – but he was sceptical of a secret organisation, and feared it. He accordingly wrote in his memoirs that 'this country wanted no Gestapo under any guise for any reason'.[37] Some conservatives in Congress and the Department of State were even more sceptical than Truman, while the most hostile 'had no comprehension as to what purposes intelligence was to serve'.[38] Others did support the whole idea of intelligence, but mistrusted the 'OSS men who were to constitute the core of central intelligence'.[39] Nevertheless, the CIA was established by President Truman in July 1947.[40] President Eisenhower did, by contrast, understand the importance of high-quality intelligence, and 'believed in the importance of unbiased intelligence and its neutral role in policy making'.[41] These descriptions illustrate that intelligence is in its essence controversial and that it exists in the realm of state power, although on the outskirts, since it is supposed to be objective, advisory, and therefore not directly involved in policy-making.

However, intelligence institutions do perform their indirect state power[42] on the same level as executive ministries, and they carry out their duties and power across ministry boundaries, and therefore execute a potential power that may constitute a threat to these ministries. This can easily create an atmosphere of mistrust and protection, and 'for a long time conventional Foreign Service officers looked upon intelligence as a distasteful but temporary burden, which would disappear once the world returned to sanity'.[43] Such a situation undoubtedly does not create a situation that fosters the development of constructive dialogue between intelligence producers and their consumers. Whether the Foreign Service officers were sceptical based on bureaucratic protectionism or justified mistrust is difficult to evaluate, but it is likely that professionalism, high-quality products and open dialogue would have increased the level of positive communication. Laqueur elucidates this in clarifying that US intelligence became acceptable when it was 'recognized as a profession'.[44]

Recognition as professionals may be based on respect, and respect may be based on mutual recognition of the quality of the performed profession. Carpenters and masons do not respect each other solely because they are craftsmen. They respect and recognise each other based on the quality of their work, and they may describe poor work by saying that it has not been done by a proper craftsman. Respect among professionals is therefore a question of quality; likewise for intelligence institutions. The relation between intelligence institutions, trust and mutual respect, must be based on the quality of the product the intelligence services disseminate to the consumer, and Herman illustrates this: 'the effect of intelligence therefore depends on its institutional reputation and the personal chemistry between practitioners and users'.[45] Intelligence must therefore be accurate, timely, reliable, relevant and unique, and dissemination must be based on the same principles. This presupposes a highly professional and effective intelligence process, meaning that both the intelligence consumer and the intelligence producer must understand the process and its limitations. The intelligence consumers must comprehend the strengths and weaknesses of intelligence; only then can they fully comprehend the intelligence product and use it properly. However, it is the intelligence institutions' responsibility to disseminate and present the product so that it can be properly understood.[46]

Whether the intelligence consumers and the decision-makers did understand the products, and consequently the threat to the USA prior to 9/11, is hard to say, simply because the 9/11 Commission Report and the Joint Inquiry tell us little about it. The inquiry focused primarily on the intelligence community, and 'the Inquiry's focus on the Intelligence Community limited the extent to which it explored these issues'.[47] Nevertheless, Rice's statement to the 9/11 Commission clarifies that President Bush knew there was a terrorist threat to US, since he 'was asking for [a strategy] and wondering what was happening to it'.[48] The President knew about the threat, he was asking for a strategy, but he never asked for a meeting with Clarke, 'one of the consummate experts that never [had] the opportunity to brief the president of the United States on one of the most lethal, dynamic and agile threats to the United States of America'.[49] The only plausible explanation is that the President did not take the threat seriously enough, and this illustrates that dissemination as such is not enough. Intelligence services and terrorist experts alike need to have access to the consumers. They need to have the opportunity, the climate, the chemistry and enough time to communicate the message so that the consumers/decision-makers can properly comprehend the message. President Bush did not give himself and Clarke the opportunity to communicate the threat, and this decreased the President's ability to properly comprehend it. The Commission Report implicitly indicates that Rice's decisions and leadership on the use of Clarke contributed to decreased dissemination and discourse between Clarke and the President:

> Because even though Dick is a very fine counterterrorism expert, he was not a specialist on Afghanistan. That's why I brought somebody in who really understood Afghanistan. He was not a specialist on Pakistan. That's why I brought somebody in to deal with Pakistan. He had some very good ideas. We acted on them. Dick Clarke – let me just step back for a second and say we had a very – we had a very good relationship.[50]

Rice's statement illustrates that the administration did not fully comprehend the threat, as well as demonstrating that they could have understood it, had they listened to Clarke. Rice and the administration understood the threat in classical terms as a threat from nation states, and she was accordingly not able to accumulate and use Clarke's ability to think differently and innovatively. Clarke took the threat from al Qaeda seriously, and wanted to counter it beyond the lines of classical warfare. Rice was inductively trapped in a classic understanding of world politics that made it challenging for her to comprehend and take seriously a threat from a non-state terrorist group. She therefore focused on Afghanistan and Pakistan, and not on the essence of the threat: the existence of al Qaeda and bin Laden, and their willingness and ability to strike against the US. The result was that Clarke was not given the opportunity to disseminate his knowledge directly to the President. This demonstrates that the qualities of leaders are often shaped by those who control their front offices.

The threat from al Qaeda was known. It had been reported on since the mid-nineties, and the intelligence had been disseminated among the intelligence services and between the services and the decision-makers. Both President Bush and President Clinton had been informed about the threat, but the attack had to happen before robust and effective measures against it were implemented.

The tragic irony is that '[t]he Administration finalized its review of policy on al Qaeda at an NSC Principals Committee meeting on September 4, 2001. President Bush had not reviewed the draft policy before September 11.'[51] President Bush had also been briefed on the threat by the CIA when he was president-elect:

> Early in 2001, DCI Tenet and Deputy Director for Operations James Pavitt gave an intelligence briefing to President-elect Bush, Vice President-elect Cheney, and Rice; it included the topic of al Qaeda. Pavitt recalled conveying that Bin Ladin was one of the gravest threats to the country.[52]

The Bush administration nevertheless did not manage to counter the threat effectively or with enough knowledge of the enemy. The administration's paradoxical response to the threat discloses itself in its ambivalent relation to and treatment of Clarke. He had served President Clinton well, and the new administration decided to keep Clarke.[53] Rice described 'Clarke and his Counterterrorism Security Group (CSG) [as] "the nerve center" in coordinating responses but that principals were also involved'.[54]

Clarke was given the opportunity to provide advice. He was given power and influence, but Rice's statement indicates another serious weakness related to the responsibility given to Clarke. He was not given enough power. The new administration had only given him advisory power.[55] He was not one of the Principals, and therefore did not have direct and routine access to the President – a factor that critically hampered the dissemination of terrorism-related intelligence, and more importantly, made it more challenging for Clarke to give President Bush direct advice. This was in contrast to his Clinton years, when he chaired the Counterterrorism and Security Group (CSG) and was also one of the Principals who frequently met in the 'Small Group' (a select group of Principals who handled sensitive security matters).[56] These factors gave Clarke more power than he later had in the Bush administration, and this shift undoubtedly reduced his ability to serve President Bush as he could have done had he been given more principal influence. Nevertheless, nor was the administration of national security and intelligence policies during Clinton ideal, as the 'Small Group' did not sufficiently communicate their decisions:

> There were few paper records. One tradeoff in such a system was that other senior officials in agencies around the government sometimes had little knowledge about what was being decided in this group, other than what they could obtain from the principals or Clarke. This sometimes led to misunderstandings and friction.[57]

There were thus also weaknesses in the Clinton administration's strategy against terrorism. However, the Clinton administration gave Clarke principal power that provided him with direct access to the President. This direct principal responsibility for security and terrorism was reduced under President Bush, although Clarke served President Bush as national coordinator for security and terrorism. His advisory role under the Principals created a negative condition that actually serves as a good example of the negative consequences on poor communication and dissemination if the dialogue between intelligence producers and decision-makers is poor. The practical effect of Clarke's degrading under President Bush was not only to reduce dissemination in the White House, but also to reduced coordination of the intelligence community, cause unfocused requirements, and negatively shape dissemination in the intelligence community. Lowenthal illustrates the challenges unfocused priorities create for intelligence organisations: 'if the policymakers do not establish a firm set of priorities, or if they fail to update their priorities regularly, the intelligence officers are left in a difficult position'.[58] Whether the situation would have been different had Clarke been given genuine principal power related to security and terrorism is difficult to judge, although this demonstrates that coordination is challenging without direct executive power.

The presented arguments illustrate that dissemination alone is not enough. There also need to be dialogue and good chemistry between the intelligence producer and the intelligence consumer. Herman illustrates this: 'close relationships between intelligence and users play a major part in determining intelligence's credibility and educating them on how to use it properly'.[59] Decision-makers receive an enormous amount of information every day and important information easily disappears in noise, or its importance is overlooked simply because there are limits to how much the human brain can accumulate. It is easier to understand and take seriously that which is known and experienced, and much more challenging to observe, take seriously and acknowledge the unexperienced.

The threat from al Qaeda was a carrier of the unexperienced and the unknown, and as such a threat to established truths, orthodoxies and political assumptions. It hence stimulated cognitive closure and discourse failure, and created a dissemination atmosphere that did not facilitate innovation and imagination. The security-focused and restrictive need-to-know culture therefore prevailed, even though some of the available information was actually disseminated between the services and to the administration. These facts illustrate that dissemination cultures are often shaped by orthodoxies and political assumptions. They must therefore be understood and fought against. Only then can effective dissemination prevail and stimulate positive and effective discourse.

Conclusion

Threats in general, and terrorist threats as such, are complex in their structures and dynamics. They are hard to comprehend and foresee, and therefore highly challenging to communicate and disseminate. Intellectual courage is therefore called for, since intelligence is useless unless the intelligence producer at some point delivers a product that reduces uncertainty to the decision-maker. However, that does not mean that intelligence institutions provide definite answers. But they must seek to increase the decision-maker's decision basis, and intelligence 'is [therefore] always about informing policy, not prescribing policy'.[60] The problems related to this challenge are illustrated by President Clinton stating that 'he was very frustrated that he could not get a definitive enough answer to do something about the *Cole* attack'.[61] The intelligence institutions could have provided a definite answer related to the *Cole* attack, because the attack had already taken place. It was therefore not a mystery, and lent itself to clearer answers. However, intelligence is both secrets and mysteries, and demands intellectual courage and imagination. Intelligence communities should therefore facilitate a courage-to-share strategy that develops a culture based on constructive discourse and intelligence dialogue. Complexity is demanding to comprehend, and therefore challenging to communicate and disseminate. It is challenging to communicate the unknown, and even harder to communicate vague indications or assessments that are based on few indicators and operators' intuition. Intelligence institutions should hence do their utmost to stimulate courage, intuition and imagination. They should develop a culture that is intellectually courageous and free, and in which operators feel safe to debate in an open atmosphere, since 'open societies, by contrast [to closed societies], are societies in which everything – policies, institutions, traditions, rulers – is open to criticism, and open to criticism from anyone'.[62] Robert Kennedy demonstrates the consequence if intellectual integrity, honesty and courage are given space:

> The task of communicating intelligence to decision makers involves a great deal of judgement and a high degree of emotional detachment and honesty on the part of the Intelligence Community. Assumptions must be made explicit. The quality and freshness of the information must be revealed. Limitations in collection and analysis must be outlined. Conclusions must be well supported and well reasoned.[63]

This quote illustrates that the quality of an intelligence product depends on the quality of the internal discourse in the intelligence institution where it has been produced, as well as the discourse between the intelligence producer and the decision-maker. The discourse needs to be critical. The sources, methods and the information itself need to be constantly and critically examined. There is no room for slacking. High-quality intelligence production therefore demands discipline. It can be terribly boring and unglamorous. It is hard work, and demands concentration and precision. It is impossible without wisdom and imagination, and it is when wisdom and imagination harmonise with discipline and precision in a perfect balance that it is possible to discern truth from lies.

Intelligence institutions should therefore replace the need-to-share principle with a courage-to-share strategy. The courage-to-share strategy facilitates and stimulates the intelligence operators' willingness and ability to believe in their own assessments, and therefore also their cognitive capability to approach complex threats. Intelligence is, in its essence, the bearer of uncertainty and complexity. Threats and the future are by their nature dubious and intelligence institutions should not try to present them as something else, since 'communicating certainty when only uncertainty is warranted'[64] is the greatest disservice intelligence institutions can perform. There must hence be created a common understanding among intelligence institutions and between these institutions and decision-makers/consumers that elucidates the true nature of threats, threat perception and intelligence, so that these communities can 'stay ahead of evolving threats to the United States, exploiting risk while recognizing the impossibility of eliminating it'.[65]

Dissemination of the intelligence product is vital, and 'delivering the product in appropriate ways is an art in itself'.[66] High-quality intelligence products are therefore worthless if they are not communicated properly and understood by the intelligence consumer. That said, it is the action/decision by the intelligence consumer that is important. The knowledge disseminated to the consumer is worthless if it is not acted on. Let it be clear that action/decision does not necessarily mean action as such. Sometimes an action could imply doing nothing, although an action could not be said to be an action if it is a result of apathy. Inaction is rational when it is based on sound and informed judgement, and irrational when it is based on ignorance. The three-dimensional force of cognition, secrecy and intelligence tribal language not only shapes and hampers effective and focused dissemination, but also severely influences the intelligence consumer's ability to react effectively and profoundly to new threats. The next chapter will hence evaluate this negative trinity against the specific findings in the 9/11 Commission Report and how it affected the actions and decisions of the intelligence consumers.

7   On Action and Decisions by the Intelligence Consumer

The use of intelligence is the 'final payoff'[1] of intelligence activity, and the quality of intelligence is never better than the decision-maker's understanding and use of it. Indeed,

> how senior policymakers use intelligence depends largely on the poli-cymakers themselves, their background, knowledge of the subject matter, previous experiences with the intelligence processes, under-standing of the strengths and weaknesses of collection methods, and so on.[2]

This suggests that the strengths and limitations of intelligence develop in the interplay between the product and the decision-makers' ability to understand it, and their consequent capacity to build on this. The Butler Report illustrates this:

> These limitations [of intelligence] are best offset by ensuring that the ultimate users of intelligence, the decision-makers at all levels, prop-erly understand its strengths and limitations and have the opportunity to acquire experience in handling it. It is not easy to do this while preserving the security of sensitive sources and methods. But unless intelligence is properly handled at this final stage, all preceding effort and expenditure is wasted.[3]

This suggests that '[intelligence] can be a dangerous tool if its limitations are not recognised by those who seek to use it'.[4] However, the limitations and strengths of a phenomenon cannot be comprehended if it is not understood in the first place, and the consequences of deficient intelligence theory and inadequate definitions are thus disclosed. The following analysis will therefore be based on the hypothesis that the quality of action/decision by the decision-makers before 9/11 was seriously reduced because the nature of intelligence was not properly understood, because the lack of intelligence theory and definitions reduced the understanding of the strengths and limitations of intelligence. The decision-makers did not pay enough attention to the problem of induction, and when this problem interplayed with secrecy and a threat appearing in new variations, an already restricted and limiting intelligence tribal language could continue to evolve. Accordingly, an already inductively limiting environment continued to develop, and 'in such an environment, it is easy to develop resolute beliefs, attitudes, and predispositions, which ultimately limit one's ability to comprehend, absorb, and react to information that runs counter to those beliefs'.[5] This culture reduced threat perception among decision-makers and reduced their capacity and willingness to understand, accept and communicate the existing threat.[6] Policy was thus often 'based on half-buried assumptions. To counter this tendency, intelligence would need to interrogate policy about its assumptions or mind-sets, then try to validate or discredit the assumptions.'[7] The following analysis will thus evaluate how the problem of induction, in its interaction with secrecy and intelligence tribal language, shaped threat perception and seemed to confirm preconceived assumptions. The analysis will also shed light on the consequences for action/decision by decision-makers.

The Analysis and its Structure

This chapter is in two main parts. Part one analyses how the problem of induction shaped decision-makers' threat perception, and how this problem increased when it was faced with a threat appearing in new variations. Part two explores how the interplay between the problem of induction, secrecy and intelligence tribal language shaped action/decision by the decision-makers. The term 'decision-makers' will be used in this chapter to describe users of intelligence, intelligence consumers and decision-makers.

The Threat and the Problem of Induction

Former US Secretary of Defense Donald Rumsfeld demonstrates a profound understanding of the al Qaeda and Salafi jihadist threat in his statement to the 9/11 Commission Report:

> The global war on terror will, in fact, be long. And I am convinced that victory in the war on terror will require a positive effort as well as an aggressive battle. We need to find creative ways to stop the next generation of terrorists from being recruited, trained and deployed to kill innocent people. For every terrorist that coalition forces capture or kill, still others are being recruited and trained. To win the war on terror, we have to win the war of ideas: the battle for the minds of those who are being recruited and financed by terrorist networks across the globe . . . [8]

Rumsfeld's statement is a precise description of how terrorism should be countered, as it acknowledges that it is the root problem that must be addressed and deterred. Below, however, we can read Rumsfeld's answer to Bob Kerrey's question about why there was a need for a full-blown war plan on Afghanistan. This answer presents a paradox when compared to his precise statement above: it also indicates that his thinking was shaped by the problem of induction.

> Afghanistan was harboring the al Qaeda. Afghanistan was something like 8,000 miles from the United States. It was surrounded by countries that were not particularly friendly to the United States of America. Afghanistan, as I said publicly on one occasion, didn't have a lot of targets. I mean, you can go from overhead and attack Afghanistan, and in a very short order, you run out of targets that are lucrative. You can pound the rubble in al Qaeda training camps 15 times and not do much damage. They can put tents right up. [9]

The above illustrates that Rumsfeld remained shaped by the Cold War paradigm: he did not believe bombing was useful, not because it would not destroy al Qaeda, but because there were not enough lucrative targets. Rumsfeld, despite communicating a firm understanding of al Qaeda's transnational identity, still believed it was possible to defeat the organisation using classical warfare. His first statement given to the Commission, however, indicates that Rumsfeld did seem to understand the complexity of the al Qaeda threat. Nonetheless, his answer to Kerrey's question indicates that he had a strong belief in a robust, full-scale retaliation on Afghanistan, the Taliban and al Qaeda, and was therefore waiting for a full-blown war plan before he could attack. The contradictory qualities of his first statement and his answer to Kerrey's question hence indicate that he did not understand the nature of the threat from al Qaeda, either before or after their terrorist attacks on the US. This assumption is strengthened by the following statement by Rumsfeld:

> Killing bin Laden would not have removed al Qaeda's sanctuary in Afghanistan. Moreover, the sleeper cells that flew the aircraft into the World Trade Towers and the Pentagon were already in the United States months before the attack. Indeed, if actionable intelligence had appeared – which it did not – 9/11 would likely still have happened.[10]

Rumsfeld's statements and answers are clearly paradoxical. On the one hand, he communicates that he understood the complex terrorist threats from networks such as al Qaeda; but he also denies that he had any information prior to 9/11 that could have given him a rational reason for comprehending the threat and countering it. Despite this contradiction, however, he is right in asking rhetorically: 'why wasn't bin Laden taken out? And if he had been hit, could it have prevented September 11th?'[11] The answer is probably no; Rumsfeld is therefore precise and right in emphasising that killing bin Laden and conducting grand-scale attacks on targets in Afghanistan would probably neither have stopped the terrorist attacks nor crushed al Qaeda. But he is right for the wrong reasons, since the right reasons would have led to a fundamentally different approach to the terrorists. A firm understanding of the terrorist threat should have resulted in an asymmetric strategy with the terrorists countered on different levels and different tactics used, such as arresting the suspected terrorists or simply preventing them from boarding the planes. Flight 93 did get hijacked, but by only four terrorists. The other planes were hijacked by five-man teams. 'The operative likely intended to round out the team for this flight [flight 93], Mohamed al Kahtani, had been refused entry by a suspicious immigration inspector at Florida's Orlando International Airport in August.'[12] This example illustrates that had all the terrorists been refused entry to the US or to the airplanes, the atrocities could have been avoided. This would not have countered the threat from al Qaeda, but it would have stopped the first grand-scale attack by foreign terrorists on American soil. Rumsfeld's statement to the 9/11 Commission thus indicates that his understanding of the threat and the response to it was shaped by the problem of induction, and a consequent classical understanding of threats and how they should be met. Rumsfeld illustrates that his threat perception was shaped by a nation-to-nation-state paradigm in claiming that the terrorists could not be countered because they 'were already in the United States months before the attack'.[13] This indicates that his mind is inductively programmed to regard threats as a phenomenon which exists only outside US borders, and which accordingly must be countered abroad. He and other decision-makers remained shaped by the Cold War, with its focus on threats from long-range missiles. The strategy against long-range missiles did not actually distinguish between domestic and international territory, but NORAD (North American Aerospace Defence Command), the US and Canadian bi-national command responsible for the defence of North American airspace, did focus abroad because 'NORAD was created to counter the Soviet threat, [and] came to define its job as defending against external attacks.'[14] This demonstrates that the Cold War still shaped NORAD, since 'the threat of terrorists hijacking commercial airlines within the United States – and using them as guided missiles – was not recognized by NORAD before 9/11'.[15]

These examples illustrate that the pre-existing is hard to change. Custom, orthodoxies and political assumptions shape human cognition and are difficult to challenge, and 'the root of the failure in policy is assumptions unknown to, hence unchallenged by, intelligence'.[16] One therefore needs to explore why NORAD, Rumsfeld and other decision-makers, despite the threat from al Qaeda, continued to focus on classic threats from long-range missiles and consequently did not fully comprehend the threat. The following analysis will thus investigate whether the character and nature of the threat were simply too challenging to comprehend within the limits of induction: in which case, it is necessary to evaluate the capabilities of cognition compared to the challenge posed by threats appearing in new variations.

The Capabilities of Cognition

Why did the decision-makers underestimate the enemy; why did they not comprehend the true nature and the lethal danger of al Qaeda? President Clinton had experienced atrocities throughout his eight-year tenure. Events in Somalia and the Balkans had taught him that humans can be gruesome. Although President Bush had not long been incumbent when the United States was attacked, he was no greenhorn and both he and Clinton knew that 'killing and cruelty may be shocking, but it is familiar'.[17] So why did they not comprehend and accept the threat, or react sufficiently against it? The answer may be found in the nature of the threat and its interaction with the human cognitive tendency to displace threatening complexity. The threat from al Qaeda not only appeared in new variations; it also marked a radical shift in warfare. It dispersed old comprehensions of terrorism and war, and arose in a new world order of terror and atrocities. Wolfgang Sofsky illustrates this in explaining how the bloodbath in the Balkans superseded classical warfare:

> The massacre marks a watershed in the history of violence. It stands at the point of transition from terrorism to a new kind of war. The old logic of terrorism is not in force any more; the calculations of provocation have been superseded. The bloodbath is no longer a measure of political communication by other means.[18]

The tactics of terror are not new, but the terrorism that arose after the Cold War appeared in a new form beyond the limits of inductive logic, and hence challenged cognition. It was when this new threat logic interacted with the human tendency to displace cognitively challenging phenomena that cognitive closure emerged. This then fuelled discourse failure and '[steered] the [intelligence] process toward desirable knowledge structures'.[19] Accordingly, decision-makers displaced the apparent, underestimated the threat, and thus did not accept that a significant threat existed.[20] Arguably, both the Clinton and the Bush administrations saw the threat, but they probably did not acknowledge its true lethal danger; and even if they did, they certainly displaced it. The 9/11 Commission Report illustrates this:

> As best we can determine, neither in 2000 nor in the first eight months of 2001 did any polling organization in the United States think the subject of terrorism sufficiently on the minds of the public to warrant asking a question about it in a major national survey. Bin Ladin, al Qaeda, or even terrorism was not an important topic in the 2000 presidential campaign. Congress and the media called little attention to it.[21]

The 9/11 Commission Report thereby supports the discourse failure theory. This theory calls attention to collective national orthodoxies and political assumptions. It clarifies that intelligence operatives are not separate from the societies they serve, nor do they conduct their duties in complete cognitive isolation. The discourse on terrorism prior to 9/11 was, as the Commission points out, limited, and it is considered likely that the public discourse on terrorism shaped the terrorism discourse in the intelligence community. This is because 'intelligence agencies reflect national priorities, and in democratic states, especially, they will invariably exhibit all the characteristics that mold a particular culture and civilization. In this respect, intelligence agencies often mirror their own societies.'[22] The arguments presented have illustrated that the intelligence agencies and decision-makers in the US were influenced by a limited terrorism discourse shaped by induction.

The lack of a proper, constructive discourse on terrorism, and especially the terrorist threat from al Qaeda, greatly decreased the decision-makers' ability to acknowledge and sufficiently react to this.

The threat identified a new logic to warfare. The new variation of previous threats did therefore not fit the old threat discourse; there was no culture or language that could be used to identify, communicate or comprehend the new threat variations. The damaging result was that the imminent threat was not on the intelligence communities' and decision-makers' cognitive radar. As illustrated by the Commission Report, the national political interest in the threat was minimal,[23] and the search for more knowledge about the threat was therefore only of moderate extent, since 'persons [and consequently also intelligence institutions and their decision-makers] do not seek just any knowledge, only knowledge in which they have some special interest'.[24] The complex identity of the threat introduced something new, and therefore constituted a threat because '[political] actors need to understand the world in a certain way in order to avoid painful value trade-offs'.[25] The decision-makers did not have a special interest in the threat, nor did they have an appropriate discourse to communicate the identity of the threat. It was when this reductive discourse interacted with the human tendency to drift into cognitive closure[26] that the decision-makers became handicapped, and accordingly they did not manage to comprehend and counter the lethal threat from al Qaeda.

This section will now conclude by highlighting that the evaluation of the interaction between terrorist threats, the problem of induction, cognition and collective discourse has not only demonstrated the immense complexity of threat perception, but has also drawn attention to the real danger to free societies: the domination of reason over imagination. Herbert Marcuse elucidates this:

> It is no longer imagination which speaks here, but Reason, in a reality which justifies everything and absolves everything – except the sin against its spirit. Imagination is abdicating to this reality, which is catching up with and overtaking imagination.[27]

Marcuse captures the important, circular relation between sensation and imagination on the one hand, and calculation and reason on the other. He implicitly suggests that they are interwoven and equally interdependent. Fromm echoes Marcuse in clarifying that man has lost his 'unity with nature'.[28] This has created a contradictory human character torn between sensation and reason, and the human 'is driven to overcome this inner split, tormented by a craving for "absoluteness," for another kind of harmony which can lift the curse by which he was separated from nature, from his fellow men, and from himself'.[29]

The force of reason over imagination shapes many modern Western societies and their discourses. This may suggest that profane societies are vulnerable to threats from sacred societies since, for those who believe in holiness, 'the *sacred* is equivalent to a *power*, and, in the last analysis, to *reality*'.[30] However, the 22/7 attacks in Oslo illustrate that it is not the distinction between the profane and the sacred that creates tension and potential terror, but the distinction between democratic and totalitarian ideologies, since it is from 'the Occidentalism discourses that some of the most dramatic political violence in our time have its roots. Whether extreme communities are leftist, rightist or religious is of less importance than whether they spread Occidentalism.'[31] All radically volatised militants with a predisposition for resorting to violence, whether al Qaeda or the Oslo bomber, therefore represent something fundamentally different to the societies they hate and want to destroy, and one has to ask whether their discourse is in any way possible to understand for intelligence institutions built on democratic values. If not, this implies that the threat is thus highly difficult to acknowledge, especially since al Qaeda's and the Oslo bomber's extremist comprehension of reality is fundamentally different to democratic values. These arguments demonstrate that not only were the threats to the US and Norway complex, they also originated from a political discourse that is alien to democratic values and is therefore challenging to comprehend and acknowledge for societies where reason dominates over imagination, since Occidentalism worships 'divine leadership, and [has] a deep faith in the superiority of instinct over reason'.[32] It is therefore difficult for decision-makers shaped by reason and democratic values to comprehend a threat shaped by instinct, since:

> Desacralization pervades the entire experience of the nonreligious man of modern societies and that, in consequence, he finds it increasingly difficult to rediscover the existential dimensions of religious man in the archaic societies.[33]

This illustrates that it is challenging to acknowledge a threat without comprehending its origin. Treverton highlights that the Israelis 'were surprised because they could not fathom Sadat's logic'.[34] An understanding of the threat posed by al Qaeda to the USA would therefore presuppose the decision-makers comprehending the nature of al Qaeda. Clearly, both the Bush administration and Congress underestimated bin Laden and al Qaeda, since 'the issue was never joined as a collective debate by the US government, including the Congress, before 9/11'.[35] May concurs, and highlights that 'terrorism was a second- or third-order priority within the committees of Congress responsible for national security'.[36] This demonstrates that the intelligence services and threat perception are products of the public and political debates and discourses in the societies of which they are a part. Prior to 9/11, Western intelligence services were predominantly shaped by their belief in the supremacy of reason over imagination; they were therefore doomed to misconceive the threat, especially when the discourse of reason interplayed with a modern, non-sacred culture. These two factors accordingly created a culture among intelligence institutions and their decision-makers which made it challenging to comprehend the discourse that shaped al Qaeda, and the threat that arose from its ideology.

The problem of induction and the consequent lack of cognitive ability to comprehend the threat, the belief in the supremacy of reason over imagination, and the nature of the threat developed a limiting and restrictive discourse in and among the intelligence institutions, and between these institutions and decision-makers. The discourse made it difficult to communicate the threat, and the discourse fuelled a specific intelligence tribal language that further contributed to cognitive closure and discourse failure. All these factors increased a discourse that was already shaped by secrecy, and this created a self-fuelling spiral that intensified a security-focused culture.

How the Interplay between the Problem of Induction, Secrecy and Intelligence Tribal Language Shaped Action and Decisions by Decision-Makers

The Clinton Administration

Attention will first be given to the Clinton administration, and the focus will be on three conditions: the Small Group; coordination and cooperation; and, the Presidential Decision Directive 62.

The Small Group

President Clinton had a political focus on terrorism, and 'when announcing his new national security team after being reelected in 1996, President Clinton mentioned terrorism first in a list of several challenges facing the country'.[37] This illustrates that terrorism was on the President's agenda, and 'on August 20, 1998, in an address to the nation on military action against terrorist sites in Afghanistan and Sudan, President Clinton declared: "A few months ago, and again this week, Bin Ladin publicly vowed to wage a terrorist war against America."'[38] The Clinton administration's consciousness of the threat from al Qaeda was thus high, and counterterrorism was coordinated in what was called the 'Small Group'. This group was an exclusive forum of selected Principals who discussed important questions related to terrorism. The group produced only limited written records, and the information discussed at its meetings was treated highly confidentially. The decisions taken and the important topics discussed were not routinely formally disseminated, and those who wanted to know about this had to approach members of the group.[39]

Cooperation and coordination

The Clinton administration wanted to strengthen coordination and cooperation between key agencies: in 1998 it implemented a 'new presidential directive on counterterrorism'.[40] A new position as counterterrorism coordinator was created, and Clarke, who filled this post, had principal power on counterterrorism topics.[41] He had direct access to President Clinton, and he could 'set the agenda and [lay] out the options, but he did not help run any of the executive departments of the government. Final decision-making responsibility resided with others.'[42] The result was a non-integrated response to the threat, and 'the Joint Inquiry found leadership and structural failings in the Intelligence Community's response to the Bin Ladin threat'.[43]

The Presidential Decision Directive 62

This directive (Protection against Unconventional Threat to the Homeland and Americans Overseas)[44] was ambitious, and President Clinton wanted to increase the coordination of counterterrorism as well as strengthen cooperation between important agencies. The new directive did not, though, change the established budget process and the counterterrorism coordinator could therefore not coordinate actual change or cooperation between agencies or departments. The Joint Inquiry concluded that 'the PDD does not appear to have had much impact'.[45]

The Clinton administration's general approach to terrorism

The character of the Small Group and its restrictive culture of dissemination capture the substantial problem in the Clinton administration. The President certainly focused on terrorism. He took the threat seriously, and he implemented measures and changes demonstrating that the administration wanted more coordination and cooperation. Even so, the presidential decision directive did not change the established bureaucracy, and Clarke did not therefore have the authority to implement coordination that challenged the executive influence of governmental departments. Clarke was thus not able to implement real, radical coordination between agencies and departments. The exclusive culture that identified the Small Group was effective in 'overseeing fast-developing but sensitive operations, moving issues quickly to the highest levels, and keeping secrets'.[46] Yet the culture proved ineffective when countering potentially grand-scale attacks on the nation that needed cooperation between huge and culturally different agencies and departments. This was because the Small Group's process and culture 'created a challenge for integrating counterterrorism issues into the broader agenda of these agencies and the US government'.[47] Accordingly, 'no other Joint Inquiry witness [except Clarke] pointed to PDD-62 as the policy guiding the government's response to the growing al-Qa'ida threat'.[48]

The Bush Administration

The Bush administration approached terrorism differently from the Clinton administration. However, it did '[decide] to retain Clarke and his core counterterrorism staff'.[49] Rice knew he was regarded as controversial, but she was also aware of his immense practical experience, and she needed 'an experienced crisis manager in place during the first part of the administration'.[50] She therefore decided to keep Clarke, and her decision proved to be right when she chose Clarke on September 11 to lead and coordinate the crisis management.[51] But it was all too late. Clarke had been chosen to continue working on terrorism, but he was no longer 'a de facto principal on terrorism'.[52] He had no direct access to the President or routine access to Rice, although he could go to Rice to discuss operational matters.[53] Despite Clarke's demotion, he did propose actions against the terrorism threat, and suggested for example that the Bush administration covertly assist the Northern Alliance, increase budgeting for counterterrorism, prepare and carry out Predator reconnaissance operations and arm the unmanned aircraft.[54] These proposals could not be initiated without Principal decisions, but no meetings on these matters were scheduled by the administration, although 'Clarke asked on several occasions for early Principals Committee meetings on these issues and was frustrated that no early meeting was scheduled'.[55] However, Deputy National Security Advisor Steve Hadley stated to the Joint Inquiry that four senior-level meetings on al Qaeda had been conducted 'between May and the end of July 2001'.[56] Whether this illustrates a contradiction between the Joint Inquiry and the 9/11 Commission Report is challenging to say, but the 9/11 Commission Report states that 'no Principals Committee meetings on al Qaeda were held until September 4, 2001'.[57] This may indicate that no Principals attended the senior-level meetings to which Hadley refers. The reality of the decisions and actions performed by the Bush administration, however, illustrates that it did not take the threat seriously enough. The first Principals Committee meeting that focused solely on the threat from al Qaeda was held seven days before 9/11.

The Bush administration had not long been in power when the US was attacked, a factor that partly explains its decisions and actions, and 'the Deputies Committees met seven times from April to September 10 on issues related to al Qaeda, Afghanistan and Pakistan'.[58] Al Qaeda was on the agenda, it was prioritised, and 'shortly after the Bush Administration took office in January 2001, the National Security Council undertook a review of existing policy for dealing with al-Qa'ida'.[59] The administration also 'proposed a 27 percent increase in CIA counterterrorism spending'.[60] Nonetheless, these priorities also seemed to have been unfocused, and the administration never dealt with al Qaeda on a presidential level:

> Rice and Hadley said this was because the Deputies Committee needed to work through the many issues related to new policy on al Qaeda. The Principals Committee did meet frequently before 9/11 on other subjects, Rice told [the 9/11 Commission], including Russia, the Persian Gulf, and the Middle East peace process.[61]

The Bush administration's dealing with the al Qaeda threat is characterised by its contradictions. The threat was prioritised. It was also certainly on the agenda, and the administration had indications that could have warned of imminent danger, since 'from April through July, alarming threat reports were pouring in'.[62] On the other hand, the administration did not undertake any actions that could have stopped the terrorists from conducting their attacks. Accordingly, one important question needs posing: did the Principals in the Bush administration have any direct access to actionable intelligence that could have indicated that the USA

249

was threatened domestically? They did know there was a threat looming, and 'on July 27 Clarke reported to Rice and Hadley that the spike in intelligence indicating a near-term attack appeared to have ceased, but he urged them to keep readiness high; intelligence indicated that an attack had been postponed for a few months'.[63] On 6 July 2001 the CIA had 'told CSG participants that al Qaeda members "believe the upcoming attack will be a 'spectacular', qualitatively different from anything they have done to date"'.[64] This illustrates that the Bush administration did receive intelligence that indicated an attack. However, little of that information was actionable or could have stopped the terrorists.

> Neither the White House nor the CSG received specific, credible information about any threatened attacks in the United States. Neither Clarke nor the CSG were informed about the August 2001 investigations that produced the discovery of suspected al Qaeda operatives in the United States. Nor did the group learn about the arrest or FBI investigation of [student pilot] Zacarias Moussaoui in Minnesota.[65]

These findings indicate that the Bush administration did not have access to intelligence that could have provided them with a substantial and holistic acknowledgement of the reality of the domestic threat to the USA. Yet they also illustrate that the administration had created an overburdened, bureaucratic system incapable of acknowledging or reacting sufficiently to the intelligence it actually had, as well as reducing effective dissemination of intelligence information and advice on counterterrorism. In addition, '[Clarke] never briefed or met with President Bush on counterterrorism, which was a significant contrast from the relationship he had enjoyed with President Clinton'.[66]

The Bush administration's focus on and priority of terrorism were certainly high on its list of priorities, although it was classic, and consequently focused on terrorism abroad and nation states; and the fact that 'The Principals Committee did meet frequently before 9/11 on other subjects, Rice told us, including Russia, the Persian Gulf, and the Middle East peace process,'[67] is illustrative. However, the Principals did at last listen to Clarke after he had written 'to Rice summarizing many of his frustrations. He urged policymakers to imagine a day after a terrorist attack, with hundreds of Americans dead at home and abroad, and ask themselves what they could have done earlier'.[68] The threat from al Qaeda was finally discussed by the Principals Committee on September 4. The draft directive and actions against al Qaeda were approved, but it was all too late, and Clarke's prophetic warning was soon realised.

Clarke had served many American presidents well. Although he was known to be controversial, his successive eleven-year service at the White House demonstrates that he was more than merely experienced. He had developed gut instinct and the ability to acknowledge the vague. He was therefore able to imagine, despite actionable intelligence, the essence of the threat from al Qaeda. Nevertheless, he was not understood, and Paul Wolfowitz, Deputy Secretary of Defence, said prior to 9/11 that Clarke had overestimated the threat from Bin Laden.[69]

Clarke could probably have said anything. He was doomed to lose against the rest of the administration, as they did not want to believe him. A discourse and a culture had been created and developed where the unavailability of the President and other Principals made the dissemination of actionable intelligence difficult. However, 'President Bush received his counterterrorism briefings directly from DCI Tenet, who began personally providing intelligence updates at the White House each morning.'[70] The content of these briefings is unknown, but the 9/11 Commission Report clarifies that the President was not given information about the arrest of Zacarias Moussaoui in Minnesota.[71] Whether this information would have changed history is difficult to evaluate, but it illustrates that the coordination and cooperation between the CIA and FBI were challenging. Nonetheless, it is clear that President Bush himself thought that President Clinton's focus on al Qaeda was excessive, and Clarke 'recalled that on his administration's taking office, Bush perceived Clinton's recommendation that 'eliminating Al Qaeda be one of their highest priorities' as 'rather odd, like so many of the Clinton administration's actions'.[72] He thereby not only criticised Clarke, his new national security and counterterrorism coordinator, but also downgraded a war plan against al Qaeda which had been on the agenda since August 1998, and which culminated in 1999 when 'CTC reviewed its covert action program against Bin Ladin and developed "The Plan."'[73]

The President of any administration shapes the language, communication, discourse, and also the focus and priorities of the administration. This surely influences not only political priorities, but also intelligence requirements and priorities. The President therefore has the staff and the services he deserves. High-quality intelligence calls for courage, and ultimately the courage to tell decision-makers what they may not want to hear.[74] This is the essence of a real intelligence service, since it illustrates the whole idea of being and providing a service. Intelligence to please is not proper intelligence, and it is certainly no proper service. Nevertheless, intelligence institutions can only provide knowledge and unwelcome news if the decision-makers want to hear this.

The argument presented and the findings from the 9/11 Commission Report illustrate that the Bush Administration 'systematically pushed [the threat from al Qaeda] to the sidelines'.[75] However, the Bush administration can be excused for some of its failures inasmuch as it, as demonstrated, did not have access to vital information. However, the Bush administration had more than enough to acknowledge that al Qaeda was lethal. The administration knew that the organisation had killed before, and it knew that al Qaeda was well organised, equipped and motivated, but the administration refused to accept the magnitude of the threat. The Bush administration did not want to acknowledge that the USA, the greatest superpower in history, could be under threat from a non-governmental organisation led by a banished radical Islamite who dwelt in a cave in Afghanistan. Hence, the administration made the same mistake as the Israelis in 1973 and '*assumed* that no nation [or groups] would start a war it could not win'.[76] Jervis illustrates the problem of these sorts of mindsets in emphasising that 'the fundamental cause of intelligence errors is that in many if not most cases countries see the world and one another very differently'.[77] The greatest threat to the Bush administration therefore came from its own mindsets and discourses. Its orthodoxies, national inherited ideologies and threat perception were shaped by the problem of induction, and created a limiting and severely restrictive language that decreased intelligence dissemination, as well as influencing the comprehension of intelligence that could in fact have warned of the threat, had it been properly understood and accepted.

The discourse in the Bush administration was thus restricted and limiting, and therefore decreased its ability to identify, analyse and accept the apparent. Nevertheless, arguably there was a more developed secrecy culture in the Clinton administration, and the findings in the 9/11 Commission Report implicitly indicate that 'the Small Group culture' of the Clinton administration shaped a distinct discourse of secrecy. Such an environment arguably does not stimulate dialogue, important self-examination or constructive criticism, and can easily create an environment where the members of the group share 'similar predispositions' and 'such an environment of mutual reinforcing beliefs is detrimental to the effective use of intelligence'.[78] But elite groups that are identified by secrecy and the exclusion of others not only decrease critical rationalism; they may also decrease coordination and consequently the quality of an integrated response to the threat. This is because 'secrecy shapes the organizational cultures at all stages; handling secret material determines procedures and sets attitudes even where analysis is based largely on open data'.[79]

Clarke was a member of the inner circle, so the lack of communication created few problems for him, although it created challenges for intelligence dissemination in general and therefore for action/decisions within agencies and executive departments outside the White House. The Bush administration, however, restricted Clarke's opportunities to offer the advice he was tasked with providing, and the administration did not listen before it was too late. Arguably, therefore, secrecy was a greater challenge within Clinton's administration than within Bush's. But the challenge created by secrecy in the Clinton administration was outweighed by the fact that the threat from al Qaeda was taken seriously. The intelligence that was disseminated was therefore also taken seriously. The Bush administration, however, outweighed less secrecy with more cognitive closure. This accordingly contributed to discourse failure.

There undoubtedly existed a limiting and restrictive culture within both the Clinton and the Bush administrations. They were different but simultaneously similar, as they contributed to and shaped discourse failure. The Clinton administration, however, escapes the harshest historical judgment because it did try to understand and take the threat seriously. Whether it did enough to counter it is more challenging to say. The Bush administration, though, did not accept what was apparent, and contributed most to discourse failure. The 'Small Group culture of elitism' that existed within the Clinton administration, on the other hand, did arguably decrease communication between decision-makers and agencies, as well as between key players in the administration that did not belong to the 'Small Group'. This undoubtedly shaped a discourse that decreased effective dissemination of intelligence and distribution of orders. In addition, it can be argued that such systems and cultures of elitism can facilitate suspicion and jealousy which in turn contribute to a culture where knowledge and information are used as tools of power.

The argument presented above has illustrated that there existed limiting mindsets and secrecy-driven cultures within both the Clinton and Bush administrations. This certainly shaped the whole political system and national policies, as well as the political climate. But the US President is not supreme. The political system is powerful; the culture and conflict between Democrats and Republicans, as well as the daily power struggles in Washington, shape the President more than he shapes Washington, and 'Republican-Democratic conflict had come to be less about interests – farmers vs. businesses vs. labor and so on – than about moral beliefs'.[80] It was in this conscious moral climate that Clinton especially had to fight terrorism. Bush came to power on a neo-conservative political wind, and most of what Clinton stood for was seen as 'rather odd'[81] by President Bush.

The culture of neo-conservatism under Bush and the culture of elite secrecy under Clinton certainly shaped threat perception, as well as arguably shaping the intelligence community, and thus the relation between intelligence producers and decision-makers. The result was less focus, less coordination and less communication, and 'the Joint Inquiry has determined that the Intelligence Community as a whole was not on a war footing before September 11'.[82] The final, damaging result was that political actions and decisions were not properly informed by intelligence.

Conclusion

The lack of proper intelligence theory and definitions shaped an intelligence community and decision-makers, which lacked a common understanding of the strengths and limitations of intelligence. The consequence was decision-makers who tried to understand the enemy blindfolded, and 'questions that go unasked by policy are not likely to be answered by intelligence. If intelligence does provide the answers without being asked, those answers are not likely to be heard by policy.'[83] The intelligence community and the decision-makers were therefore unable to identify their intelligence needs, since it is challenging to choose a route if one does not know the destination. Consequently, the intelligence community could create neither effective intelligence requirements nor priorities. The intelligence requirements that were shaped by policy were hence unfocused, and President Bush's Deputy National Security Advisor, Hadley, told the Joint Inquiry 'that Bush Administration officials were told during the transition [from Clinton to Bush] that "this priority-setting process [PDD-35] . . . was not effective for communicating changing priorities over time"'.[84] The practical, negative effect of this unfocused requirement and priority system was demonstrated, as crucial Sigint about suspected al Qaeda facilities in the Middle East was not disseminated by Sigint summaries, since the information did not 'meet NSA reporting thresholds'.[85] The damaging effect was that the decision-makers did not receive intelligence that could have given them the knowledge they needed to take appropriate decisions and conduct proportional countermeasures against the threat.

The nature of the threat, the political situation during the Clinton years, the problem of induction and the fact that intelligence as a phenomenon was not properly understood combined to create a cognitive climate in which the threat became increasingly challenging to comprehend within the limits of inductive logic. This situation could develop because the interplay between the threat and the problem of induction facilitated cognitive closure, and it was when the consequence of this interplay interacted with secrecy and intelligence tribal language that discourse failure evolved. The final result was that the decision-makers did not manage to analyse the situation and the threat properly, and they thus did not have a language that was sophisticated and precise enough to communicate the complexity of the threat from al Qaeda. The Clinton and Bush administrations therefore became cognitively and politically handicapped and could thus not implement effective policy, and 'neither President Clinton nor President Bush nor their National Security Councils put the Government or the Intelligence Community on a war footing before September 11'.[86] The intelligence community therefore drifted without a course, and hence did not know what it should search for or comprehend, and thus, on the day, the 9/11 attackers succeeded.

Conclusion

Intelligence failures cause inquiries, which cause debates, which lead to literature, facilitating books such as this. With intelligence, it is difficult to know whether the literature or available sources are valuable enough or valid. Intelligence studies are therefore not fundamentally different from other academic studies, apart from the danger that some of the literature available may be part of an intelligence institution's attempt to mislead and dictate the public debate. Intelligence studies thus easily become a part of the intelligence culture that they seek to explore, and intelligence studies may thus turn out to be a part of the reciprocal nature of intelligence. Intelligence academics must therefore remember that their products become indivisible parts of the communities that they describe.

This book has therefore already become a part of the discourse on the US intelligence community and the 9/11 attacks and its prolonged aftermath. It is coloured by the 9/11 Commission Report and the Joint Inquiry, and its validity is shaped by the quality of the sources used: accordingly, it has become a part of the problem of induction.

Literature about intelligence must therefore be used carefully, not only because it may be part of deception, but also because it is mostly about the failures and seldom about the successes of intelligence. This is because discussion and debate of the successes would disclose the methods, capacities and sources of intelligence services. However, although the amount of intelligence literature has increased as a result of 9/11, little has focused on the effects of the Intelligence Reform and Terrorism Prevention Act of 2004, and even less has focused on the subsequent reform's effect on collection, analysis, dissemination and action/decision by the intelligence consumer. But the greatest gap in the intelligence literature is the lack of intelligence theory and definitions, and quality analysis on whether and how this weakness influences the performance of intelligence activity and hence shapes intelligence failure.

The Problem of Induction and Secret Intelligence

The aim of this book has been to bridge this gap. The analysis has illustrated how the lack of intelligence theory has hindered a critical comprehension of the damaging effect of the problems of induction, secrecy and intelligence tribal language on the intelligence process, which has hindered an adequate understanding of the strengths and weaknesses of intelligence. This lack of understanding of the quintessential capacity of intelligence has contributed to discourse failure, and the book has demonstrated that if intelligence is understood as the art of knowing beyond the limits of inductive logic, the problem of induction will be diminished and discourse failure can be reduced. Evidently, what a good intelligence theory '[needs] for this is a quality of insight [that goes] beyond any particular fixed form of reaction and associated reflective thought'. High-quality intelligence is hence *free of conditioning to previously existing patterns, otherwise it will, of course, ultimately be just an extension of mechanical reaction*.[1] However, this does not imply that good intelligence theory is not influenced by history or understandings of the past. Qualitative intelligence and theorising about it must of course be developed and 'evaluated through empirical investigation. Here there may be important gains from incorporating some well-developed ideas from the social sciences about how to evaluate propositions with rigorous research designs.'[2]

Intelligence, intelligence failure and discourse failure can therefore only be sufficiently understood if one has developed an intelligence theory that has withstood empirical investigation but that is not shaped by the inductive, mechanical reactions that the problem of induction and history can so easily create. A good intelligence theory must therefore be developed with a sensible understanding of history, but without being shaped by it. Intelligence is therefore an infinite art, since as art it seeks to understand and describe the indescribable. It seeks to probe beyond the limits of history and induction, and ultimately beyond the limits set by language and discourse. This implies that art is art when it portrays sensation beyond language and experience, and art and good intelligence are per definition always original. They go beyond cognitive understanding and mirror feelings communicable only through poetry, music, visual art and so forth, and the artist and therefore the intelligence operator must always be willing to learn, even when existing ideas and theories are challenged.[3] High-quality intelligence should always aspire to be original, and seek to identify, comprehend and communicate an understanding of threats appearing in new variations beyond the limits set by inductive logic.

Good art and good intelligence are therefore original because they describe those phenomena that cannot be described within the limits of formal language; and this understanding of intelligence is essential, since it ensures that intelligence institutions acknowledge the problem of induction. It is only when intelligence institutions acknowledge this problem that they can develop and appreciate the importance of an intelligence theory that facilitates an intelligence discourse which stimulates those cognitive processes (attentiveness, alertness, awareness and sensitivity) that exist beyond the limits of inductive logic, and thus facilitate intuition and originality.

Dictating the Discourse and Conquering the Opponent

Intelligence theory that is based on and stimulates these cognitive processes will further shape an intelligence discourse that is imaginative and creative, and intelligence institutions that manage to develop and capitalise on these qualitative factors will increase their cognitive and discursive ability to comprehend threats appearing in new discursive variations.

259

This suggests that intelligence is essentially the art of understanding the limitation of discourse, a notion illustrated by Mehren. He emphasises that 'the ideological battle is not determined by the durability and the strength of the arguments, but because one can choose the language that the arguments are expressed in. The one that dictates the parlance [discourse] is halfway to conquering its opponent.'[4]

However, the one who controls the parlance and the discourse can then easily be misled to believe that one understands something that one does not in fact understand. It is therefore the comprehension of the constant margins of language and its limitations to communicate that which exists beyond the limits of induction that constitutes victory. But language must not be understood as finite. Language is, like human cognition, infinite. Human creativity and fantasy are endless, and language is therefore also essentially and potentially endless. Nonetheless, language will at any given point always be limited to objects that appear in infinite and new orders and variations. It is against this challenge that intelligence institutions must safeguard. Mehren is also therefore demonstrative in illustrating the importance of understanding and controlling the discourse if one wants to win.

The Threat from Threat Perception

That said, discourse, like intelligence, is reciprocal. Intelligence must therefore never forget that discourse failure first develops when humans think that human action is easy to understand, or that discourse can be controlled. But that does not exclude the substantial importance of Mehren's argument, since it is a reminder of the importance and force of language and communication, and as such also of discourse. Mehren's argument thus illustrates the importance of a profound understanding of not only the opponent's discourse, but also our own, and lastly and most importantly a deep comprehension of the discourse evolving from the interaction between the threat perception conducted by intelligence services, and the threats they attempt to comprehend. Intelligence institutions that understand this discourse have not only diminished the danger of discourse failure, they have also increased their understanding of the opponent, and are consequently more qualified to comprehend threats.

The argument presented seems logical and straightforward, and it is, but it does not tell the whole story. It is important to understand the synergy between intelligence institutions and their opponents, but such a one-dimensional focus can easily mislead, resulting in a spy-hunt-spy game. The game and the intelligence methods can easily become the objective, and in such an environment one may forget that intelligence services' prime goal is to produce wisdom and insight. Intelligence services must therefore not focus solely on their opponents: they must also go beyond the strict bureaucratic boundaries of the intelligence process.[5] They must not search only for that which is requested by the intelligence consumer, since such mindsets and procedures seriously limit the intelligence institution's ability to detect and warn of threats existing outside the inductive boundaries of threat structures. This means that the essence of intelligence method is the search for those swans that are not white,[6] as they reflect the real threats and are the ones that need to be understood. Their nature must be analysed, and intelligence institutions must remember that the real danger develops when threats meet threat perception, contributing to discourse failure.

Threats are essentially simple, but they become complex when they interact with their targets, and against the intelligence services that try to comprehend them. Threats are as such not dissimilar to the silent majority of the population, because the masses and the threats reflect all references, orthodoxies, political assumptions, beliefs and opinions that have not become compelling and understandable to humans.[7] Threats can therefore be understood as phenomena that by their nature inhale and abstract societal orthodoxies and political assumptions. This implies that intelligence services are threatened by their own threat perception, and consequently they easily and unconsciously choose a limited, reductive discourse, ultimately leading to discourse failure.

It is damaging and dangerous if opponents understand this quintessential threat character and use the window of opportunity that will always exist as a result of the misbalance emerging from the disparity between the infinity of the objects that are to be understood, and the finite language that intelligence institutions have to understand these objects. All this suggests that the real threat is the fear and uncertainty created by threats, since 'the real target . . . is the unstable psychological infrastructure of above all the Western countries. By attacking this psychological infrastructure the political will of the country attacked is to be exhausted.'[8] The most important countermeasure to such threats is that societies and intelligence services attempt to reduce this unstable psychological infrastructure by understanding, detecting and warning of any disparity between reality, observation and the level of precision in the communication of these observations. Such detection is challenging, however, since it is difficult if not impossible for humans to fully understand the complexity of the world around them. Believing otherwise would not only be wishful thinking: it would also be arrogant.

Understanding Fear

Intelligence intuitions and their operators must try to understand their fear, personal weaknesses and the institutional weaknesses of their organisations. They must methodically question their own belief systems, orthodoxies and political assumptions. The result of such self-critical analysis is that intelligence institutions will start to understand not only their own organisational weaknesses, but also and most importantly the psychological weaknesses of the societies they serve: they will hence be better tooled to protect these societies. Discourse failure therefore appears where vagueness, duality, uncertainty, unhealthy secrecy and intelligence tribal language rule, and diminishes where openness and critical rationalism are given a serious chance. Societies and intelligence institutions that nurture freedom, opinions and criticism will reduce the danger of fear, as well as the disparity between reality and observation, and the communication of these observations. This reduces the 'unstable psychological infrastructure'[9] in any society, and it will become more challenging for opponents to exploit the disparity that results from the misbalance between reality and the observations and communication of these, because an awareness of limited, restrictive discourse expressed as unstable psychological infrastructure reduces the possibilities for discourse failure.

Towards a Theory on Intelligence

Good intelligence is attentive to the limitations of the tripartite force of cognition, secrecy and intelligence tribal language, and thereby also acknowledges and embraces the possibilities of cognition and intelligence. Such a system of intelligence, which acknowledges its own constraints, also embraces and exploits the possibilities of cognition. This form of intelligence certainly increases its possibilities to comprehend the nature of threats and change, as well as having the discourse to communicate it, and it is hence worth illustrating why threats have such a damaging effect on human cognition.

To reiterate, threats in general, and the threat from violent sub-state actors of the kind that struck on 9/11 in particular, are similar to the masses of a society: this is because the threats not only identify and elucidate the innate fear of freedom and the lust for submission, but also because the threats abstract these human weaknesses and therefore increase them. Arguably, this seems a very theoretical approach to an understanding of threats and the dangers posed by violent extremes, and it can probably also be claimed that the argument is postmodernistic and constructive, and therefore disregards issues like terrorism as an extreme political instrument. However, understanding terrorism as a practical and extreme political instrument is insufficient; one must also comprehend the reciprocal nature between threats, threat perception and the fear created by such terroristic acts. The force and effects of terrorism are fuelled by fear. Attacks are conducted, and targets are carefully selected with the aim of increasing fear, and thereby paralyse the collective cognition and discourse in free societies. This implies that the attacks in themselves are not only instrumental – they also serve a higher, more devastating and damaging purpose: they seek to undermine healthy and creative societal discourse. The result is cognitive closure and discourse failure. Threat perception is therefore challenging, since it is itself a victim and target of the threats it seeks to comprehend. Thus, the perceptions of threat and danger, terrorist or otherwise, also shape the world view of intelligence employees and the resulting intelligence products they generate.

Intelligence operatives are therefore not unlike the members of the society they serve: they also fear freedom and have an innate lust to submit. It is these psychological tendencies that constitute the real danger to any society, and it is these tendencies that have a likely propensity to increase discourse failure. The quintessence of the discourse failure theory elucidates the relation between the nature of threats and the innate weaknesses of human cognition. It highlights that humans, and therefore also intelligence operatives, are not only receptive to, but increase the collective orthodoxies and political assumptions in their own societies. The discourse failure theory therefore highlights that discourse failure is a phenomenon that increases and develops in the shadows and as a result of the force of the silent majorities.[10] Discourse failure is given a chance and fuels its negative force when intelligence services and their operatives submit to cognitive closure. They then also submit to the forces of the masses of their societies, and become part of a silent consensus that has disregarded critical thinking. Intelligence operatives and intelligence institutions have consequently come to reject the possibilities to comprehend the wholeness of threats, since their rejection of a critical social order also implies that they have rejected a comprehension of the dialectical meaning[11] of threats.

The discourse failure theory therefore elucidates that threats and dangers develop and are not properly comprehended and, at worst, rejected and overlooked because intelligence operatives reject the wholeness and harmony of their own minds. Intelligence operatives and institutions therefore fail to understand the dynamics and wholeness of threats. Threats are therefore a phenomenon that must be understood in its relationship to threat perception, since threats increase as a result of decreased perception and fragmented thinking. Intelligence has traditionally not appreciated the importance of an understanding of the relationship between threats and threat perception, and how the problem of induction shapes cognition, and makes it impossible to understand threats that appear beyond the limits of induction.

But threats never operate within the limits of induction: they constantly change and will always appear in new variations. Threats therefore also operate beyond the limits of traditional science, and intelligence must hence be understood as art. It is only when intelligence is understood as art that the problem of induction and discourse failure can be diminished.

A Definition of Intelligence

Intelligence is *secretly generated wisdom beyond the limits of formal reasoning that makes uncertain estimates less uncertain, and that consequently generates political, strategic and operational advantages over adversaries.*

However, an acknowledgement of intelligence as art and the use of critical rationalism cannot solve the problem of induction. It only reduces the problem, since humans can never free themselves from their own history and experiences. Critical rationalism can therefore be understood as critical induction, and hence illustrates how thinking, and therefore decisions, are shaped by each person's history and experiences. It is in this spirit of humility and self-awareness that intelligence as art must be understood. Intelligence is not static. It cannot provide facts, and it cannot increase certainty. Intelligence can only make uncertain estimates less uncertain, and can therefore only decrease uncertainty. It is this understanding of the limitations of intelligence that constitutes the strengths of intelligence, ensuring an understanding of intelligence as the art that seeks to comprehend and describe threats that appear in new variations and thus beyond the limits of inductive logic. An understanding of intelligence as art thus reduces the challenges posed by the problem of induction and discourse failure because it acknowledges that the wisdom that makes uncertainty less uncertain cannot be generated and advanced within the limits of formal reasoning.

Notes

Introduction

1. The term should be understood as the misconceptions caused by an opponents' targeted use of digital platforms for the sake of deception. Digideceptionalisation increases when misunderstood secrecy, intelligence tribal language and the conventional belief in historical reproduction mutate and interact with the opponent's digital deception. The term will not be analysed further, other than to be used as an introductory explanation of why the plethora of misleading and confusing data is a bigger challenge now than ever before.
2. Kahn, 'An Historical Theory of Intelligence', p. 4.
3. Kuhns, 'Intelligence Failures: Forecasting and the Lessons of Epistemology', p. 88.
4. Blackburn, *Oxford Dictionary of Philosophy*, p. 192.
5. This definition was first presented to the Research Advisory Board at the Norwegian Defence Intelligence School, 1 April 2012.
6. Ibid.
7. Musgrave, 'How Popper (Might Have) Solved the Problem of Induction', pp. 18–23.
8. Hatlebrekke, *Towards a Theory on Intelligence*, p. 275. See also Hatlebrekke and Smith, 'Towards a New Theory of Intelligence Failure? The Impact of Cognitive Closure and Discourse Failure', p. 158.
9. Hatlebrekke, *Towards a Theory on Intelligence*, p. 275.
10. Blackburn, *Oxford Dictionary of Philosophy*, p. 320.
11. Ibid. p. 142.
12. Kruglanski, *Lay Epistemics and Human Knowledge: Cognitive and Motivational Bases*, p. 14. See also Bar-Joseph, 'Intelligence Failure and the Need for Cognitive Closure: The Case of Yom Kippur', p. 182.
13. Neumann and Smith, 'Missing the Plot? Intelligence and Discourse Failure', pp. 95–107.

14. Kruglanski, *Lay Epistemics and Human Knowledge: Cognitive and Motivational Bases*, p. 14. See also Bar-Joseph, 'Intelligence Failure and the Need for Cognitive Closure: The Case of Yom Kippur', p. 182.

15. The Butler Report, *Review of Intelligence on Weapons of Mass Destruction*, p. 14, para. 51.

16. Omand, lecture to the Professional Advanced Intelligence course, The Norwegian Defence University College, Oslo (7 October 2008). Omand presented elucidation as a way of looking afresh at the classical processes of analysis and assessment that seek to shed light on the real world seen through the prism of intelligence.

17. Blackburn, *Oxford Dictionary of Philosophy*, p. 221.

18. Kuhns, 'Intelligence Failures: Forecasting and the Lessons of Epistemology', p. 88.

19. Popper, *Unended Quest*, p. 168.

20. Ibid.

21. Omand, *Securing the State*, p. 122.

22. Treverton, *Intelligence for an Age of Terror*, p. 146.

23. Omand, *Securing the State*, p. 46.

24. Ibid.

25. Blackburn, *Oxford Dictionary of Philosophy*, p. 192.

26. Treverton, *Reshaping National Intelligence for an Age of Information*, p. 12.

27. Treverton, *Intelligence for an Age of Terror*, p. 146.

28. Ibid.

29. Ibid.

30. Kent, *Strategic Intelligence for American World Policy*, p. vii.

31. Jones, *Reflections on Intelligence*, p. 155.

32. Blackburn, *Oxford Dictionary of Philosophy*, p. 153.

33. Popper, *Unended Quest*, p. 168.

34. Bohm, *On Creativity*, p. 11.

35. Smith, lecture to the Professional Advanced Intelligence course, The Norwegian Defence University College, Oslo (26 September 2008).

36. Neumann and Smith, 'Missing the Plot? Intelligence and Discourse Failure', p. 106.

37. Ibid. p. 96.

38. Bohm, *On Dialogue*, p. 3.

39. Herman, *Intelligence Power in Peace and War*, p. 234. See also Wirtz, 'Theory of Surprise', p. 106.

40. Blackburn, *Oxford Dictionary of Philosophy*, p. 67.

41. Oakeshott, 'Rationalism in Politics', p. 6.

42. Oakeshott, 'On Being Conservative', p. 409.

43. Ibid. See also Popper, *Unended Quest*, p. 171.
44. Sun Tzu, *The Art of War*, p. 271.
45. Omand, *Securing the State*, p. 22.
46. Fromm, *The Fear of Freedom*, p. 4.
47. Musgrave, 'How Popper (Might Have) Solved the Problem of Induction', p. 26.
48. Blackburn, *Oxford Dictionary of Philosophy*, p. 14, see analysis. See also holism, p. 177.
49. Kent, *Strategic Intelligence for American World Policy*, p. vii.
50. Bohm, *On Creativity*, p. 5.
51. Sinclair, *Thinking and Writing: Cognitive Science and Intelligence Analysis*, p. ix.
52. Herman, *Intelligence Services in the Information Age*, p. 4.
53. Herman, *Intelligence Power in Peace and War*, p. 103. See also p. 295.
54. Agrell and Treverton, 'The Science of Intelligence: Reflections on a Field that Never Was', p. 265.
55. Sims, 'Understanding Friends and Enemies: The Context for American Intelligence Reform', p. 15.
56. Heuer, 'Limits of Intelligence Analysis', pp. 78–9. See also Coker, 'The Future of War: What Are the New Complexities?', p. 86.
57. Popper, *The Open Society and Its Enemies: Volume Two*, p. 289.
58. Ibid.
59. Wittgenstein, *Philosophical Investigations*, p. 10.
60. Shulsky and Schmitt, *Silent Warfare: Understanding the World of Intelligence*, p. 63.
61. Kuhns, 'Intelligence Failures: Forecasting and the Lessons of Epistemology', p. 81.
62. Heuer, 'Limits of Intelligence Analysis', p. 78.
63. Betts, 'Analysis, War, and Decision: Why Intelligence Failures are Inevitable', p. 122.
64. Ibid.
65. Ibid.
66. Ibid.
67. Treverton, Jones, Boraz and Lipscy, *Toward a Theory of Intelligence*, p. 27.
68. Betts, 'Analysis, War, and Decision: Why Intelligence Failures are Inevitable', p. 134.
69. Hatlebrekke and Smith, 'Towards a New Theory of Intelligence Failure? The Impact of Cognitive Closure and Discourse Failure', p. 158.

70. Treverton, Jones, Boraz and Lipscy, *Toward a Theory of Intelligence: Workshop Report*, p. 2.
71. Ibid.
72. Ibid. p. 4.
73. Ibid.
74. Ibid. p. 7.
75. Ibid. p. 14.
76. Ibid.
77. Ibid.
78. Sun Tzu, *The Art of War: The New Illustrated Edition*, p. 232.
79. Treverton, Jones, Boraz and Lipscy, *Toward a Theory of Intelligence, Workshop Report*, p. 23.
80. Ibid. p. 16.
81. Ibid. p. 18.
82. Ibid. p. 20.
83. Johnson, 'Preface to a Theory of Strategic Intelligence', p. 648. Quoted in Treverton, Jones, Boraz and Lipscy, *Toward a Theory of Intelligence: Workshop Report*, p. 7. See also Gill, 'Theories of Intelligence: Where Are We, Where Should We Go and How Might We Proceed?', p. 214.
84. Gill, 'Theories of Intelligence: Where Are We, Where Should We Go and How Might We Proceed?', p. 214.
85. Treverton, Jones, Boraz and Lipscy, *Toward a Theory of Intelligence: Workshop Report*, p. 23.
86. Ibid.
87. Ibid.
88. Bohm, *On Creativity*, p. 52.
89. Ibid. p. 57.
90. Johnson, 'Sketches for a Theory of Strategic Intelligence', p. 52.
91. Herman, *Intelligence Services in the Information Age*, p. 4.
92. Handel, 'Intelligence and the Problem of Strategic Surprise', p. 15.
93. Sims, 'A Theory of Intelligence and International Politics', p. 61.
94. Kahn, 'An Historical Theory of Intelligence', p. 4.
95. Herman, *Intelligence Power in Peace and War*, p. 234.
96. Wirtz, 'Theory of Surprise', p. 106.
97. Handel, 'Intelligence and the Problem of Strategic Surprise', p. 9.
98. Coker, 'The Future of War: What are the New Complexities?', p. 86.
99. Bohm, *On Creativity*, p. 12.
100. Davis, 'Strategic Warning: Intelligence Support in a World of Uncertainty and Surprise', p. 178.

101. Kuhns, 'Intelligence Failures: Forecasting and the Lessons of Epistemology', pp. 90–6. See also Musgrave, 'How Popper (Might Have) Solved the Problem of Induction', p. 26.
102. Handel, 'Intelligence and the Problem of Strategic Surprise', p. 9.
103. Coker, lecture to the Norwegian Naval Special Operations Conference, Bergen (27–8 August 2007). Coker lends support to the presented argument when he emphasises that threats are in constant change, and that this in itself creates a challenge for cognition and thus poses a threat to perception.
104. Heuer, 'Limits of Intelligence Analysis', p. 76.
105. Oakeshott, 'Rationalism in Politics', p. 38.
106. Kruglanski, *Lay Epistemics and Human Knowledge: Cognitive and Motivational Bases*, p. 14. See also Bar-Joseph, 'Intelligence Failure and the Need for Cognitive Closure: The Case of Yom Kippur', p. 182.
107. Turner, *Why Secret Intelligence Fails*, p. 173.
108. Bar-Joseph, 'Intelligence Failure and the Need for Cognitive Closure: The Case of Yom Kippur', p. 182.
109. Shulsky and Schmitt, *Silent Warfare: Understanding the World of Intelligence*, p. 72.
110. Brady, 'Intelligence Failures: *Plus ça change . . .* ', p. 86. Quoted in Kuhns, 'Intelligence Failures: Forecasting and the Lessons of Epistemology', p. 81.
111. Friedman, 'The Crisis in the CIA', p. 3.
112. Laqueur, *The Uses and Limits of Intelligence*, p. 269.

Chapter 1

1. Bohm, *Wholeness and the Implicate Order*, p. xiii.
2. Ibid.
3. Bohm, *On Creativity*, p. 2.
4. Blackburn, *Oxford Dictionary of Philosophy*, p. 67.
5. Ibid.
6. Evans, Over and Handley, 'A Theory of Hypothetical Thinking', p. 3.
7. Bohm, *On Creativity*, p. 62.
8. Ibid.
9. Sun Tzu, *The Art of War*, p. 267.
10. Bohm, *On Creativity*, p. 67.

11. Blackburn, *Oxford Dictionary of Philosophy*, p. 187.
12. Ibid. p. 320.
13. Ibid. p. 142.
14. Ibid. p. 67.
15. Ibid. p. 320.
16. Ibid. p. 192.
17. Musgrave, 'How Popper (Might Have) Solved the Problem of Induction', p. 16.
18. Blackburn, *Oxford Dictionary of Philosophy*, p. 119.
19. Bohm, *On Creativity*, p. 74.
20. Baron, *Thinking and Deciding*, p. 7.
21. Bohm, *On Creativity*, p. 3.
22. Herman, *Intelligence Services in the Information Age*, p. 11.
23. Bohm, *On Creativity*, p. 3.
24. Ibid. p. 50.
25. Ibid. p. 5.
26. Midgley, *Heart and Mind*, p. 40.
27. Bohm, *Wholeness and the Implicate Order*, p. xiii.
28. Ibid. p. 4.
29. Petersen, 'The Challenge for the Political Analyst', p. 305.
30. Ibid. p. 306.
31. Eliade, *The Sacred and the Profane*, p. 13.
32. Neumann and Smith, 'Missing the Plot? Intelligence and Discourse Failure', p. 106.
33. Ibid.
34. May, *The 9/11 Commission Report*, p. 344.
35. Blackburn, *Oxford Dictionary of Philosophy*, p. 187.
36. Ibid. p. 377.
37. McLean and McMillan, *Concise Dictionary of Politics*, p. 342.
38. Kruglanski, *Lay Epistemics and Human Knowledge: Cognitve and Motivational Bases*, p. 14.
39. May, *The 9/11 Commission Report*, p. 153.
40. Ibid. p. 130.
41. Ibid.
42. Ibid. p. 131.
43. Ibid.
44. Neumann and Smith, 'Missing the Plot? Intelligence and Discourse Failure', p. 96.
45. The 9/11 Commission Report, p. 131.
46. Wirtz, 'Déjà Vu? Comparing Pearl Harbor and September 11', p. 188.

47. Ibid. p. 187.
48. Wohlstetter, *Pearl Harbor: Warning and Decision*, p. 397.
49. Ibid. p. 401.
50. Strasser, *The 9/11 Investigations*, p. 495.
51. Ibid.
52. Moynihan, *Secrecy*, p. 169.
53. MacGaffin, 'Clandestine Human Intelligence: Spies, Counterspies, and Covert Action', p. 80.
54. Ibid.
55. Ibid.
56. The Joint Inquiry, Abridged Findings and Conclusions, Systemic Findings, Finding 5.
57. Davis, 'Strategic Warning: Intelligence Support in a World of Uncertainty and Surprise', p. 183.
58. Ibid.
59. Bar-Joseph, 'Intelligence Failure and the Need for Cognitive Closure: The Case of Yom Kippur', p. 174.
60. Oakeshott, 'Rationalism in Politics', p. 39.
61. Oakeshott, *The Voice of Liberal Learning*, p. 180.
62. Ibid. p. 179.
63. Bohm, *Wholeness and the Implicate Order*, p. 4.
64. Popper, *The Logic of Scientific Discovery*, p. 4.
65. Ibid.
66. Popper, *Conjectures and Refutations: The Growth of Scientific Knowledge*, p. 64.
67. Blackburn, *Oxford Dictionary of Philosophy*, p. 192.
68. Ibid. See also Popper, *Unended Quest*, p. 168.
69. Musgrave, 'How Popper (Might Have) Solved the Problem of Induction', p. 20.
70. Ibid. p. 21.
71. Ibid. p. 23.
72. Mehren, *The Myth and the Irrational Reason* (Norwegian title: *Myten og den irrasjonelle fornuft*), p. 12.
73. Oakeshott, 'Rationalism in Politics', p. 6.
74. Knut Aasberg, former Director of Division in the Norwegian Intelligence Service, argued in a discussion at the Norwegian Defence University College (28 April 2010) that intelligence services can only hope to reduce the danger of intelligence failure if they search for the swans that are not white.
75. Blackburn, *Oxford Dictionary of Philosophy*, p. 192. See also p. 142.

76. Popper, *Conjectures and Refutations: The Growth of Scientific Knowledge*, p. 64.
77. Bohm, *On Creativity*, p. 32.

Chapter 2

1. Bohm, *Wholeness and the Implicate Order*, p. 8.
2. Ibid.
3. Bohm, *On Creativity*, p. 12.
4. Neumann and Smith, 'Missing the Plot? Intelligence and Discourse Failure', p. 106.
5. Bohm, *On Creativity*, p. 9–11.
6. Ibid. p. 9.
7. Ibid.
8. Ibid. p. 12.
9. Ibid.
10. Ibid. p. 11.
11. Sun Tzu, *The Art of War*, p. 265.
12. Ibid. p. 266.
13. Herman, *Intelligence Services in the Information Age*, p. 11.
14. Musgrave, 'How Popper (Might Have) Solved the Problem of Induction', pp. 18–23.
15. Anjum (2011). The Norwegian philosopher Rani Lill Anjum argues in her work *Our Conditional World: A Critique of the Formal Logical Approach* that formal logic is illogical since it fails to elucidate logical coherence as well as meaning and context. Available at <https://sites.google.com/site/ranilillanjum/home/research/our-conditional-worldhttps://sites.google.com/site/ranilillanjum/home/research/our-conditional-world> (accessed 7 October 2018).
16. Bohm, *Wholeness and the Implicate Order*, p. 4.
17. Kerr, 'The Track Record: CIA Analysis from 1950 to 2000', p. 51. See also Jackson, 'On Uncertainty and the Limits of Intelligence', pp. 456–8, and Hollister Hedley, 'Analysis for Strategic Intelligence', p. 221.
18. Bohm, *On Creativity*, p. 61.
19. Bohm, *Wholeness and the Implicate Order*, p. 4.
20. Herman, *Intelligence Services in the Information Age*, p. 3.
21. Scott and Jackson, 'Journeys in Shadows', p. 3.

22. Herman, *Intelligence Services in the Information Age*, p. 4.
23. Sims, 'A Theory of Intelligence and International Politics', p. 87.
24. Sun Tzu, *The Art of War*, pp. 266–7.
25. Ibid. p. 97.
26. Ibid. p. 273.
27. Kent, *Strategic Intelligence for American World Policy*, p. ix.
28. Ibid. p. viii.
29. Herman, *Intelligence Services in the Information Age*, p. 4.
30. Ibid. Herman emphasises the importance of understanding the fundamental difference between the twin skills of intelligence: collection and analysis.
31. Johnson, 'Sketches for a Theory of Strategic Intelligence', p. 33.
32. Herman, *Intelligence Power in Peace and War*, p. 93.
33. Moynihan, *Secrecy*, p. 180.
34. Herman, *Intelligence Services in the Information Age*, p. 8.
35. Herman, *Intelligence Power in Peace and War*, p. 93.
36. Gill and Phythian, *Intelligence in an Insecure World*, p. 103.
37. Marrin, 'Adding Value to the Intelligence Product', p. 206.
38. Petersen, 'What We Should Demand from Intelligence', p. 428.
39. Aasberg, lecture to the Professional Advanced Intelligence course, Norwegian Defence University College, Oslo (16 September 2008).
40. Betts, *Enemies of Intelligence: Knowledge and Power in American National Security*, p. 190.
41. Herman, *Intelligence Power in Peace and War*, p. 45.
42. Bruce and Bennett, 'Foreign Denial and Deception: Analytical Imperatives', p. 134.
43. Herman, *Intelligence Services in the Information Age*, p. 4.
44. Størmer Thaulow (2008). Størmer Thaulow was a student on the Professional Advanced Intelligence course, Norwegian Defence University College, who argued that the intelligence product is substantially the service intelligence organizations provide to their decision-makers and the society of which they form a part. See also Warner, 'Intelligence as Risk Shifting', p. 18.
45. Omand, 'Reflections on Secret Intelligence', p. 99.
46. Treverton, Jones, Boraz and Lipscy, *Toward a Theory of Intelligence*, p. 3. See also Warner, 'Wanted: A Definition of "Intelligence"', p. 3.
47. Scott and Jackson, 'Journeys in Shadows', p. 2.
48. Omand, lecture to the Professional Advanced Intelligence course, Norwegian Defense University College, Oslo (7 October 2008). Omand holds that inductive analytic methods are likely to fail to

comprehend complex future situations, especially low-probability, high-impact events. His use of the term 'elucidation' is intended to guide intelligence organisations to rethink how they produce their estimates through a threefold process of establishing situational awareness, arriving at the best explanation of the situation consistent with the available evidence, and then predicting possible outcomes and their relative likelihood. See also Omand, *Securing the State*, p. 122.

49. Omand, *Securing the State*, p. 23.
50. Herman, *Intelligence Services in the Information Age*, pp. 12–13.
51. Betts, 'Politization of Intelligence: Costs and Benefits', pp. 60–2; Russell, 'Achieving All-Source Fusion in the Intelligence Community', p. 195; and Omand, *Securing the State*, pp. 178–82.
52. Davies, 'Theory and Intelligence Reconsidered', p. 189.
53. Russell, 'Achieving All-Source Fusion in the Intelligence Community', p. 195.
54. Ibid.
55. Gill and Phythian, *Intelligence in an Insecure World*, p. 117.
56. The 9/11 Commission Report (2004), p. 419.
57. Ibid. p. 417.
58. May, *The 9/11 Commission Report*, p. 29.
59. The 9/11 Commission Report (2004), pp. 8 and 10.
60. Omand, *Securing the State*, p. 184.
61. Ibid.
62. Herman, *Intelligence Services in the Information Age*, p. 12.
63. Omand, 'Reflections on Secret Intelligence', p. 99.
64. Ibid.
65. Ibid.
66. Robertson, *Routledge Dictionary of Politics*, p. 382.
67. Ibid. p. 383.
68. McLean and McMillan, *Concise Dictionary of Politics*, p. 417.
69. Oakeshott, *The Voice of Liberal Learning*, p. 160.
70. Phythian, 'Intelligence Theory and Theories of International Relations: Shared World or Separate Worlds?', p. 57.
71. Herman, *Intelligence Services in the Information Age*, p. 6.
72. Phythian, 'Intelligence Theory and Theories of International Relations: Shared World or Separate Worlds?', p. 57.
73. Herman, *Intelligence Services in the Information Age*, pp. 6 and 10.
74. Cradock, *In Pursuit of British Interests: Reflections on Foreign Policy under Margaret Thatcher and John Major*, p. 37. Quoted in Herman, *Intelligence Services in the Information Age*, p. 8.

75. Ibid.
76. Herman, *Intelligence Services in the Information Age*, p. 11.
77. McLean and McMillan, *Concise Dictionary of Politics*, p. 399.
78. Phythian, 'Intelligence Theory and Theories of International Relations: Shared World or Separate Worlds?', p. 55.
79. Clausewitz, *On War*, p. 117.
80. Ibid.
81. Kuhns, 'Intelligence Failures: Forecasting and the Lessons of Epistemology', p. 89.
82. Popper, *The Logic of Scientific Discovery*, p. 4. Popper highlights that there is no inference between observed singular premises and universal statements, which means that there is no inference between history and future.
83. Kruglanski, *Lay Epistemics and Human Knowledge: Cognitive and Motivational Bases*, p. 14.
84. Ibid.
85. Kahana, 'Early Warning versus Concept: The Case of the Yom Kippur War 1973', p. 184.
86. Bar-Joseph, 'Intelligence Failure and the Need for Cognitive Closure: The Case of Yom Kippur', p. 182.
87. Ibid. p. 166.
88. Ibid. p. 167.
89. Branch 3+5+6+Israeli Air Force (IAF) Intelligence Division + Israeli Navy (IN) Intelligence Division, Immediate Military Intelligence Review, 'Alert Status and Activity in Syria and Egypt as of 051000 Oct. 7', para. 40 (private collection). Quoted in Bar-Joseph, 'Intelligence Failure and the Need for Cognitive Closure: The Case of Yom Kippur', p. 166.
90. Bar-Joseph, 'Intelligence Failure and the Need for Cognitive Closure: The Case of Yom Kippur', p. 167.
91. Ibid. p. 166.
92. Ibid. p. 167.
93. Clarke, *Against All Enemies: Inside America's War on Terror*, pp. 231–2.
94. Plato, *Complete Works*, p. 27, para. 29 b–c. Socrates contends that he is the wisest man in Athens because he knows that 'it is the most blameworthy ignorance to believe that one knows what one does not know'.
95. Bar-Joseph, 'Intelligence Failure and the Need for Cognitive Closure: The Case of Yom Kippur', p. 177.
96. Arie Braun, *Moshe Dayan and the Yom Kippur War*, p. 83. Estimate by Major General (ret.) Avram Adan. Quoted in Bar-Joseph,

'Intelligence Failure and the Need for Cognitive Closure: The Case of Yom Kippur', p. 170.

97. The Joint Inquiry, Abridged Findings and Conclusions, Factual Findings, Finding 4, p. xi. See also Bar-Joseph, 'Intelligence Failure and the Need for Cognitive Closure: The Case of Yom Kippur', p. 181.

98. Bar-Joseph, 'Intelligence Failure and the Need for Cognitive Closure: The Case of Yom Kippur', p. 172.

99. Smith, lecture to the Professional Advanced Intelligence course, Norwegian Defense University College, Oslo (26 September 2008).

100. Agrell, 'Intelligence Analysis after the Cold War: New Paradigm or Old Anomalies', p. 114.

101. Shulsky and Schmitt, *Silent Warfare: Understanding the World of Intelligence*, p. 64.

102. Ibid. pp. 64–7.

103. Plato, *Complete Works*, p. 27, para. 29 b–c.

104. Sun Tzu, *The Art of War*, p. 97.

105. Omand, 'Reflections on Secret Intelligence', p. 99.

106. McLean and McMillan, *Concise Dictionary of Politics*, p. 425.

107. Ibid. p. 426.

108. Sims, 'A Theory of Intelligence and International Politics', p. 62.

109. Clausewitz, *On War*, p. 101.

110. Ibid. p. 105.

111. Kuhns, 'Intelligence Failures: Forecasting and the Lessons of Epistemology', p. 96.

112. Blackburn, *Oxford Dictionary of Philosophy*, p. 67.

113. Clausewitz, *On War*, p. 101.

114. Herman, *Intelligence Services in the Information Age*, p. 12.

115. Riste, 'The Intelligence–Policy Maker Relationship and the Politicization of Intelligence', p. 208.

116. Gardiner, 'Squaring the Circle: Dealing with Intelligence-Policy Breakdowns', p. 136.

117. Omand, 'The Limits of Avowal: Secret Intelligence in an Age of Public Scrutiny', p. 261.

118. Gardiner, 'Squaring the Circle: Dealing with Intelligence-Policy Breakdowns', p. 136.

119. Omand, *Securing the State*, p. 185.

120. Hennessy, *The Prime Minister: The Office and its Holders Since 1945*, p. 71. Quoted in Herman, *Intelligence Services in the Information Age*, p. 16.

121. Timeliness, relevance and reliability are the vision and ethos of the Norwegian Intelligence Service.

122. Sims, 'A Theory of Intelligence and International Politics', p. 62.
123. Blackburn, *Oxford Dictionary of Philosophy*, p. 67.
124. Bohm, *On Creativity*, p. 75.
125. Blackburn, *Oxford Dictionary of Philosophy*, p. 197.
126. Ibid. p. 198.
127. Ibid. p. 197.
128. Handel, 'Intelligence and the Problem of Strategic Surprise', p. 23.
129. Blackburn, *Oxford Dictionary of Philosophy*, p. 67.
130. George and Kline, *Intelligence and the National Security Strategist: Enduring Issues and Challenges*, p. 357.
131. Handel, 'Intelligence and the Problem of Strategic Surprise', p. 17.
132. Bruce, 'Denial and Deception in the 21st Century: Adaptation Implications for Western Intelligence', p. 16.
133. Popper, *Conjectures and Refutations: The Growth of Scientific Knowledge*, p. 39.
134. Russell, *The Problems of Philosophy*, p. 1.
135. Popper, *The Logic of Scientific Discovery*, p. 4.
136. Omand, lecture to the Professional Advanced Intelligence course, Norwegian Defense University College, Oslo (7 October 2008). The former UK Intelligence and Security Coordinator suggested elucidation as a way of looking afresh at the classical processes of analysis and assessment that seek to shed light on the real world seen through the prism of intelligence.
137. Omand, *Securing the State*, p. 122.
138. Sims, 'A Theory of Intelligence and International Politics', p. 62.
139. Popper, *Conjectures and Refutations: The Growth of Scientific Knowledge*, p. 39.
140. Feyerabend, *Against Method*, p. 7.
141. Kuhns, 'Intelligence Failures: Forecasting and the Lessons of Epistemology', p. 88.
142. Omand, *Securing the State*, pp. 158–9. See also Jackson, 'On Uncertainty and the Limits of Intelligence', p. 456.
143. Betts, *Enemies of Intelligence: Knowledge and Power in American National Security*, p. 111.
144. Blackburn, *Oxford Dictionary of Philosophy*, p. 192.
145. Ibid.
146. Ibid. p. 136.
147. Popper, *Conjectures and Refutations: The Growth of Scientific Knowledge*, p. 64.
148. The 9/11 Commission Report, p. 417.

149. Midgley, *Beast and Man: The Roots of Human Nature*, p. 339.
150. The 9/11 Commission Report, p. 416.
151. Midgley, *Beast and Man: The Roots of Human Nature*, p. 339.
152. Bar-Joseph and McDermott, 'The Intelligence Analysis Crisis', p. 372.
153. Midgley, *Beast and Man: The Roots of Human Nature*, p. 340.
154. Jones, 'It's a Cultural Thing: Thoughts on a Troubled CIA', p. 27.
155. Laqueur, *The Uses and Limits of Intelligence*, p. 344.
156. Omand, *Securing the State*, p. 150.
157. Herman, *Intelligence Services in the Information Age*, p. 12.
158. Laqueur, *The Uses and Limits of Intelligence*, p. 319.
159. The 9/11 Commission Report, p. 426.
160. Ibid. p. 427.
161. Laqueur, *The Uses and Limits of Intelligence*, p. 321.
162. The Joint Inquiry, Abridged Findings and Conclusions, Systemic Findings, Finding 5, p. xvi.
163. Clarke, *Your Government Failed You: Breaking The Cycle of National Security Disasters*, p. 120.
164. Byman, 'Strategic Surprise and the September 11 Attacks', p. 165.
165. Laqueur, *The Uses and Limits of Intelligence*, p. 314.
166. Ibid. pp. 314–15.
167. Clarke, *Your Government Failed You: Breaking The Cycle of National Security Disasters*, p. 120.
168. British Joint Operational Intelligence, Annex 1A, p. 1. Quoted in Herman, *Intelligence Services in the Information Age*, pp. 12 and 13.
169. Cradock, *Know Your Enemy: How the Joint Intelligence Committee Saw the World*, p. 296. Quoted in House of Commons – Foreign Affairs – Ninth Report, article 155, available at <http://www.publications.parliament.uk/pa/cm200203/cmselect/cmfaff/813/81309.htm> (accessed 7 October 2018). See also Omand, *Securing the State*, p. 180.
170. Jones, 'It's a Cultural Thing: Thoughts on a Troubled CIA', p. 27.
171. Betts, *Enemies of Intelligence: Knowledge and Power in American National Security*, p. 111.
172. Jervis, *Why Intelligence Fails: Lessons from the Iranian Revolution and the Iraq War*, p. 195. See also Gardiner, 'Squaring the Circle: Dealing with Intelligence-Policy Breakdowns', p. 136; Sinclair, *Thinking and Writing: Cognitive Science and Intelligence Analysis*, p. 26.

Chapter 3

1. Sun Tzu, *The Art of War: The New Illustrated Edition*, p. 235.
2. Rutland, 'Sovietology: Notes for a Post-Mortem', p. 116. Quoted in Jones and Smith, 'Is There a Sovietology of South-East Asian Studies?', p. 856.
3. Sun Tzu, *The Art of War: The New Illustrated Edition*, p. 236.
4. Whaley, *Stratagem, Deception and Surprise in War*, p. 135. Quoted in Handel, 'Intelligence and Deception', p. 359.
5. Næss, *History of Philosophy*, p. 549.
6. Sun Tzu, *The Art of War*, p. 271.
7. Herman, *Intelligence Power in Peace and War*, pp. 103 and 295.
8. MacGaffin, 'Clandestine Human Intelligence: Spies, Counterspies, and Covert Action', p. 79.
9. Ibid. p. 87.
10. Fromm, *The Fear of Freedom*, p. 3.
11. Ibid. p. 4.
12. Ibid.
13. Bohm, *Wholeness and the Implicate Order*, p. 4.
14. Bohm, *On Dialogue*, p. 6.
15. Ibid. p. 7.
16. Ibid.
17. Ibid.
18. Ibid.
19. Gill and Phythian, *Intelligence in an Insecure World*, p. 106.
20. Gadamer, *Truth and Method*, p. 189.
21. Ibid.
22. Williams, *Truth and Truthfulness*, p. 212.
23. The 9/11 Commission Report, p. 342.
24. Popper, *The Open Society and Its Enemies: Volume Two*, p. 289.
25. The 9/11 Commission Report, p. 343.
26. Ibid. p. 416.
27. Ibid. p. 417.
28. Ibid.
29. The Joint Inquiry, Abridged Findings and Conclusions, Systemic Findings, Findings 1, 2, 3, 4 and 5, p. xvi. See also The 9/11 Commission Report, pp. 342, 347 and 417.
30. The 9/11 Commission Report, p. 342.
31. Ibid. p. 417.

32. Ibid. p. 343.
33. Ibid. p. 344.
34. Ibid. p. 343.
35. The Joint Inquiry, Abridged Findings and Conclusions, Systemic Findings, Finding 9, p. xvii.
36. Ibid.
37. Herman, *Intelligence Power in Peace and War*, p. 98.
38. The 9/11 Commission Report, p. 353.
39. Ibid. p. 416.
40. Neumann and Smith, 'Missing the Plot? Intelligence and Discourse Failure', p. 96.
41. Ibid.
42. The 9/11 Commission Report, p. 356.
43. Herman, *Intelligence Power in Peace and War*, p. 329.
44. Ibid.
45. Ibid. p. 93.
46. Ibid. p. 329.
47. Strasser, *The 9/11 Investigations*, p. 199.
48. The 9/11 Commission Report, p. 344.
49. Fromm, *The Fear of Freedom*, pp. 3 and 4.
50. Herman, *Intelligence Power in Peace and War*, p. 98.
51. Bohm, *On Creativity*, p. 50.
52. Ibid. p. 53.
53. Sun Tzu, *The Art of War*, p. 267.
54. Strasser, *The 9/11 Investigations*, p. 187.
55. Herman, *Intelligence Power in Peace and War*, pp. 39, 43, 103 and 295.
56. Turner, *Why Secret Intelligence Fails*, revised edition, p. 94.
57. Ibid.
58. Ibid.
59. The 9/11 Commission Report, p. 355.
60. Ibid. pp. 416–17.
61. Ibid. p. xvi.

Chapter 4

1. Herman, *Intelligence Power in Peace and War*, pp. 103 and 295.
2. Omand, *Securing the State*, p. 117.
3. Ibid. pp. 118–19.

4. Aasberg, lecture to the Professional Advanced Intelligence course, Norwegian Defence University College, Oslo (16 September 2008). Aasberg is former Director of Division in the Norwegian Intelligence Service and clarified that the intelligence process must be understood as function and not organization.
5. Omand, *Securing the State*, p. 119.
6. Ibid.
7. Herman, *Intelligence Power in Peace and War*, p. 39.
8. Lowenthal, *Intelligence: From Secrets to Policy*, p. 60.
9. Betts, 'Analysis, War, and Decision: Why Intelligence Failures are Inevitable', p. 129.
10. The Joint Inquiry, Abridged Findings and Conclusions, Systemic Findings, Finding 6, p. xvi.
11. Gill and Phythian, *Intelligence in an Insecure World*, p. 72.
12. Lowenthal, *Intelligence: From Secrets to Policy*, p. 61.
13. Treverton, Jones, Boraz and Lipscy, *Toward a Theory of Intelligence*, p. 14.
14. Aid, 'The Time of Troubles: The US National Security Agency in the Twenty-First Century', p. 99.
15. Gill and Phythian, *Intelligence in an Insecure World*, p. 72.
16. Hitz, 'Human Source Intelligence', p. 127.
17. The 9/11 Commission Report, p. 342.
18. Lowenthal, *Intelligence: From Secrets to Policy*, p. 60.
19. Davies, 'Intelligence, Complexity, the Media and Public Understanding', p. 65.
20. Lowenthal, *Intelligence: From Secrets to Policy*, p. 61.
21. House of Commons Hansard Debates, 22 June 2000, Part 30, Column 543, available at <https://publications.parliament.uk/pa/cm199900/cmhansrd/vo000622/debtext/00622-30.htm> (accessed 7 October 2018). Quoted in Aid, 'All Glory is Fleeting: SIGINT and the Fight against International Terrorism', p. 67.
22. Lowenthal, *Intelligence: From Secrets to Policy*, p. 100.
23. The 9/11 Commission Report, p. 415.
24. Aid, 'All Glory is Fleeting: SIGINT and the Fight against International Terrorism', p. 43.
25. Ibid.
26. The 9/11 Commission Report, pp. 343 and 416.
27. Gill and Phythian, *Intelligence in an Insecure World*, p. 81.
28. Herman, *Intelligence Services in the Information Age*, p. 5.
29. Davies, 'Intelligence, Complexity, the Media and Public Understanding', p. 51.

30. Lowenthal, *Intelligence: From Secrets to Policy*, p. 94.
31. The 9/11 Commission Report, p. 415.
32. Herman, *Intelligence Power in Peace and War*, p. 43.
33. Lowenthal, *Intelligence: From Secrets to Policy*, p. 70.
34. Herman, *Intelligence Power in Peace and War*, p. 101.
35. Omand, *Securing the State*, p. 149.
36. The Joint Inquiry, Abridged Findings and Conclusions, Systemic Findings, Finding 6, p. xvi.
37. Aid, 'All Glory is Fleeting: SIGINT and the Fight against International Terrorism', p. 66.
38. The 9/11 Commission Report, p. 352.
39. Ibid. p. 350.
40. The Joint Inquiry, Abridged Findings and Conclusions, Factual Findings, Finding 1, p. xi.
41. Gerber, 'Managing HUMINT: The Need for a New Approach', p. 193.
42. Monnier, 'Managing Domestic, Military, and Foreign Policy Requirements: Correcting Frankenstein's Blunder', p. 158.
43. Sims, 'Understanding Friends and Enemies: The Context for American Intelligence Reform', p. 14.
44. Monnier, 'Managing Domestic, Military, and Foreign Policy Requirements: Correcting Frankenstein's Blunder', p. 160.
45. Bar-Joseph, 'Intelligence Failure and the Need for Cognitive Closure: The Case of Yom Kippur', p. 182.
46. Sims, 'Understanding Friends and Enemies: The Context for American Intelligence Reform', p. 15.
47. Betts, 'Analysis, War, and Decision: Why Intelligence Failures are Inevitable', p. 127.
48. Jervis, *Why Intelligence Fails: Lessons from the Iranian Revolution and the Iraq War*, p. 131.
49. The Joint Inquiry, Abridged Findings and Conclusions, Conclusion – Factual Findings, p. xv.
50. Ibid.
51. Fulghum, 'Computer Combat Rules Frustrates the Pentagon', p. 68. Quoted in Aid, 'All Glory is Fleeting: SIGINT and the Fight against International Terrorism', p. 57.
52. Aid, 'All Glory is Fleeting: SIGINT and the Fight against International Terrorism', p. 57.
53. The Joint Inquiry, Abridged Findings and Conclusions, Systemic Findings, Finding 1, p. xv.
54. Ibid.

55. Strasser, *The 9/11 Investigations*, p. 492.
56. The Joint Inquiry, Abridged Findings and Conclusions, Systemic Findings, Finding 15, p. xviii.
57. Ibid. Finding 1, p. xv.
58. Ibid.
59. Ibid.
60. Ibid. Finding 5, p. xvi.
61. Herman, *Intelligence Power in Peace and War*, p. 329.
62. Ibid. p. 330.
63. Ibid.
64. Cogan, 'The In-Culture of the DO', p. 211.
65. The Joint Inquiry, Abridged Findings and Conclusions, Systemic findings, Finding 5, p. xvi.
66. The 9/11 Commission Report, p. 347.
67. Popper, *The Poverty of Historicism*, p. 43.
68. The 9/11 Commission Report, p. 342.
69. Ibid. p. 347.
70. Rolington, 'Objective Intelligence or Plausible Denial: An Open Source Review of Intelligence Method and Process since 9/11', p. 91.
71. Handel, 'Intelligence and the Problem of Strategic Surprise', p. 16.
72. Betts, 'Analysis, War, and Decision: Why Intelligence Failures are Inevitable', p. 131.
73. The 9/11 Commission Report, p. 346. See also May, *The 9/11 Commission Report*, p. 153.
74. Kuhns, 'Intelligence Failures: Forecasting and the Lessons of Epistemology', p. 88.
75. Popper, *The Poverty of Historicism*, p. 149.
76. Clausewitz, *On War*, p. 85.
77. Ibid. p. 87.
78. Omand, lecture to the Professional Advanced Intelligence course, Norwegian Defense University College, Oslo (7 October 2008).
79. The Joint Inquiry, Abridged Findings and Conclusions, Systemic Findings, Finding 16, p. xviii.
80. The 9/11 Commission Report, p. 263. See also Byman, 'Strategic Surprise and the September 11 Attacks', p. 171.
81. Byman, 'Strategic Surprise and the September 11 Attacks', p. 172.
82. Hitz, 'Human Source Intelligence', p. 125.
83. Pillar (2009), 'Adapting Intelligence to Changing Issues', p. 161.
84. Hitz, 'Human Source Intelligence', p. 126.

85. The 9/11 Commission Report, p. 353.
86. Rolington, 'Objective Intelligence or Plausible Denial: An Open Source Review of Intelligence Method and Process since 9/11', p. 92.
87. Hitz, 'Human Source Intelligence', p. 125.
88. Strasser, *The 9/11 Investigations*, p. 501.
89. The 9/11 Commission Report, p. 355.
90. Strasser, *The 9/11 Investigations*, p. 499.
91. Blackburn, *Oxford Dictionary of Philosophy*, p. 192.
92. Neumann and Smith, 'Missing the Plot? Intelligence and Discourse Failure', p. 106.
93. Blackburn, *Oxford Dictionary of Philosophy*, p. 192.
94. Strasser, *The 9/11 Investigations*, p. 91.
95. Frank J. Cilluffo, Ronald A. Marks and George C. Salmoiraghi, 'The Use and Limits of US Intelligence', p. 66. Quoted in Aid, 'All Glory is Fleeting: SIGINT and the Fight against International Terrorism', p. 46.
96. Hitz, 'Human Source Intelligence', p. 128.
97. Rolinton, 'Objective Intelligence or Plausible Denial: An Open Source Review of Intelligence Method and Process since 9/11', p. 88.
98. Aid, 'All Glory is Fleeting: SIGINT and the Fight against International Terrorism', p. 45.
99. The 9/11 Commission Report, Intelligence Policy, Staff Statement No. 7, p. 3.
100. Ibid. p. 4.
101. Ibid.
102. Ibid. p. 5.
103. Ibid. p. 4.
104. The 9/11 Commission Report, Intelligence Policy, Staff Statement No. 7, p. 5.
105. Ibid.
106. Strasser, *The 9/11 Investigations*, p. 457.
107. Ibid. pp. 457 and 494.
108. Strasser, *The 9/11 Investigations*, p. 495. See also The Joint Inquiry, Abridged Findings and Conclusions, Systemic Findings, Findings 9 and 10, p. xvii.
109. Ibid. p. 457.
110. The Joint Inquiry, Abridged Findings and Conclusions, Systemic Findings, Finding 11, p. xvii.

111. Kruglanski, *Lay Epistemics and Human Knowledge: Cognitive and Motivational Bases*, p. 14.
112. The 9/11 Commission Report, Intelligence Policy, Staff Statement No. 7, p. 5.
113. Ibid.
114. Ibid. p. 6.
115. Ibid.
116. Ibid. p. 7.
117. The Joint Inquiry, Findings and Conclusions, Systemic Finding, Finding 1, Discussion, p. 34.
118. The 9/11 Commission Report, Intelligence Policy, Staff Statement No. 7, p. 5.
119. Ibid.
120. The Joint Inquiry, Abridged Findings and Conclusions, Systemic Findings, Finding 5, p. xvi.
121. Ibid. Related Findings, Finding 17, p. xviii.
122. The 9/11 Commission Report, Intelligence Policy, Staff Statement No. 7, p. 6.
123. Ibid.
124. Friedman, 'The Crisis in the CIA', p. 3.
125. The Joint Inquiry, Findings and Conclusions, Systemic Findings, Finding 1, Discussion, p. 34.
126. The 9/11 Commission Report, p. 184.
127. Ibid.
128. Ibid.
129. Ibid.
130. Ibid. p. 185.
131. Friedman, 'The Problem with the CIA', p. 3.
132. Ibid. p. 4.
133. Rolington, 'Objective Intelligence or Plausible Denial: An Open Source Review of Intelligence Method and Process since 9/11', p. 88.
134. Strasser, *The 9/11 Investigations*, p. 492.
135. The 9/11 Commission Report, p. 184.
136. Strasser, *The 9/11 Investigations*, p. 493.
137. The Joint Inquiry, Part One, Findings and Conclusions, Factual Findings, Finding 5a, Discussion, p. 11.
138. The 9/11 Commission Report, p. 186.
139. Ibid. pp. 186–87.
140. Ibid. p. 187.

141. The 9/11 Commission Report, p. 188.
142. Ibid.
143. Hitz, 'Human Source Intelligence', p. 125.
144. The Joint Inquiry, Abridged Findings and Conclusions, Factual Findings, Finding 3, p. xi.
145. Popper, *Unended Quest*, p. 169.

Chapter 5

1. Russell, *The Problems of Philosophy*, p. 1.
2. Omand, *Securing the State*, p. 158.
3. Ibid. p. 122.
4. Blackburn, *Oxford Dictionary of Philosophy*, p. 192.
5. Ibid.
6. Heuer, *Psychology of Intelligence Analysis*, p. 1.
7. Blackburn, *Oxford Dictionary of Philosophy*, p. 192.
8. Ibid.
9. Kuhns, 'Intelligence Failures: Forecasting and the Lessons of Epistemology', p. 88.
10. Popper, *Unended Quest*, p. 168.
11. Ibid.
12. Kim, 'Events as Property Exemplifications', p. 160.
13. Popper, *Unended Quest*, p. 168.
14. Ibid. p. 169.
15. Musgrave, 'How Popper (Might Have) Solved the Problem of Induction', pp. 17–18.
16. Ibid.
17. Popper, *Unended Quest*, p. 169.
18. Ibid. p. 170.
19. Goodman, *Fact, Fiction, and Forecast*, p. 65. Quoted in Popper, *Unended Quest*, p. 171.
20. Popper, *Unended Quest*, p. 171.
21. Ibid.
22. Ibid.
23. Ibid.
24. Musgrave, 'How Popper (Might Have) Solved the Problem of Induction', p. 18.
25. Ibid. p. 21.
26. Ibid. p. 25.

27. Ibid. p. 20.
28. Ibid. p. 23.
29. Ibid. p. 19.
30. Blackburn, *Oxford Dictionary of Philosophy*, p. 14.
31. Musgrave, 'How Popper (Might Have) Solved the Problem of Induction', p. 19.
32. Johnson, 'Sketches for a Theory of Strategic Intelligence', p. 34.
33. Blackburn, *Oxford Dictionary of Philosophy*, p. 14.
34. Musgrave, 'How Popper (Might Have) Solved the Problem of Induction', pp. 17–18.
35. Ibid. p. 18.
36. Lowenthal, *Intelligence: From Secrets to Policy*, p. 133.
37. Ibid.
38. Kuhns, 'Intelligence Failures: Forecasting and the Lessons of Epistemology', p. 96.
39. Hatlebrekke. The idea was first presented to the Professional Advanced Intelligence course at the Norwegian Defence University College, Oslo, 21 October 2009.
40. Strasser, *The 9/11 Investigations*, p. 497.
41. Agrell, 'Intelligence Analysis after the Cold War – New Paradigm or Old Anomalies', p. 94.
42. Ibid.
43. Ibid. p. 113.
44. Richards, *The Art and Science of Intelligence Analysis*, p. 3.
45. Popper, *Unended Quest*, p. 171.
46. Strasser, *The 9/11 Investigations*, p. 498.
47. The National Intelligence Strategy of the United States of America, *Transformation through Integration and Innovation* (October 2005), Strategy Guidance, Mission Objectives, p. 6.
48. Davies, 'Theory and Intelligence Reconsidered', p. 200.
49. Bohm, *On Creativity*, p. 52.
50. Ibid. p. 61.
51. Ibid. pp. 57–61.
52. Ibid. p. 4.
53. Ibid.
54. Popper, *The Logic of Scientific Discovery*, p. 92.
55. Kerr, 'The Track Record: CIA Analysis from 1950 to 2000', p. 51.
56. Russell, *Sharpening Strategic Intelligence: Why the CIA Gets It Wrong, and What Needs to Be Done to Get It Right*, p. 121.
57. Sinclair, *Thinking and Writing: Cognitive Science and Intelligence Analysis*, p. ix.

58. Davis, 'Defining the Analytic Mission: Facts, Findings, Forecasts, and Fortunetelling', p. 298.

59. Omand, lecture to the Professional Advanced Intelligence course, Norwegian Defense University College, Oslo (7 October 2008). Omand holds that most external intelligence agencies now have functions both in actionable intelligence and covert action, as well as in more traditional long-term agent running. Such duality presupposes officers with different personality types: adventurers (camel drivers) and chess masters (playing by 'Moscow rules').

60. Bruce and Bennet, 'Foreign Denial and Deception: Analytical Imperatives', p. 133. See also Petersen, 'The Challenge for the Political Analyst', p. 305.

61. Kerr, 'The Track Record: CIA Analysis from 1950 to 2000', p. 51.

62. Kent, *Strategic Intelligence for American World Policy*, p. 74. Quoted in Russell, *Sharpening Strategic Intelligence: Why the CIA Gets It Wrong, and What Needs to Be Done to Get It Right*, p. 119.

63. The 9/11 Commission Report, pp. 339–48.

64. Posner, *Preventing Surprise Attacks: Intelligence Reform in the Wake of 9/11*, p. 77.

65. The 9/11 Commission Report, p. 213.

66. Ibid. p. 209.

67. Zegart, *Spying Blind: The CIA, The FBI, and the Origins of 9/11*, p. 63.

68. May, *The 9/11 Commission Report*, p. 131.

69. The 9/11 Commission Report, pp. 340–41. See also Posner, *Preventing Surprise Attacks: Intelligence Reform in the Wake of 9/11*, p. 20.

70. The 9/11 Commission Report, p. 342.

71. Ibid. p. 345.

72. Ibid. p. 341.

73. May, *The 9/11 Commission Report*, p. 154.

74. Ibid. p. 152.

75. Davis, 'Strategic Warning: Intelligence Support in a World of Uncertainty and Surprise', p. 177.

76. Adorno, *The Culture Industry*, p. 200.

77. Fromm, *The Fear of Freedom*, p. 3.

78. Ibid. p. 4.

79. Adorno, *The Culture Industry*, p. 202.

80. Kerr, 'The Track Record: CIA Analysis from 1950 to 2000', p. 37.

81. Treverton, *Intelligence for an Age of Terror*, p. 141.

82. Zegart, *Spying Blind: The CIA, The FBI, and the Origins of 9/11*, p. 63.

83. Treverton, *Intelligence for an Age of Terror*, p. 147.
84. Adorno, *The Culture Industry*, p. 202.
85. Jervis, *Why Intelligence Fails: Lessons from the Iranian Revolution and the Iraq War*, p. 194.
86. Laqueur, *The Uses and Limits of Intelligence*, p. 257.
87. Ibid. p. 259.
88. Davis, 'Why Bad Things Happens to Good Analysts', p. 161.
89. Adorno, *The Culture Industry*, p. 203.
90. Dixon, *On the Psychology of Military Incompetence*, p. 166.
91. The Joint Inquiry, Abridged Findings and Conclusions, Systemic Findings, Finding 19, p. xix.
92. The 9/11 Commission Report, p. 184.
93. Ibid.
94. Johnson, 'Sketches for a Theory of Strategic Intelligence', p. 40.
95. The Joint Inquiry, Abridged Findings and Conclusions, Systemic Findings, Finding 3, p. xvi.
96. Wohlstetter, *Pearl Harbor: Warning and Decision*, p. 393.
97. Hollister Hedley, 'Analysis for Strategic Intelligence', p. 221.
98. The 9/11 Commission Report, p. 186.
99. Ibid.
100. Ibid.
101. Ibid. p. 204.
102. Ibid. p. 255.
103. Ibid.
104. Ibid. p. 256.
105. Ibid. p. 257.
106. Wohlstetter, *Pearl Harbor: Warning and Decision*, p. 387.
107. Hollister Hedeley, 'Analysis for Strategic Intelligence', p. 215.
108. Ibid. p. 212.
109. Ibid.
110. Petersen, 'The Challenge for the Political Analyst', p. 304.
111. Omand, *Securing the State*, p. 150.
112. Ibid. p. 153.
113. Zegart, *Spying Blind*, p. 121.
114. Posner, *Preventing Surprise Attacks: Intelligence Reform in the Wake of 9/11*, p. 25.
115. Ibid.
116. Hollister Hedley, 'Analysis for Strategic Intelligence', p. 213.
117. Popper, *Conjectures and Refutations: The Growth of Scientific Knowledge*, p. 38.

118. Davis, 'Defining the Analytic Mission: Facts, Findings, Forecasts, and Fortunetelling', p. 299.
119. Hollister Hedley, 'Analysis for Strategic Intelligence', p. 215.
120. Davis, 'Defining the Analytic Mission: Facts, Findings, Forecasts, and Fortunetelling', p. 299.
121. George, 'Fixing the Problem of Analytical Mindsets: Alternative Analysis', p. 312.
122. Jackson, 'On Uncertainty and the Limits of Intelligence', p. 454.
123. George, 'Fixing the Problem of Analytical Mindsets: Alternative Analysis', p. 312.
124. Jackson, 'On Uncertainty and the Limits of Intelligence', p. 457.
125. Kent, 'A Crucial Estimate Relived', p. 6. Quoted in George, 'Fixing the Problem of Analytical Mindsets: Alternative Analysis', p. 313.
126. Aasberg, lecture to the Professional Advanced Intelligence course, Norwegian Defence University College, Oslo (16 September 2008). Aasberg is former Director of Division in the Norwegian Intelligence Service and holds that the intelligence cycle must be understood as function and not organisation.
127. Omand, *Securing the State*, p. 119.
128. Ibid.
129. Hollister Hedley, 'Analysis for strategic intelligence', p. 213.
130. Omand, *Securing the State*, p. 131.
131. Ibid. p. 149.
132. The 9/11 Commission Report, p. 260.
133. Ibid. p. 342.
134. Hollister Hedley, 'Analysis for Strategic Intelligence', p. 213.
135. Omand, *Securing the State*, p. 149.
136. The 9/11 Commission Report, p. 342.
137. Davis, 'Strategic Warning: Intelligence Support in a World of Uncertainty and Surprise', p. 180.
138. The 9/11 Commission Report, p. 341.
139. Ibid.
140. Ibid. p. 353.
141. The Joint Inquiry, Abridged Findings and Conclusions, Systemic Findings, Finding 5, p. xvi.
142. Ibid. Finding 9, p. xvii.
143. Byman, 'Strategic Surprise and the September 11 Attacks', p. 165.
144. Clarke, *Your Government Failed You: Breaking The Cycle of National Security Disasters*, p. 131.
145. Ibid.

146. May, *The 9/11 Commission Report*, p. 152.
147. George, 'Fixing the Problem of Analytical Mindsets: Alternative Analysis', p. 315.
148. Heuer, *Psychology of Intelligence Analysis*, p. 5. Quoted in George, 'Fixing the Problem of Analytical Mindsets: Alternative Analysis', p. 315.
149. The 9/11 Commission Report, p. 359.
150. Ibid. p. xvi.
151. Handel, 'Intelligence and the Problem of Strategic Surprise', p. 1. See also Davis, 'Strategic Warning: Intelligence Support in a World of Uncertainty and Surprise', p. 176, and Hollister Hedley, 'Analysis for Strategic Intelligence', p. 223.
152. Betts, 'Analysis, War, and Decision: Why Intelligence Failures are Inevitable', p. 133.

Chapter 6

1. Herman, *Intelligence Power in Peace and War*, p. 45.
2. Kennedy, *Of Knowledge and Power: The Complexities of National Intelligence*, p. 111.
3. Friedman, 'The Crisis in the CIA', p. 2.
4. Laqueur, *The Uses and Limits of Intelligence*, p. 71.
5. Herman, *Intelligence Power in Peace and War*, p. 44.
6. Kennedy, *Of Knowledge and Power: The Complexities of National Intelligence*, p. 111.
7. Lowenthal, 'The Policymaker-Intelligence Relationship', p. 437.
8. The Joint Inquiry, Abridged Findings and Conclusions, Systemic Findings, Finding 10, p. xvii.
9. Strasser, *The 9/11 Investigations*, p. 501.
10. Gill and Phythian, *Intelligence in an Insecure World*, p. 91.
11. Kennedy, *Of Knowledge and Power: The Complexities of National Intelligence*, p. 119.
12. Ibid. p. 111.
13. The Joint Inquiry, Findings and Conclusions, Recommendations, p. 6.
14. The 9/11 Commission Report, p. 417.
15. McLaughlin, 'Serving the National Policymaker', p. 75.
16. Steinberg, 'The Policymaker's Perspective: Transparency and Partnership', p. 84.
17. Pillar, 'The Perils of Politicization', p. 483.

18. Ibid.
19. Kennedy, *Of Knowledge and Power: The Complexities of National Intelligence*, p. 126.
20. The 9/11 Commission Report, p. 417.
21. The National Intelligence Strategy of the United States of America (October 2005), *Transformation through Integration and Innovation*, Strategy Guidance, Mission Objectives, p. 6.
22. Omand, 'Reflections on Secret Intelligence', p. 120. Omand has borrowed the phrase from Senator Pat Roberts, former Chair of the US Senate Intelligence Committee.
23. Johnson and Wirtz, *Intelligence and National Security: The Secret World of Spies*, p. 189.
24. Strasser, *The 9/11 Investigations*, p. 181.
25. The Joint Inquiry, p. 359.
26. Ibid. p. 364.
27. Ibid.
28. The Joint Inquiry, p. 236.
29. Ibid.
30. Ibid. p. 362.
31. Ibid. Abridged Findings and Conclusions, Systemic Findings, Finding 9, p. xvii.
32. Clarke, *Your Government Failed You: Breaking The Cycle of National Security Disasters*, p. 136.
33. Sun Tzu, *The Art of War*, p. 204.
34. Gill and Phythian, *Intelligence in an Insecure World*, p. 92.
35. Aspin-Brown Commission, 'The Need for Policy Guidance', p. 255.
36. Herman, 'Intelligence and National Action', p. 239.
37. Truman, *Year of Decision*, p. 226. Quoted in Laqueur, *The Uses and Limits of Intelligence*, p. 72.
38. Laqueur, *The Uses and Limits of Intelligence*, p. 72.
39. Ibid.
40. Ibid.
41. Ibid. p. 75.
42. Ransom, 'The Politicization of Intelligence', p. 193.
43. Laqueur, *The Uses and Limits of Intelligence*, p. 108.
44. Ibid.
45. Herman, 'Intelligence and National Action', p. 239.
46. Hollister Hedley, 'Analysis for Strategic Intelligence', p. 216.
47. The Joint Inquiry, Abridged Findings and Conclusions, Systemic Findings, Finding 10, p. xvii.
48. Strasser, *The 9/11 Investigations*, p. 236.

49. Ibid.
50. Ibid.
51. Ibid. p. 474.
52. The 9/11 Commission Report, p. 348.
53. Ibid.
54. Strasser, *The 9/11 Investigations*, p. 274.
55. Ibid. pp. 163–64.
56. Ibid. p. 153.
57. Ibid. p. 154.
58. Lowenthal, 'The Policymaker–Intelligence Relationship', p. 441.
59. Herman, *Intelligence Power in Peace and War*, p. 45.
60. McLaughlin, 'Serving the National Policymaker', p. 75.
61. The 9/11 Commission Report, p. 193. Quoted in Gill and Phythian, *Intelligence in an Insecure World*, p. 93.
62. O'Hear, 'The Open Society Revisited', p. 189.
63. Kennedy, *Of Knowledge and Power: The Complexities of National Intelligence*, p. 124.
64. Ibid. p. 126.
65. The National Intelligence Strategy of the United States of America (October 2005), *Transformation through Integration and Innovation*, p. 3.
66. Turner, *Why Secret Intelligence Fails*, p. 124.

Chapter 7

1. Kennedy, *Of Knowledge and Power: The Complexities of National Intelligence*, p. 111.
2. Ibid. p. 129.
3. The Butler Report, *Review of Intelligence on Weapons of Mass Destruction*, p. 15.
4. Ibid. p. 14.
5. Kennedy, *Of Knowledge and Power: The Complexities of National Intelligence*, p. 135.
6. Neumann and Smith, 'Missing the Plot? Intelligence and Discourse Failure', p. 96.
7. Treverton, *Reshaping National Intelligence for an Age of Information*, p. 208.
8. Strasser, *The 9/11 Investigations*, p. 125.
9. Ibid. p. 127.

10. Ibid. p. 125.
11. Ibid. p. 124.
12. The 9/11 Commission Report, p. 11.
13. Strasser, *The 9/11 Investigations*, p. 125.
14. The 9/11 Commission Report, p. 16.
15. Ibid. p. 17.
16. Treverton, *Reshaping National Intelligence for an Age of Information*, p. 210.
17. Bourke, *An Intimate History of Killing: Face-To-Face Killing in Twentieth-Century Warfare*, p. 369.
18. Sofsky, *Violence, Terrorism, Genocide, War*, p. 181.
19. Kruglanski, *Lay Epistemics and Human Knowledge: Cognitive and Motivational Bases*, p. 16.
20. Neumann and Smith, 'Missing the Plot? Intelligence and Discourse Failure', p. 96.
21. The 9/11 Commission Report, p. 341.
22. Neumann and Smith, 'Missing the Plot? Intelligence and Discourse Failure', p. 95.
23. The 9/11 Commission Report, p. 343.
24. Kruglanski, *Lay Epistemics and Human Knowledge: Cognitive and Motivational Bases*, p. 14.
25. Jervis, *Why Intelligence Fails: Lessons from the Iranian Revolution and the Iraq War*, p. 177.
26. Kruglanski, *Lay Epistemics and Human Knowledge: Cognitive and Motivational Bases*, p. 14.
27. Marcuse, *One-Dimensional Man*, p. 251.
28. Fromm, *Man for Himself*, p. 29.
29. Ibid.
30. Eliade, *The Sacred and the Profane: The Nature of Religion*, p. 12.
31. Borchgrevink, 'What kind of ideas kill?'. Aage Borchrevink, a Norwegian author and columnist argued in the Norwegian newspaper *Aftenposten* on 4 August 2011 that Occidentalism may explain the real danger from terrorism today, since Occidentalism highlights that it is the hatred against Western values such as liberalism, individualism, capitalism and secularism that is al Qaeda's and the Oslo bomber's real motivation. The term Occidentalism used by Borchrevink originates from Ian Buruma's and Avishai Margalit's book: *Occidentalism: The West in the Eyes of its Enemies* (2004).
32. Buruma and Margalit, 'Occidentalism', *The New York Review of Books*, 17 January 2002.
33. Eliade, *The Sacred and the Profane: The Nature of Religion*, p. 13.

34. Treverton, *Reshaping National Intelligence for an Age of Information*, p. 209.
35. The 9/11 Commission Report, p. 343.
36. May, *The 9/11 Commission Report*, p. 76.
37. Ibid. p. 75.
38. The Joint Inquiry, p. 230.
39. The 9/11 Commission Report, National Policy Coordination, Staff Statement No. 8, p. 2.
40. Ibid. p. 3. See also May, *The 9/11 Commission Report*, p. 75.
41. Ibid.
42. Ibid.
43. The Joint Inquiry, p. 241.
44. Ibid. p. 234.
45. Ibid. p. 235.
46. The 9/11 Commission Report, National Policy Coordination, Staff Statement No. 8, p. 3.
47. Ibid.
48. The Joint Inquiry, p. 235.
49. The 9/11 Commission Report, National Policy Coordination, Staff Statement No. 8, p. 8.
50. Ibid.
51. Clarke, *Against All Enemies: Inside America's War on Terror*, pp. 2 and 3.
52. The 9/11 Commission Report, National Policy Coordination, Staff Statement No. 8, p. 9.
53. Ibid.
54. Ibid.
55. Ibid.
56. The Joint Inquiry, p. 235.
57. The 9/11 Commission Report, National Policy Coordination, Staff Statement No. 8, p. 9.
58. Ibid. p. 10.
59. The Joint Inquiry, p. 235.
60. The 9/11 Commission Report, National Policy Coordination, Staff Statement No. 8, p. 10.
61. Ibid.
62. Ibid. p. 11.
63. Ibid.
64. Ibid.
65. Ibid.
66. Ibid. p. 9.

67. Ibid. p. 10.
68. Ibid. p. 12.
69. Clarke, *Against All Enemies: Inside America's War on Terror*, pp. 231–2.
70. The 9/11 Commission Report, National Policy Coordination, Staff Statement No. 8, p. 9.
71. Ibid. p. 11.
72. Neumann and Smith, 'Missing the Plot? Intelligence and Discourse Failure', p. 104. See Clarke, *Against All Enemies: Inside America's War on Terror*, p. 226.
73. The Joint Inquiry, p. 298. See also p. 231.
74. Jones, *Reflections on Intelligence*, p. 149. See also Jones, 'Intelligence and Command', p. 291.
75. Neumann and Smith, 'Missing the Plot? Intelligence and Discourse Failure', p. 105.
76. Treverton, *Reshaping National Intelligence for an Age of Information*, p. 209.
77. Jervis, *Why Intelligence Fails: Lessons from the Iranian Revolution and the Iraq War*, p. 175.
78. Kennedy, *Of Knowledge and Power: The Complexities of National Intelligence*, p. 135.
79. Herman, *Intelligence Power in Peace and War*, p. 92.
80. May, *The 9/11 Commission Report*, p. 2.
81. Neumann and Smith, 'Missing the Plot? Intelligence and Discourse Failure', p. 104.
82. The Joint Inquiry, p. 232.
83. Treverton, *Reshaping National Intelligence for an Age of Information*, p. 192.
84. Strasser, *The 9/11 Investigations*, p. 457.
85. Ibid. p. 402.
86. The Joint Inquiry, p. 236.

Conclusion

1. Bohm, *On Creativity*, p. 74.
2. Walsh, *Confidential: The International Politics of Intelligence Sharing*, p. 139.
3. Bohm, *On Creativity*, p. 4.
4. Mehren, *The Myth and the Irrational Reason*, p. 15.

5. Discussion with Bar-Joseph in Oslo, October 2008.
6. The argument has been developed together with Knut Aasberg, former Director of Division in the Norwegian Intelligence Service, 28 April 2010.
7. Baudrillard, *In the Shadow of the Silent Majorities*, p. 11.
8. Münkler, 'What is Really New about The New Wars? A Reply to the Critics', p. 82.
9. Ibid.
10. Baudrillard, *In the Shadow of the Silent Majorities*, p. 11.
11. Ibid. p. 13.

Bibliography

Adorno, Theodor W., *The Culture Industry* (London and New York: Routledge Classics, [1991] 2008).

Agrell, Wilhelm, 'Intelligence Analysis after the Cold War – New Paradigm or Old Anomalies', in Gregory F. Treverton and Wilhelm Agrell (eds), *National Intelligence Systems: Current Research and Future Prospects* (Cambridge: Cambridge University Press, 2009), pp. 93–114.

Agrell, Wilhelm, and Gregory F. Treverton, 'The Science of Intelligence: Reflections on a Field That Never Was', in Gregory F. Treverton and Wilhelm Agrell (eds), *National Intelligence Systems: Current Research and Future Prospects* (Cambridge: Cambridge University Press, 2009), pp. 265–80.

Aid, Matthew, 'All Glory is Fleeting: SIGINT and the fight against international terrorism', in Christopher Andrew, Richard J. Aldrich and Wesley K. Wark (eds), *Secret Intelligence: A Reader* (London and New York: Routledge, Taylor & Francis Group, 2009), pp. 40–77.

Aid, Matthew M., 'The Time of Troubles: The US National Security Agency in the Twenty-First Century', in Loch K. Johnson and James J. Wirtz (eds), *Intelligence and National Security: The Secret World of Spies* (New York and Oxford: Oxford University Press, 2008), pp. 88–105.

Anjum, Rani Lill, *Our Conditional World: A Critique of the Formal Logical Approach*, PhD thesis (Tromsø: University of Tromsø, 2005), <https://sites.google.com/site/ranilillanjum/home/research/our-conditional-world> (last accessed 20 January 2019).

Aspin-Brown Commission, 'The Need for Policy Guidance', in Loch K. Johnson and James J. Wirtz (eds), *Intelligence and National Security: The Secret World of Spies* (New York and Oxford: Oxford University Press, 2008), pp. 255–9.

Bar-Joseph, Uri, 'Intelligence Failure and the Need for Cognitive Closure: The Case of Yom Kippur', in Richard K. Betts and Thomas G.

Mahnken (eds), *Paradoxes of Strategic Intelligence: Essays in Honor of Michael I. Handel* (London and Portland, OR: Frank Cass, 2003), pp. 166–89.

Bar-Joseph, Uri, and Rose McDermott, 'The Intelligence Analysis Crisis', in Loch K. Johnson (ed.), *The Oxford Handbook of National Security Intelligence* (Oxford: Oxford University Press, 2010), pp. 359–74.

Baron, Jonathan, *Thinking and Deciding* (Cambridge: Cambridge University Press, [1998] 2004).

Baudrillard, Jean, *In the Shadow of the Silent Majorities* (*I skyggen av de tause majoriteter*) (Oslo: J.W. Cappelens Forlag AS, 2005).

Betts, Richard K., 'Politization of Intelligence: Costs and Benefits', in Richard K. Betts and Thomas G. Mahnken (eds), *Paradoxes of Strategic Intelligence: Essays in Honor of Michael I. Handel* (London and Portland, OR: Frank Cass, 2003), pp. 59–79.

Betts, Richard K., *Enemies of Intelligence: Knowledge and Power in American National Security* (New York: Colombia University Press, 2007).

Betts, Richard K., 'Analysis, War, and Decision: Why Intelligence Failures are Inevitable', in Loch K. Johnson and James J. Wirtz (eds), *Intelligence and National Security: The Secret World of Spies* (New York and Oxford: Oxford University Press, 2008), pp. 122–36.

Blackburn, Simon, *The Oxford Dictionary of Philosophy* (Oxford and New York: Oxford University Press, 1996).

Bohm, David, *On Creativity*, ed. Lee Nichol (London and New York: Routledge Classics, [1996] 2005).

Bohm, David, *On Dialogue*, ed. Lee Nichol (London and New York: Routledge Classics, [1996] 2006).

Bohm, David, *Wholeness and the Implicate Order* (London and New York: Routledge Classics, 2007).

Borchgrevink, Aage, 'What Kind of Ideas Kill?', *Aftenposten (Norwegian Evening Post)*, 4 August 2011.

Bourke, Joanna, *An Intimate History of Killing: Face-To-Face Killing in Twentieth-Century Warfare* (London: Granta Books, 2000).

Brady, Christopher, 'Intelligence Failures: *Plus ça change ...*', *Intelligence and National Security* vol. 4, no. 8 (October 1993): 86–96.

Branch 3+5+6+Israeli Air Force (IAF) Intelligence Division + Israeli Navy (IN) Intelligence Division, Imediate Military Intelligence Review, 'Alert Status and Activity in Syria and Egypt as of 051000 Oct.7', para. 40 (private collection).

Braun, Arie, *Moshe Dayan and the Yom Kippur War* (Tel Aviv: Edanim, 1992).

300

Bruce, James B., 'Denial and Deception in the 21st Century: Adaptation Implications for Western Intelligence', *Defense Intelligence Journal* vol. 15, no. 2 (2006): 13–28.

Bruce, James B., and Michael Bennet, 'Foreign Denial and Deception: Analytical Imperatives', in Roger Z. George and James B. Bruce (eds), *Analyzing Intelligence: Origins, Obstacles, and Innovations* (Washington, DC: Georgetown University Press, 2008), pp. 122–39.

Buruma, Ian, and Avishai Margalit, 'Occidentalism', *The New York Review of Books*, [2002] 17 January 2011, <https://www.nybooks.com/articles/2002/01/17/occidentalism/> (last accessed 20 January 2019).

Byman, Daniel, 'Strategic Surprise and the September 11 Attacks', in Christopher Andrew, Richard J. Aldrich and Wesley K. Wark (eds), *Secret Intelligence: A Reader* (London and New York: Routledge, Taylor & Francis Group, 2009), pp. 164–85.

Cilluffo, Frank J., Ronald A. Marks and George C. Salmoiraghi, 'The Use and Limits of US Intelligence', *The Washington Quarterly* vol. 25, issue 1 (2002): pp. 61–74.

Clarke, Richard A., *Against All Enemies: Inside America's War on Terror* (London: Simon & Schuster Ltd, 2004).

Clarke, Richard A., *Your Government Failed You: Breaking the Cycle of National Security Disasters* (New York: Harper Collins Publishers, 2008).

Clausewitz, Carl, *On War*, ed. and trans. Michael Howard and Peter Paret (Princeton: Princeton University Press, 1989).

Cogan, Charles G., 'The In-Culture of the DO', in Roger Z. George and Robert D. Kline (eds), *Intelligence and the National Security Strategist: Enduring Issues and Challenges* (Lanham, Boulder, New York, Toronto and Oxford: Rowman & Littlefield Publishers, Inc., 2006), pp. 209–16.

Coker, Christopher, 'The Future of War: What are the New Complexities?', in John Andreas Olsen (ed.), *On New Wars* (Oslo: Norwegian Institute for Defence Studies, 2007), pp. 83–103.

Cradock, Percy, *In Pursuit of British Interests: Reflections on Foreign Policy under Margaret Thatcher and John Major* (London: John Murray, 1997).

Cradock, Percy, *Know Your Enemy: How the Joint Intelligence Committee Saw the World* (London: John Murray, 2002).

Davies, Philip H. J., 'Theory and Intelligence Reconsidered', in Peter Gill, Stephen Marrin and Mark Phytian (eds), *Intelligence Theory: Key questions and Debates*, Studies in Intelligence Series (London and New York: Routledge, Taylor & Francis Group, 2009), pp. 208–26.

Davies, Philip H. J., 'Intelligence, Complexity, the Media and Public Understanding', in Patrick Major and Christopher R. Moran (eds), *Spooked: Britain, Empire and Intelligence since 1945* (Newcastle: Cambridge Scholars Publishing, 2009), pp. 51–71.

Davis, Jack, 'Defining the Analytic Mission: Facts, Findings, Forecasts, and Fortunetelling', in Roger Z. George and Robert D. Kline (eds), *Intelligence and the National Security Strategist: Enduring Issues and Challenges* (Lanham, Boulder, New York, Toronto and Oxford: Rowman & Littlefield Publishers, Inc., 2006), pp. 295–301.

Davis, Jack, 'Why Bad Things Happens to Good Analysts', in Roger Z. George and James B. Bruce (eds), *Analyzing Intelligence: Origins, Obstacles, and Innovations* (Washington, DC: Georgetown University Press, 2008), pp. 157–70.

Davis, Jack, 'Strategic Warning: Intelligence Support in a World of Uncertainty and Surprise', in Loch K. Johnson (ed.), *Handbook of Intelligence Studies* (London and New York: Routledge, Taylor and Francis Group, 2009), pp. 173–88.

Dixon, Norman, *On the Psychology of Military Incompetence* (London: Pimlico, [1976] 1994).

Eliade, Mircea, *The Sacred and the Profane: The Nature of Religion*, trans. Willard R. Trask (San Diego, New York and London: A Harvest Book, Harcourt, Inc. [1957] 1987).

Evans, Jonathan St. B.T., David E. Over and Simon J. Handley, 'A Theory of Hypothetical Thinking', in David Hardman and Laura Macchi (eds), *Thinking: Psychological Perspectives on Reasoning, Judgment and Decision Making* (Chichester: John Wiley & Sons, Ltd., 2005), pp. 3–21.

Feyerabend, Paul, *Against Method* (London and New York: Verso, [1975] 2002).

Friedman, George, 'The Problem with the CIA', Stratfor, 13 July 2004, pp. 1–4.

Friedman, George, 'The Crisis in the CIA', *Strategic Forecasting*, Stratfor, 18 November 2004, pp. 1–4.

Fromm, Eric, *The Fear of Freedom* (London and New York: Routledge Classics, [1942] 2006).

Fromm, Eric, *Man for Himself* (London and New York: Routledge Classics, [1947] 2006).

Fulghum, David A., 'Computer Combat Rules Frustrate the Pentagon', *Aviation Week & Space Technology*, 15 September 1997: 67–8.

Gadamer, Hans-Georg, *Truth and Method*, revised edition, trans. revised by Joel Weinsheimer and Donald G. Marshall (London and New York: Continuum [1975] 2006).

Gardiner, K. L., 'Squaring the Circle: Dealing with Intelligence-Policy Breakdowns', in Christopher Andrew, Richard J. Aldrich and Wesley K. Wark (eds), *Secret Intelligence: A Reader* (London and New York: Routledge, Taylor & Francis Group, 2009), pp. 129–39.

George, Roger Z., 'Fixing the Problem of Analytical Mindsets: Alternative Analysis', in Roger Z. George and Robert D. Kline (eds), *Intelligence and the National Security Strategist: Enduring Issues and Challenges* (Lanham, Boulder, New York, Toronto and Oxford: Rowman & Littlefield Publishers, Inc., 2006), pp. 311–26.

George, Roger Z., and Robert D. Kline (eds), *Intelligence and the National Security Strategist: Enduring Issues and Challenges* (Lanham, Boulder, New York, Toronto and Oxford: Rowman & Littlefield Publishers, Inc., 2006).

Gerber, Burton, 'Managing HUMINT: The Need for a New Approach', in Jennifer E. Sims and Burton Gerber (eds), *Transforming US Intelligence*, in cooperation with the Center for Peace and Security Studies, Edmund A. Walsh School of Foreign Service, Georgetown University (Washington, DC: Georgetown University Press, 2005), pp. 180–97.

Gill, Peter, 'Theories of Intelligence: Where Are We, Where Should We Go and How Might We Proceed?', in Peter Gill, Stephen Marrin and Mark Phytian (eds), *Intelligence Theory: Key Questions and Debates* (London and New York: Routledge, Taylor & Francis Group, 2009), pp. 208–26.

Gill, Peter, and Mark Phythian, *Intelligence in an Insecure World* (Cambridge: Polity Press, 2006).

Goodman, Nelson, *Fact, Fiction, and Forecast* (Cambridge, MA: Harvard University Press, 1955).

Handel, Michael I., 'Intelligence and the Problem of Strategic Surprise', in Richard K. Betts and Thomas G. Mahnken (eds), *Paradoxes of Strategic Intelligence: Essays in Honor of Michael I. Handel* (London and Portland, OR: Frank Cass, 2003), pp. 1–58.

Handel, Michael I., 'Intelligence and Deception', in Roger Z. George and Robert D. Kline (eds), *Intelligence and the National Security Strategist: Enduring Issues and Challenges* (Oxford: Rowman & Littlefield Publishers, Inc., 2006), pp. 359–87.

Hatlebrekke, Kjetil A., *Towards a Theory on Intelligence: The Art of Knowing Beyond the Limits of Formal Logic, Why Intelligence is Art and its Impact on the Problem of Induction and Discourse Failure* (London: King's College London, 2011).

Hatlebrekke, Kjetil A., and M. L. R. Smith, 'Towards a New Theory of Intelligence Failure? The Impact of Cognitive Closure and Discourse

Failure', *Intelligence and National Security* vol. 25, no. 2 (April 2010): 147–82.

Hennessy, Peter, *The Prime Minister: The Office and Its Holders Since 1945* (London: Penguin Books, 2001).

Herman, Michael, *Intelligence Services in the Information Age* (London and Portland, OR: Frank Cass, [2001] 2002).

Herman, Michael, *Intelligence Power in Peace and War* (Cambridge: Cambridge University Press and The Royal Institute of International Affairs, [1996] 2003).

Herman, Michael, 'Intelligence and National Action', in Loch K. Johnson and James J. Wirtz (eds), *Intelligence and National Security: The Secret World of Spies* (New York and Oxford: Oxford University Press, 2008), pp. 237–46.

Heuer, Richards J., Jr., *Psychology of Intelligence Analysis* (Central Intelligence Agency: Center for the Study of Intelligence, 1999).

Heuer, Richards J., Jr., 'Limits of Intelligence Analysis', *Orbis* (Winter 2005): 75–94.

Hitz, Frederick P., 'Human Source Intelligence', in Loch K. Johnson (ed.), *Handbook of Intelligence Studies* (London and New York: Routledge, Taylor & Francis Group, 2009), pp. 118–28.

Hollister Hedley, John, 'Analysis for Strategic Intelligence', in Loch K. Johnson (ed.), *Handbook of Intelligence* (London and New York: Routledge, Taylor & Francis Group, 2009), pp. 211–26.

House of Commons – Foreign Affairs – Ninth Report, article 155, <http://www.publications.parliament.uk/pa/cm200203/cmselect/cmfaff/813/81309.htm> (last accessed 20 January 2019).

House of Commons Hansard Debates, 22 June 2000, Part 30, Column 543, <https://publications.parliament.uk/pa/cm199900/cmhansrd/vo000622/debtext/00622-30.htm> (last accessed 20 January 2019).

Jackson, Peter, 'On Uncertainty and the Limits of Intelligence', in Loch K. Johnson (ed.), *The Oxford Handbook of National Security Intelligence* (Oxford: Oxford University Press, 2010), pp. 452–71.

Jervis, Robert, *Why Intelligence Fails: Lessons from the Iranian Revolution and the Iraq War* (Ithaca, NY and London: Cornell University Press, 2010).

Johnson, Loch K., 'Preface to a Theory of Strategic Intelligence', *International Journal of Intelligence and Counterintelligence* vol. 16, no. 4 (October–December 2003): 638–63.

Johnson, Loch K., 'Sketches for a Theory of Strategic Intelligence', in Peter Gill, Stephen Marrin and Mark Phytian (eds), *Intelligence Theory: Key Questions and Debates*, Studies in Intelligence Series

(London and New York: Routledge, Taylor & Francis Group, 2009), pp. 33–53.

Johnson, Loch K., and James J. Wirtz (eds), *Intelligence and National Security: The Secret World of Spies* (New York and Oxford: Oxford University Press, 2008).

Joint Warfare Publication, *British Joint Operational Intelligence*, 2–00, Annex 1A, 2000.

Jones, David Martin, and Michael L. R. Smith, 'Is There a Sovietology of South-East Asian Studies?' *International Affairs* vol. 77, no. 4 (2001): 843–66.

Jones, Garret, 'It's a Cultural Thing: Thoughts on a Troubled CIA', in Christopher Andrew, Richard J. Aldrich and Wesley K. Wark (eds), *Secret Intelligence: A Reader* (London and New York: Routledge, Taylor & Francis Group, 2009), pp. 26–39.

Jones, R. V., 'Intelligence and Command', in Michael I. Handel (ed.), *Leaders and Intelligence* (Abingdon, Milton Park: Frank Cass & Co., 1989), pp. 288–98.

Jones, R. V., *Reflections on Intelligence* (London: Heinemann, 1989).

Kahana, Ephraim, 'Early Warning versus Concept: The Case of the Yom Kippur War 1973', in Loch K. Johnson and James J. Wirtz (eds), *Intelligence and National Security: The Secret World of Spies* (New York and Oxford: Oxford University Press, 2008), pp. 176–88.

Kahn, David, 'An Historical Theory of Intelligence', in Peter Gill, Stephen Marrin and Mark Phytian (eds), *Intelligence Theory: Key Questions and Debates* (London and New York: Routledge, Taylor & Francis Group, 2009), pp. 4–15.

Kennedy, Robert, *Of Knowledge and Power: The Complexities of National Intelligence* (Westport, CT and London: Praeger Security International, 2008).

Kent, Sherman, *Strategic Intelligence for American World Policy* (Princeton: Princeton University Press, 1951).

Kent, Sherman, 'A Crucial Estimate Relived', *Studies in Intelligence* 8, no. 2 (Spring 1964): 1–18.

Kerr, Richard J., 'The Track Record: CIA Analysis from 1950 to 2000', in Roger Z. George and James B. Bruce (eds), *Analyzing Intelligence: Origins, Obstacles, and Innovations*, in cooperation with the Center for Peace and Security Studies, Edmund A. Walsh School of Foreign Service, Georgetown University (Washington, DC: Georgetown University Press, 2008), pp. 35–54.

Kim, Jaegwon, 'Events as Property Exemplifications', in Myles Brand and Douglas Walton (eds), *Action Theory*, Proceedings of the Winnipeg

Conference on Human Action, held at Winnipeg, Manitoba, Canada, 9–11 May 1975 (Dordrecht: Springer, D. Reidel Publishing Company, 1975), pp. 159–77.

Kruglanski, Arie W., *Lay Epistemics and Human Knowledge: Cognitive and Motivational Bases* (New York and London: Plenum Press, 1989).

Kuhns, Woodrow J., 'Intelligence Failures: Forecasting and the Lessons of Epistemology', in Richard K. Betts and Thomas G. Mahnken (eds), *Paradoxes of Strategic Intelligence: Essays in Honor of Michael I. Handel* (London and Portland, OR: Frank Cass, 2003), pp. 80–100.

Laqueur, Walter, *The Uses and Limits of Intelligence* (New Brunswick and London: Transaction Publishers, [1985] 1995).

Lowenthal, Mark M., *Intelligence: From Secrets to Policy* (Washington, DC: CQ Press, a division of Congressional Quarterly Inc., 2006).

Lowenthal, Mark M., 'The Policymaker–Intelligence Relationship', in Loch K. Johnson (ed.), *The Oxford Handbook of National Security Intelligence* (Oxford: Oxford University Press, 2010), pp. 437–51.

MacGaffin, John, 'Clandestine Human Intelligence: Spies, Counterspies, and Covert Action', in Jennifer E. Sims and Burton Gerber (eds), *Transforming US Intelligence*, in cooperation with the Center for Peace and Security Studies, Edmund A. Walsh School of Foreign Service, Georgetown University (Washington, DC: Georgetown University Press, 2005), pp. 79–95.

McLaughlin, John, 'Serving the National Policymaker', in Roger Z. George and James B. Bruce (eds), *Analyzing Intelligence: Origins, Obstacles, and Innovations* (Washington, DC: Georgetown University Press, 2008), pp. 71–81.

McLean, Iain, and Alistair McMillan, *Concise Dictionary of Politics* (Oxford: Oxford University Press, [1996] 2009).

Marcuse, Herbert, *One-Dimensional Man* (London and New York: Routledge Classics, 2006).

Marrin, Stephen, 'Adding Value to the Intelligence Product', in Loch K. Lohnson (ed.), *Handbook of Intelligence Studies* (London and New York: Routledge, Taylor & Francis Group, 2009), pp. 199–210.

May, Ernest R., *The 9/11 Commission Report*, with related documents, abridged and with an introduction by Ernest R. May (Boston and New York: Bedford/St. Martin's, 2007).

Mehren, Stein, *The Myth and the Irrational Reason* (*Myten og den irrasjonelle fornuft*), Part One: Ideology and the Perception of the Human Persona [1977]; Part Two: The Living Universe and the Crisis of Rationalism [1980] (Oslo: Aschehoug, 2005).

Midgley, Mary, *Beast and Man: The Roots of Human Nature* (London and New York: Routledge Classics, [1979] 2002).

Midgley, Mary, *Heart and Mind* (London: Routledge, [1981] 2003).

Moynihan, Daniel Patrick, *Secrecy* (New Haven and London: Yale University Press, 1998).

Munkler, Herfried, 'What Is Really New about the New Wars? A Reply to the Critics', in John Andreas Olsen (ed.), *On New Wars* (Oslo: Norwegian Institute for Defence Studies, 2007), pp. 67–82.

Musgrave, Alan, 'How Popper (Might Have) Solved the Problem of Induction', in Philip Catton and Graham MacDonald (eds), *Karl Popper: Critical Appraisals* (London and New York: Routledge, Taylor & Francis Group, 2004), pp. 16–27.

Næss, Arne, *History of Philosophy (Filosofiens Historie)* (Oslo: Universitetsforlaget, [1953] 2001).

Neumann, Peter R., and M. L. R. Smith, 'Missing the Plot? Intelligence and Discourse failure', *Orbis* (Winter 2005), pp. 95–107.

O'Hear, Anthony, 'The Open Society Revisited', in Philip Catton and Graham MacDonald (eds), *Karl Popper: Critical Appraisals* (London and New York: Routledge, Taylor & Francis Group, 2004), pp. 189–202.

Oakeshott, Michael, 'On Being Conservative', in Michael Oakeshott (ed.), *Rationalism in Politics and Other Essays* (Indianapolis: Liberty Fund, [1962] 1991), pp. 407–37.

Oakeshott, Michael, 'Rationalism in Politics', in Michael Oakeshott (ed.), *Rationalism in Politics and Other Essays* (Indianapolis: Liberty Fund, [1962] 1991), pp. 5–42.

Oakeshott, Michael, *Rationalism in Politics and Other Essays*, with a foreword by Timothy Fuller (Indianapolis: Liberty Fund, [1962] 1991).

Oakeshott, Michael, *The Voice of Liberal Learning*, with a foreword by Timothy Fuller (Indianapolis: Liberty Fund, [1989] 2001).

Omand, David, 'Reflections on Secret Intelligence', in Peter Hennesy (ed.), *The New Protective State: Government, Intelligence and Terrorism* (New York: Continuum, 2007), pp. 97–122.

Omand, David, 'The Limits of Avowal: Secret Intelligence in an Age of Public Scrutiny', in Gregory F. Treverton and Wilhelm Agrell (eds), *National Intelligence Systems: Current Research and Future Prospects* (Cambridge: Cambridge University Press, 2009), pp. 235–64.

Omand, David, *Securing the State* (London: Hurst & Company, 2010).

Petersen, Martin, 'What We Should Demand from Intelligence', in Roger Z. George and Robert D. Kline (eds), *Intelligence and the National*

Security Strategist: Enduring Issues and Challenges (Lanham, Boulder, New York, Toronto and Oxford: Rowman & Littlefield Publishers, Inc., 2006), pp. 425–30.

Petersen, Martin, 'The Challenge for the Political analyst', in Roger Z. George and Robert D. Kline (eds), *Intelligence and the National Security Strategist: Enduring Issues and Challenges* (Lanham, Boulder, New York, Toronto and Oxford: Rowman & Littlefield Publishers, Inc., 2006), pp. 303–10.

Phytian, Mark, 'Intelligence Theory and Theories of International Relations: Shared World or Separate Worlds?', in Peter Gill, Stephen Marrin and Mark Phytian (eds), *Intelligence Theory: Key questions and Debates*, Studies in Intelligence Series (London and New York: Routledge, Taylor & Francis Group, 2009), pp. 54–72.

Pillar, Paul R., 'Adapting Intelligence to Changing Issues', in Loch K. Johnson (ed.), *Handbook of Intelligence Studies* (London and New York: Routledge, Taylor & Francis Group, 2009), pp. 148–62.

Pillar, Paul R., 'The Perils of Politicization', in Loch K. Johnson (ed.), *The Oxford Handbook of National Security Intelligence* (Oxford: Oxford University Press, 2010), pp. 472–84.

Plato, *Complete Works*, in John M. Cooper (ed.) (Indianapolis and Cambridge: Hackett Publishing Company, 1997)

Popper, Karl, *The Open Society and Its Enemies, Volume Two: Hegel and Marx* (London and New York: Routledge Classics, [1945] 2003).

Popper, Karl, *The Poverty of Historicism* (London and New York: Routledge Classics, [1957] 2004).

Popper, Karl, *Conjectures and Refutations: The Growth of Scientific Knowledge* (London and New York: Routledge Classics, [1963] 2006).

Popper, Karl, *Unended Quest*, originally published as *Autobiography by Karl Popper* (London and New York: Routledge Classics, [1974] 2006).

Popper, Karl, *The Logic of Scientific Discovery* (London and New York: Routledge Classics, [1959] 2008).

Posner, Richard A., *Preventing Surprise Attacks: Intelligence Reform in the Wake of 9/11*, in cooperation with the Hoover Institution, Stanford University, Stanford, CA (Lanham, Boulder, New York, Toronto and Oxford: Rowman & Littlefield, 2005).

Ransom, Harry Howe, 'The Politicization of Intelligence', in Loch K. Johnson and James J. Wirtz (ed.), *Intelligence and National Security: The Secret World of Spies* (New York and Oxford: Oxford University Press, 2008), pp. 193–204.

Richards, Julian, *The Art and Science of Intelligence Analysis* (Oxford: Oxford University Press, 2010).

Riste, Olav, 'The Intelligence–Policy Maker Relationship and the Politicization of Intelligence', in Gregory F. Treverton and Willhelm Agrell (eds), *National Intelligence Systems: Current Research and Future Prospects* (Cambridge: Cambridge University Press, 2009), pp. 179–209.

Robertson, David, *The Routledge Dictionary of Politics*, third edition (London and New York: Routledge, Taylor & Francis Group, [2002] 2004).

Rolington, Alfred, 'Objective Intelligence or Plausible Denial: An Open Source Review of Intelligence Method and Process since 9/11', in Len V. Scott and Gerald R. Hughes (eds), *Intelligence, Crises and Security: Prospects and Retrospect* (London and New York: Routledge, Taylor & Francis Group, 2008), pp. 86–107.

Russell, Bertrand, *The Problems of Philosophy*, with an introduction by John Skorupski (Oxford: Oxford University Press, [1912] 2001).

Russell, Richard L., *Sharpening Strategic Intelligence: Why the CIA Gets It Wrong, and What Needs to Be Done to Get It Right* (Cambridge: Cambridge University Press, 2007).

Russell, Richard L., 'Achieving All-Source Fusion in the Intelligence Community', in Loch K. Johnson (ed.), *Handbook of Intelligence Studies* (London and New York: Routledge, Taylor & Francis Group, 2009), pp. 189–98.

Rutland, Peter, 'Sovietology: Notes for a Post-Mortem', *National Interest* 31 (Spring 1993): pp. 109–22.

Scott, Len V., and Peter Jackson, 'Journeys in Shadows', in Len V. Scott and Peter Jackson (eds), *Understanding Intelligence in the Twenty-First Century: Journeys in Shadows* (London and New York: Routledge, Taylor & Francis Group, 2004), pp. 1–28.

Scott, Len V., and Peter Jackson (eds), *Understanding Intelligence in the Twenty-First Century: Journeys in Shadows* (London and New York: Routledge, Taylor & Francis Group, 2004).

Shulsky, Abram, and Gary J. Schmitt, *Silent Warfare: Understanding the World of Intelligence* (Washington, DC: Brassey's Inc., [1991] 2002).

Simon, James Monnier, Jr., 'Managing Domestic, Military, and Foreign Policy Requirements: Correcting Frankenstein's Blunder', in Jennifer E. Sims and Burton Gerber (eds), *Transforming US Intelligence*, in cooperation with the Center for Peace and Security Studies, Edmund A. Walsh School of Foreign Service, Georgetown University (Washington, DC: Georgetown University Press, 2005), pp. 149–61.

Sims, Jennifer, 'Understanding Friends and Enemies: The Context for American Intelligence Reform', in Jennifer E. Sims and Burton Gerber (eds), *Transforming US Intelligence*, in cooperation with the Center for Peace and Security Studies, Edmund A. Walsh School of Foreign Service, Georgetown University (Washington, DC: Georgetown University Press, 2005), pp. 14–31.

Sims, Jennifer, 'A Theory of Intelligence and International Politics', in Gregory F. Treverton and Wilhelm Agrell (eds), *National Intelligence Systems: Current Research and Future Prospects* (Cambridge: Cambridge University Press, 2009), pp. 58–92.

Sinclair, Robert S., *Thinking and Writing: Cognitive Science and Intelligence Analysis* (Washington, DC: Center for the Study of Intelligence, [1984] 2010).

Sofsky, Wolfgang, *Violence, Terrorism, Genocide, War* (London: Granta Books, 2003).

Steinberg, James B., 'The Policymaker's Perspective: Transparency and Partnership', in Roger Z. George and James B. Bruce (eds), *Analyzing Intelligence: Origins, Obstacles, and Innovations* (Washington, DC: Georgetown University Press, 2008), pp. 82–90.

Strasser, Steven (ed.), *The 9/11 Investigations* (New York: Public Affairs Reports, 2004).

Sun Tzu, *The Art of War*, trans., essays and commentary by the Denma Translation Group (Boston and London: Shambhala, 2001).

Sun Tzu, *The Art of War: The New Illustrated Edition*, trans. Samuel B. Griffith (London: Duncan Baird Publishers, 2005).

Treverton, Gregory F., *Reshaping National Intelligence for an Age of Information* (Cambridge: Cambridge University Press, 2003).

Treverton, Gregory F., Seth G. Jones, Steven Boraz and Phillip Lipscy, *Toward a Theory of Intelligence*, Workshop Report (Santa Monica, Arlington and Pittsburgh: RAND Corporation, 2006).

Treverton, Gregory F., *Intelligence for an Age of Terror* (Cambridge: Cambridge University Press, 2009).

Truman, Harry S., *Year of Decision*, vol. 1 of *Memories by Harry Truman* (Garden City, NY: Doubleday, 1965).

Turner, Michael A., *Why Secret Intelligence Fails*, revised edn (Washington, DC: Potomac Books, Inc., 2006).

Walsh, James Igoe, *Confidential: The International Politics of Intelligence Sharing* (New York: Colombia University Press, 2010).

Warner, Michael, 'Intelligence as Risk Shifting', in Peter Gill, Stephen Marrin and Mark Phytian (eds), *Intelligence Theory: Key Questions and Debates*, Studies in Intelligence Series (London and New York: Routledge, Taylor & Francis Group, 2009), pp. 16–32.

Warner, Michael, 'Wanted: A Definition of "Intelligence"', in Christopher Andrew, Richard J. Aldrich and Wesley K. Wark (eds), *Secret Intelligence: A Reader* (London and New York: Routledge, Taylor & Francis Group, 2009), pp. 3–11.

Whaley, Barton, *Stratagem: Deception and Surprise in War* (Cambridge, MA: MIT Center for International Studies, 1969).

Williams, Bernard, *Truth and Truthfulness* (Princeton and Oxford: Princeton University Press, 2002).

Wirtz, James J., 'Theory of Surprise', in Richard K. Betts and Thomas G. Mahnken (eds), *Paradoxes of Strategic Intelligence: Essays in Honor of Michael I. Handel* (London and Portland, OR: Frank Cass, 2003), pp. 101–16.

Wirtz, James J., 'Déjà Vu? Comparing Pearl Harbor and September 11', in Christoper Andrew, Richard J. Aldrich and Wesley K. Wark (eds), *Secret Intelligence: A Reader* (London and New York: Routledge, Taylor & Francis Group, 2009), pp. 186–92.

Wittgenstein, Ludwig, *Philosophical Investigations: The German Text, with a Revised English Translation* (Oxford and Malden, MA: Blackwell Publishers, 2001).

Wohlstetter, Roberta, *Pearl Harbor: Warning and Decision* (Stanford: Stanford University Press, 1962).

Zegart, Amy B., *Spying Blind: The CIA, The FBI, and the Origins of 9/11* (Princeton and Oxford: Princeton University Press, 2007).

Inquiries, Recommendations and Strategies

Branch 3+5+6+Israeli Air Force (IAF) Intelligence Division + Israeli Navy (IN) Intelligence Division, Immediate Military Intelligence Review, 'Alert Status and Activity in Syria and Egypt as of 051000 Oct.7'.

House Permanent Select Committee on Intelligence and the Senate Select Committee on Intelligence, *Report of the Joint Inquiry into Intelligence Community Activities before and after the Terrorist Attacks of September 11, 2001* (2002).

Review of Intelligence on Weapons of Mass Destruction, Report of a Committee of Privy Councellors, Chairman: The Rt Hon. The Lord Butler of Brockwell KG GCB CVO, 2004.

The 9/11 Commission Report: Final Report of The National Commission on Terrorist Attacks upon the United States, authorized edition (New York and London: W.W. Norton & Company, 2004).

The 9/11 Commission Report: Intelligence Policy, Staff Statement No. 7.

The 9/11 Commission Report: National Policy Coordination, Staff Statement No. 8.

The Joint Inquiry into Intelligence Community Activities before and after the Terrorist Attacks of September 11, 2001, *Recommendations* (2002).

The National Intelligence Strategy of the United States of America, *Transformation through Integration and Innovation* (October 2005).

Serendipitous Sources

Aasberg, Knut, lecture to the Professional Advanced Intelligence course, Norwegian Defence University College, Oslo, 16 September 2008.

Bar-Joseph, Uri, pers. discussion in Oslo, October, 2008.

Coker, Christopher, lecture to the Norwegian Naval Special Operations Conference, Bergen, 27 August 2007.

Omand, David, lecture to the Professional Advanced Intelligence course, Norwegian Defence University College, Oslo, 7 October 2008.

Smith, M. L. R., lecture to the Professional Advanced Intelligence course, Norwegian Defence University College, Oslo, 26 September 2008.

Størmer Thaulow, Sven, discussions as a student of the Professional Advanced Intelligence course, Norwegian Defence University College, Oslo, September/October 2008.

Index

A reference in **bold** indicates a table.

and the counter-action of adversaries,
6–7
defined, 6
of intelligence, 18
presupposition of wholeness, 18–19, 28
the secrecy paradox and, 10–11
Cook, Robin, 136
Counterterrorism and Security Group
(CSG), 231–2, 250
Counter Terrorist Center (CTC), 52, 136,
147, 158, 170, 172, 252
Cradock, Sir Percy, 80, 105
creativity
as challenge to orthodoxies, 58
dialogue as creative process, 117–18
fusion of creativity with falsification
and critical rationalism, 57–62
individual creative cognitive force,
46–7
in an intelligence operative, 58, 102,
192–3
lack of within the US tell-tale indicator
system, 167–9
as limited by discourse failure, 10,
171–2
reason, creativity, imagination and
thought relationship, 2, 41–4
in relation to integrity, 58
in relation to intellectual freedom,
45–6, 51
secrecy and, 117–19
tensions with bureaucratic systems, 50
to understand threat structures, 60
critical rationalism
the critical mind, 10, 191
fusion of creativity with falsification
and critical rationalism, 57–62
need for in an intelligence operative, 58
as science and intelligence activity,
28–9, **29**, 97–9
as solution to the problem of induction,
59–62, 98–9, 178

Davies, Philip H., 23, 187, 188
Davis, Jack, 195, 198, 207–8
decision-makers
awareness of uncertainties, 221
communication of new threats to,
244–5

dissemination culture prior to 9/11,
227–33
political effects of intelligence
knowledge, 89–90
producer/consumer relationship, 22–3,
25–6, 72–3, 91–2
provision of knowledge to, 80, 226–7,
232–3, 235
realisation of the limitations of
intelligence, 236–7
see also policy-makers
dialogue
as creative process, 117–18
discourse and enriching dialogue, 9
and the dissemination of information,
223, 227–30, 232–3
between the producer/consumer, 76–8
term, 117
discourse
as creative process, 117–18
enriching dialogue, 9
and intelligence theory, 259–60
new threat discourses, 167
as presupposing dialogue, 117
between the producer/consumer, 76–8
qualitative information sharing, 76
secrecy's reductive effect on, 11, 123–4
societal discourse on terrorism, 215–16,
242–3, 245
discourse failure
9/11 attacks and, 34, 123, 195
of the Bush administration, 254–5
cognitive closure's impact on, 32–3, 35,
49–50, 242
the critical mind and, 10
defined, 8, 177
domestic threat from foreign terrorists,
52–3, 145, 153–6, 172–3, 194, 240
flawed cognitive processes and, 32–3,
35, 40, 87, 146–7
human nature and, 49, 87–8
impact of societal discourse and,
215–16, 242–3, 245, 264
intelligence failure manifested as, 86–8
intelligence tribal language and, 8, 51,
87, 146–7
lack of humility and, 85–6, 88
lack of understanding of intelligence
and, 29

The Problem of Secret Intelligence

imagination (*cont.*)
  lack of within the US tell-tale indicator
    system, 167–9
  as limited by discourse failure, 171–2
  reason, creativity, imagination and
    thought relationship, 2, 41–4
  in relation to intellectual freedom, 45–6
  tensions with bureaucratic systems, 50,
    124–5, 168–9
induction
  classic inductive intelligence analysis, 4,
    7, 97–8, 151, 175–6
  defined, 59
  within formal reasoning, 2, 43
  refutation as solution to, 60
  the relation between similar differences
    and different similarities, 8
  see also problem of induction
information sharing
  courage-to-share principle, 100–1, 222,
    233–5, 252
  cultural resistance to prior to 9/11,
    121–3, 129–30
  incentives for, 222
  lack of National Intelligence Estimates,
    120–1
  need-to-know principle, limitations of,
    121–2, 169, 221, 222, 223–7
  need-to-share culture, post-9/11, 99, 222
  qualitative information sharing, 76
  see also dissemination of information
integrity
  discourse and, 117
  of the intelligence service, 91
  in relation to creativity, 58
  value of individual integrity, 47, 226, 234
intelligence
  complexity of, 18
  as dangerous, 11
  defined, 2, 4, 18, 19, 125–6, 258, 265
  as estimation beyond formal reasoning
    and secrets, 5–6
  fourfold description of, 69, 74
  holistic nature of, 28, 30
  as intellectually and mentally
    challenging, 49, 234
  limitations of, 3–4
  as misunderstood, 17–20
  myths of, 138

the relation between similar differences
    and different similarities, 8
  specialness of, 23–5
  as the subject matter of intelligence, 28
  theoretical understanding of, 14–15
  twelve images of, 28–9, **29**
  understandings of, 18
intelligence, theory of
  characteristics of, 26–7
  constant change in, 187
  defined, 20
  and evaluation of intelligence failure, 17
  and intelligence discourse, 259–60
  lack of, 29–31, 184–7, 258
  in relation to discourse failure and
    intelligence failure, 258–9
  in relation to empirical reasoning,
    188–9, 258
  scholarship on, 15–17, 257–8
intelligence cycle
  functions of, 128
  infinite character of, 206–7
  as interactive network, 210
  need for, 127–8
  politicisation of, 85
  as technical and organisational, 134
  traditional process of, 133–4
  understanding of as functions and
    network, 134
  see also analysis; collection of
    intelligence; dissemination of
    information
intelligence failure
  defined, 16, 86
  due to lack of imagination, 118
  evaluation of, 17
  as hard to understand, 20
  human uncertainty as cause of, 16
  links with human cognition, 9, 16–17,
    30–1, 34
  manifested as discourse failure, 86–8
  Pearl Harbour, 53, 150, 198, 203
  and the problem of induction, 197–8
  relationship with intelligence theory,
    258–9
  reliance on inductive analysis, 184–5,
    186
  scholarship on, 16–17, 257
  Yom Kippur war, 57, 82–3, 85–6, 198